How to Design Optimization Algorithms by Applying Natural Behavioral Patterns

Authored by

Rohollah Omidvar

Department of Sama Technical and Vocational Training College,
Islamic Azad University,
Shiraz Branch, Shiraz,
Iran

Behrouz Minaei Bidgoli

Computer Engineering Department,
University of Science and Technology,
Iran

How to Design Optimization Algorithms by Applying Natural Behavioral Patterns

Authors: Rohollah Omidvar and Behrouz Minaei Bidgoli

ISBN (Online): 978-981-14-5959-7

ISBN (Print): 978-981-14-5957-3

Paper Back (Online): 978-981-14-5958-0

Published by Bentham Science Publishers Pte. Ltd. Singapore. All Rights Reserved.

need for a court order if at any point you breach any terms of this License Agreement. In no event will any delay or failure by Bentham Science Publishers in enforcing your compliance with this License Agreement constitute a waiver of any of its rights.

3. You acknowledge that you have read this License Agreement, and agree to be bound by its terms and conditions. To the extent that any other terms and conditions presented on any website of Bentham Science Publishers conflict with, or are inconsistent with, the terms and conditions set out in this License Agreement, you acknowledge that the terms and conditions set out in this License Agreement shall prevail.

Bentham Science Publishers Pte. Ltd.
80 Robinson Road #02-00
Singapore 068898
Singapore
Email: subscriptions@benthamscience.net

BENTHAM SCIENCE

CONTENTS

FOREWORD

With the dawn of artificial intelligence (AI) and the rise of the fourth industrial revolution, it is easy to see how nature-inspired intelligent systems will play an even more fundamental role in improving and enriching human lives. While we may never agree on what constitutes AI, optimization is widely understood as one of its chief pillars. With the increasing computational processing power in modern times, nature-inspired optimization has produced considerable academic debate and successful solutions to many challenging numerical optimization problems. In my opinion, these two paths of theoretical and practical solution-oriented developments will continue to flourish in the future. And nature will continue to awe us with the treasures and beauties it holds on our way to its discovery.

Mohammad-R. Akbarzadeh-T.
Center of Excellence on Soft Computing and Intelligent Information Processing
Departments of Electrical Engineering and Computer Engineering
Ferdowsi University of Mashhad
Mashhad
Iran
E-mail: akbazar@um.ac.ir

PREFACE

Most of the books presented by respected researchers in the field of optimization have introduced algorithms. So I thought young researchers and students needed a reference to research in this area and create their own algorithm. Nature has always been full of secrets in the history of mankind, and from time to time, human beings discover some of these mysteries. But there is still much to be desired until the day that man reaches the secrets of nature. With these discoveries, he has been able to propose important mechanisms based on these mysteries of nature. In this book, I talk mostly to young people and students who are interested in science. I try to share with them the little science I have in this area.

Rohollah Omidvar
Department of Sama Technical and Vocational Training College/Islamic Azad University
Shiraz Branch
Shiraz
Iran
E-mail: r.omidvar.uni@gmail.com

DEDICATION

I dedicate this book to the soul of Ms. Narjes Khanalizadeh. She was the first Iranian nurse to die of coronavirus. Narjes was born in 1995 in the city of Rudsar in northern Iran. After graduation, she worked as a nurse at the emergency department of Lahijan city. Narjes Khanalizadeh, on February 23, 2020, after the widespread outbreak of coronavirus in Iran, with similar complications of the coronavirus, lost consciousness and fell to the ground while taking care of patients at work. Narjes Khanalizadeh died in the afternoon of February 25, 2020 at Milad Hospital in Lahijan.

CHAPTER 1

Introduction to Optimization

Abstract: Finding the best answer among the various solutions to complex and mathematical problems is called optimization. There are two types of optimization problems; continuous optimization and discrete optimization. Finding the solution in these environments is the best solution for that particular solution. Optimization exists in many fields and sciences, and it shows that if researchers provide the most quality optimization algorithms, it can have a great impact on human life. Optimization is similar to finding a treasure in an area. In this analogy, you have to mobilize a crowd to find this treasure. Since the population does not know the location of the treasure from the beginning, these populations will start searching at random and will reach near to it at a certain time. The topic of the search here is very important. It is very important to find a mechanism that can best organize the population. The search engine must follow certain ideas and rules. In the optimization problem, the most important step is proper search. In optimization issues, the concept of the best answer, best search, best solution and best organization is desired. Nowadays, optimization can be applied everywhere we deal with big data.

Keywords: Algorithm, Environments, Mathematics, Nature, Optimization, Space.

Optimization problems are called complex and mathematical problems that are more complex than other problems. There are two types of continuous and discrete variables in optimization problems. In a discrete optimization problem, we are looking for an object such as an integer, permutation or graph from a countable set. Problems with continuous variables include constrained problems and multimodal problems. It can be said that optimization is a kind of mathematical programming. As such, optimization has been able to solve many problems in the sciences, including physics, biology, engineering, economics and business. In most cases there is some kind of mathematical problem that needs to be solved It Algorithms convert and solve these problems into mathematical problems.

The historic term mathematical programming, broadly synonymous with optimization, was coined in the 1940s before programming became equated with computer programming. Mathematical programming includes the study of the mathematical structure of optimization problems, the invention of methods for

Rohollah Omidvar and Behrouz Minaei Bidgoli

solving these problems, the study of the mathematical properties of these methods, and the implementation of these methods on computers. Faster computers have greatly expanded the size and complexity of optimization problems that can be solved. The development of optimization techniques has paralleled advances not only in computer science but also in operations research, numerical analysis, game theory, mathematical economics, control theory, and combinatory.

Optimization must have to consider three main problems. The first problem is that the answer is not exactly clear what. Whether the answer is a minimum number or a range of company costs, this type of answer must be precisely specified. The second problem is that sometimes it is necessary to manipulate values rather than an answer. Examples include quantities of stock to buy or sell the amount of different resources that must be allocated to different production activities, the route followed by the vehicle through the traffic network, or the policies that must be supported by a candidate. The final problem with optimization is that the answer area or the space of the item must be specified. For example, a production process may not require more resources than the available resources and it may not use less than zero resources. In this broad framework, optimization problems can have different mathematical properties. Mathematical optimization or mathematical programming is the selection of a best element (with regard to some criterion) from some set of available alternatives [1]. Optimization problems from computer science and engineering to operations research and economics, and the development of solution methods has been of interest in mathematics [2].

In the simplest case, an optimization problem consists of maximizing or minimizing a real function by systematically choosing input values from within an allowed set and computing the value of the function. The generalization of optimization theory and techniques to other formulations constitutes a large area of applied mathematics. More generally, optimization includes finding "best available" values of some objective function given a defined domain (or input), including a variety of different types of objective functions and different types of domains.

During the optimization, the initial algorithms are studied by the different methods and the obtained information is used to improve a thought or method. An optimization is a mathematical tool, which is concerns with finding the answers to many questions about the quality of solutions of different problems. The term of "the best" implicitly suggests that there are more than one solution to a given problem, which of course the solutions don't have the identical values. The definition of the best solution depends on the discussed problem as well as the allowable error value. So, the way that the problem is formulated in which, also has a direct impact on the quality of the best solution. Some problems have a clear response; such as the best player of a sport branch, the longest day of the year and solution of an ordinary first grade differential equation are examples that can be named as easy problems. In contrast, some problems have the various maximum or minimum solutions known as the optimal or extreme points and probably would be the best answer to a relative concept. The best work of art, the most beautiful landscape and the most dulcet track of music are among examples that can be said for these problems. Optimization is changing the inputs and characteristics of a device, a mathematical process or an experimental test in a way that the best output or result achieved. Inputs are the variables of a process that are referred to as the objective function, the cost function, or the fitness function.

Optimization is a process followed to improve something. A thought, idea or plan raised by a scientist or an engineer may get better through optimization procedure. During optimization, the initial conditions are investigated through different methods, and the obtained information is used to improve a thought or the used methods. Optimization is a mathematical tool used to find answers of many questions on how various solutions to problems are used. Optimization deals with finding the best response to a problem. The word "best" implies that there is more than one response to a problem but they are of different values. The definition of the "best" response depends on the problem, the solution and the amount of the permissible error. Therefore, the formulation also affects the definition of the best answer directly. Some problems have certain responses; the best player in a sport, the longest day of the year and the answer to an ordinary differential equation of first grade are some examples of simple problems. In contrast, some problems have several maximum or minimum answers known as optimal points or Extremum, and are probably the best answer to a relative concept. The best work of art, the most beautiful landscapes and the most pleasant piece of music can be named as examples of such problems, and Swarm Intelligence is a type of artificial intelligence technique established on the basis of collective behavior in decentralized and self-organized systems. These systems have populations that are purposefully and socially connected to one another and generate search. Usually these populations are automatically connected to each other and do not require special management. This kind of self-adaptive movement of populations makes the implementation mechanism in different systems easier.

Optimization refers to changing the input and characteristics of a device, or a mathematical process or an empirical test so that the best output or result would be achieved. The inputs are the variables of the process or function, namely objective function, cost function or fitness function. The output is defined as cost, benefit or fitness. In this book, according to many articles related to the topic, all optimization problems have been considered as minimization of a cost function. We can easily show that any optimization problem can be defined as a minimization problem.

Swarm algorithms have a weakness for creating the random initial population. Also, particle swarm algorithm does not consider the quality of the problem space when the particles move in the space, and does not adjust the speed of the particles with that quality. Furthermore, choosing a point between the local and public optimums, the swarm algorithm makes the particles to spend a lot of time to reach the optimal solution.

Optimization always helps human life and makes the system from one state to a better one. The problem of optimization has existed in human minds for a long time. Optimization helps bring the system and the person closer to their goal in life [3]. In fact, in any problem, there is an objective function that must be optimized. Assume that if the optimization point is found, the problem is solved. A goal function can be in the form of fitness or performance. If we are to minimize objective performance, that process can be a cost function. If we want to maximize the performance of a goal, it can be considered as a fitness performance. The problem of optimization has been and is widely affecting all aspects of human life.

Optimization is everywhere, in various fields of production, management, business, military, and decision [4]. While in linear optimization, mathematical linear programming is the best option, it covers a few real problems; *i.e.* there are a few problems that can be expressed in the form of a linear objective function. In convex optimization, mathematical convex programming is the best option. In spite of limitation of linear objective function, the convex objective function covered much more real problems. Although there are many problems in the science that can be expressed in the form of convex objective function, almost all real problems can't be expressed in terms of convex objective function and they are a non-linear objective function. In engineering, the best product, and manufacturing parameters are considered. In the industry of selecting the right raw materials, its quantity, time and ultimately product output have always been a priority. In economics, resource allocation can best help create a quality economy [5]. Much of human discovery has been inspired by nature and has been in various forms throughout history. For example, they get help from a random mechanism. In human exploration, auxiliary parameters have been used that are often used by nature, and these parameters have been effective in the quality of the explored product [6]. Optimization is actually finding the best situation. The problem of optimization involves many areas in human life. There are also various solutions to finding human issues that have broadened this optimization problem. The algorithms that solve the optimization problem can be definitive or probabilistic. Prior to the optimization algorithms, the solutions were not very suitable and led to failure. For this reason, human beings have increasingly resorted to optimization algorithms and expanded them every day to achieve definitive calculations [7]. Science has shown that the movement of living beings is dome based on a coherent social philosophy that accuracy in these behaviors can be useful to achieve a solution to many complex problems. In Fig. (**1**), you can see some optimization resources in nature.

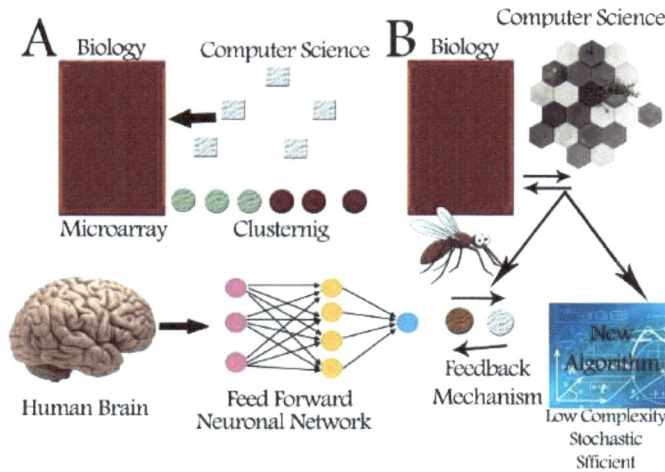

Fig. (1). Algorithms in nature [1].

Nature Inspired Algorithms is a very active research area. This is because problems with which we are normally familiar are getting more and more complex due to size and other aspects, but all optimization problems include two types of continuous optimization and discrete optimization. Finding the solution in these environments is the best solution for that particular solution. Optimization exists in many fields and sciences, showing how effective optimization can be in human life if one can find the best optimization algorithms. In optimization, most of the new problems that the existing methods do not work on are resolved. For this reason, it seems that these days and in the future they will be more inspired by nature. To answer the question whether recent algorithms inspired by Nature such as Colony Bee Colony algorithm, Firefly algorithm and Spider Social algorithm, Bet algorithm, Strawberry algorithm, Plant propagation algorithm, Plant propagation algorithm or many have not been effective? These are much more effective in most search/optimization problems than in nature-based algorithms such as genetic algorithms, annealing simulations, anti-cloning and super-optimization. Computer and Biology has a long history. In recent years, computer scientists have been using biology to build advanced computing mechanisms, such as neural networks. Computer science and biology have long been integrated to create computational mechanisms and have yielded good results. In Fig. (**2**), you can see an example of a problem space in optimization.

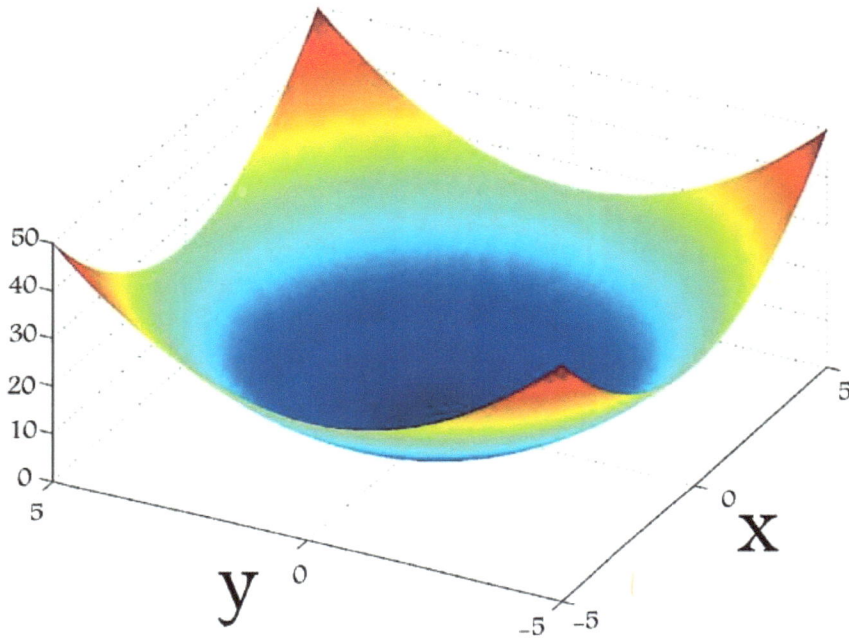

Fig. (2). A sample of optimization problem.

CHAPTER 2

Nature and Optimization Algorithms

Abstract: New algorithms have been developed to see if they can cope with these challenging optimization problems. Among these new algorithms, many algorithms, such as particle swarm optimization, cuckoo search, and firefly algorithm, have gained popularity due to their high efficiency. In the current literature, there are about 40 different algorithms. It is a challenging task to classify these algorithms systematically. In this chapter, the reader becomes familiar with the source of nature so that he can come up with an idea. Therefore, the first step in building and delivering a nature-inspired algorithm is to become familiar with nature and understand its features. Nature is a great source of inspiration for all stages of human life. In nature, creatures and structures always find solutions to their problems. Hence, it is nature that plays the leading role. Nature-inspired optimization algorithms are always some of the best mechanisms to solve complex problems. In this chapter, the reader will be introduced to a variety of nature-based optimization algorithms. Optimization algorithms are introduced and their techniques will be examined. This chapter has a history of nature-inspired algorithms whose evolution is visible. Researchers have tried to draw inspiration from natural resources as well as animals from nature that provided algorithms that have helped researchers in many problems. This chapter can also introduce readers to the history of making nature-based algorithms.

Keywords: Algorithm, Cost, Meta-heuristic, Nature, Optimization, Problem.

Nature-inspired algorithms all use a unique order in nature. These ideas have all come from field research and laboratory research on natural animals and natural phenomena. It is best to look around for ideas in nature and find the greatest effectiveness from the smallest of behaviors. How an ant moves with grain, how it carries it, and how it moves. How a bird learns to fly from a bird near it, how lions hunt in the jungle. We can even think of phenomena. How the clouds fertilize, and how it rains, and even how different generations of mankind have evolved with each other throughout history, reaching modern life. Studies have been conducted in recent years that have proposed different optimization algorithms based on different shapes of nature. Table **1** is a description of these efforts [8].

Rohollah Omidvar and Behrouz Minaei Bidgoli

Table 1. Various swarm based optimization algorithms.

AF Algorithm *Cheng et al.*	2018
whale optimization algorithm *S Mirjalili, A Lewis*	2016
SSPCO Algorithm *Omidvar et al.*	2015
Wolf search *Tang et al.*	2012
Bat Algorithm *Yang*	
Eagle Strategy *Yang and Deb*	2010
Firefly Algorithm *Yang*	
Cuckoo Search *Yang and Deb*	2009
Artificial Bee Colony *Karaboga and Basturk*	2007
Monkey Search *Mucherino and Seref*	
Cat Swarm *Chu et al.*	2006
Bees Algorithm *Pham et al.*	
Bacterial Foraging *Passino*	2002
Fish Swarm *Li et al.*	
Particle Swarm Algorithm *Kennedy and Eberhart*	1995
Ant Colony Optimization *Dorigo*	1992

Genetic algorithm is one of the most popular algorithms of the new generation and is probably one of the first evolutionary algorithms in the field of optimization. A person named John Holland and his colleagues were able to draw inspiration from the genetic evolutionary system of natural organisms and develop a genetic algorithm. This algorithm is very effective in solving problems dealing with discrete numbers [9].

Genetic algorithm is one of the algorithms inspired by the natural structure and very successful. This algorithm has become one of the best optimization algorithms because it has been able to solve many difficult problems. The initial population of this algorithm is called the chromosome. Each chromosome consists of several females. Each chromosome is then subjected to cost function and its cost is determined. The most elusive chromosomes are put into the mating phase, which consists of two main cross-sections and mutations, resulting in a new and better population using this mating. Genetic algorithm is a conception of the generation evolution of living beings that could create an applied role in many scientific fields. Evolution Strategy was an evolutionary algorithm that used the natural evolutionary process to solve its problems. This algorithm was also introduced by Rechenberg in the early 1960s [10, 11].

Another optimization algorithm this decade called Evolutionary Programming (EP) by L.J. Foggel was introduced, inspired by the evolution in the field of artificial intelligence [12]. After the personal genetic algorithm called Kosa introduced a similar algorithm called the Genetic Programming (GP) algorithm in 1990 which was an interesting way of looking for the optimal solution. This algorithm almost automatically provided a solution to the problem [68]. This algorithm created a computer program from the process of solving an optimization problem and introduced it as the optimal solution [13].

Differential Evolution Algorithm (DE) is one of the most popular algorithms in the world of optimization algorithms [14]. This algorithm was proposed by Storn and Price to solve polynomial problems and its results showed that it is an acceptable algorithm for solving optimization problems.

The particle swarm optimization algorithm was introduced in 1995 by James Kennedy and Russell Eberhert, who was inspired by the crowd of birds in flight [15].

The algorithm is inspired by the behavior of birds when searching for food. The bird algorithm has a simple mechanism for implementation and simulation and is used in many engineering sciences and so on. In this algorithm, the population is randomly initialized and then the cost of each population is determined. The best local population and the best general population are identified. Each population moves in space according to the equation of velocity and motion, and at the end the final answer is determined [16 - 18]. This algorithm solves the problem of the back gypsy best known as the SF.

Particle swarm optimization algorithms and genetic algorithms combined to solve many difficult problems [19].

In a study to solve the backpack problem, a binary particle swarm algorithm was proposed by the mutation operator [20]. Different algorithms have been proposed by researchers based on the behavior of bees in nature. One of them is the artificial bee algorithm, which is classified into two categories. These two types of behavior include foraging behavior and mating behavior of bees. The artificial bee colonization algorithm uses a set of multiple bees in nature to search for food. This algorithm was presented by Karaboga and Basturk [21].

Different food-seeking behaviors are found in bees. The first step in sending bees to nature is through a special mechanism for food search. When the bees find their desired food source, they return to their colony and declare this to other bees with their own dance. Then there are three types of information in this dance. First, it tells the distance of the food source from the colony, the direction in which all the other bees have to go and to maintain the quality of the food source. Bees are only attracted to bees that have obtained information about the best quality food source. This process provides the best food source. Inspired by the original artificial bee colony algorithm, an algorithm was developed in which the behavior of the observed bees was modified and SF was used and the values were binary [22], and a similar algorithm was used to solve the TSP problem [23].

The Harmony Search Algorithm is a music structure-based optimization algorithm in which the musical instrument is used to construct a targeted algorithm. This algorithm provides a mechanism whereby musical notes are put together as a tool to start from a basic state and to make the best of a pleasant music. These tools are placed in the target function and there the best case will be selected [24]. Bee's algorithm was first introduced by Pham *et al.*, [25] and the bee algorithm was first designed as a mathematical problem. Bees choose the best food source as the best answer to the mathematical equation. The algorithm's equilibrium exploration and exploitation is performed using a spectator bee that randomly searches for new sites and is regularly used by worker bees to search for neighbours in the site with higher qualification performance. Bees searching for the best food sources are selected as elite bees in this algorithm. Then neighbouring sources of elite sources will also be considered as valuable resources. Initially, the bee algorithm was introduced and presented by its authors as a continuous algorithm. This initial algorithm was used for scheduling and planning in the industry [26], and data clustering was also performed well by this algorithm. These binary data were well clustered in this algorithm [27].

Imperialist Competitive Algorithm is an optimization algorithm of the best evolutionary algorithms that is inspired by the political mechanism of imperialist competition and inspired by the imperialist behavior of some countries in the world to improve their country. In this algorithm, we had an initial population of two, divided into two groups. The first type of these populations are colonial and the second are the imperialist population. The power of each country is more imperialist at the expense of the opposite. This means that a stronger imperialist will dominate more colonies [28]. The colony mechanism where poor populations are brought to cultural evolution by elite populations can lead to better bad populations, and the algorithm automatically optimizes its populations using this mechanism. This political system was more prevalent in the 19th century.

A paper was presented in which the process of plant migration and reproduction was used and a single algorithm was introduced called AF. Due to its own mechanism, this algorithm can be useful in solving discrete problems. It is interesting in nature that although a plant cannot move, it can be effective in sending its seed to its offspring. In this algorithm, the location and propagation distance of the plant are first considered. Then, the propagation position and distance of the main plant are replaced as parameters in the propagation function to produce offspring plants. After this step, the elite child will be selected as the main plant. By changing the main plant, the main plant will become known as the former. This process will continue until the final answer is reached [29].

The root of the simulated annealing (SA) method is in statistical mechanics (Metropolis Algorithm [30]). It was first suggested by Kirkpatrick *et al*. [31], but originally by Cerny [32]. SA is inspired by the annealing technique used by metallurgists to obtain "regularly ordered" solid state with minimal energy (while avoiding "stable meta" structures, characteristic of local minimum energy). The method was to place the material at high temperature and then at low temperature. SA transforms the annealing process into a mechanism: then by introducing a dummy temperature T, which is a simple controllable parameter of the algorithm, the objective performance of the problem, similar to the energy of a material, is minimized [33].

In recent years, optimization algorithms have been developed by researchers to optimize various science problems. Many of these algorithms were very popular and many researchers used them.

Nature became a source of inspiration to many human beings due to its purposeful and complex order, including optimization researchers. Most optimization algorithms today are inspired by nature. These algorithms applied to all areas of nature, including biology, structure, and organisms. Collective intelligence, meanwhile, was able to handle most algorithms, and researchers realized that collective intelligence of natural beings was the source of many of the behaviors that were targeted. Many of today's algorithms in the field of artificial intelligence are from the category of collective intelligence [34].

Fig. (**3**) shows how the algorithm is inspired by nature. Order in nature is the main source of all algorithms. The concept of the new order in nature is that all the components of a set work precisely to achieve the goal of the set. The order of using the algorithms was obtained by careful examination in nature.

The world we live in is very complex and strange, and man has not yet discovered many of its secrets. If many of these secrets are found in nature, humans will be able to build more technologies. Careful study of nature can help the growth of human life.

In the religious books, this order and complexity of the structure of nature are clearly described. Daily sunrise and sunset are a simple example of this structural order. So scientists have been able to discover many of these mechanisms in many cases, especially in the field of zoology. So using them in the form of structures like an optimization algorithm can help solve many problems.

A. inspiration Source for SSPCO algorithm   B. inspiration Source for ACO algorithm

C. inspiration Source for PSO algorithm   D. inspiration Source for ABC algorithm

Fig. (3). Existing nature-inspired algorithm.

Interestingly, in the world we live in, we also see disorder. Like natural storms and more. So there is also a disorder in the world that falls into order. Therefore, one can reach an order through disorder, and this is one of the lessons that nature teaches us.

The potential for disorder is sometimes called "entropy" the tendency of a system to head toward a disordered state. The idea of entropy is embodied in the second law of thermodynamics which states that isolated systems with no influences from the outside world will exhibit increased disorder over time. It may be argued that entropy is not an appropriate phenomenon and that, instead of being disordered, life systems are transformed into highly complex and orderly structures.

Unlike the separate systems described by the second law of thermodynamics, the creatures that live in nature are not a closed phenomenon and are connected to nature and follow this structure.

Scott Camazine says that many creatures that are in one system and that this system is self-adapted, it expresses its own individual desires, and it is these tendencies that lead to the survival of the system.

By examining these examples of complex order, one concludes that social behavior is what sustains a system. Regular individual behavior and interaction with other populations causes order to be seen in many areas of nature [35].

CHAPTER 3

How to Formulate Natural Ideas in Several Algorithms

Abstract: This chapter introduces examples of nature-inspired algorithms presented by authors in recent years. These algorithms all use the source of nature, and the nature and behavior of some animals are the main basis of these algorithms. These algorithms show the orderly behavior of some natural animals and show how this targeted order becomes an algorithm. Understanding these algorithms can help the reader understand how to transform the idea of nature into meaningful equations. We present some examples of these algorithms in this chapter to familiarize the reader with the order in some natural animals. Also, in this chapter, we can understand how to transform this natural order into meaningful equations. These meaningful equations are introduced in the form of an optimization algorithm. In this chapter, the algorithm SSPCO that inspired by the behavior of See-see partridge chickens, SSPCO algorithm based on chaotic population, data clustering using algorithm SSPCO algorithm, data clustering with algorithm chaotic SSPCO, Solving the Travelling salesman problem with the help of SSPCO algorithm, escape from hunter particle swarm optimization algorithm and birds algorithm based on classical condition learning, provided. In this chapter, we are going to introduce the reader to a number of algorithms presented and published by the author of the book. We are going to understand how an idea becomes a mathematical formula. Articles are available in the magazines which can be referred to for additional details.

Keywords: Algorithm, Equations, Nature-inspired, Optimization, Order.

3.1. SSPCO ALGORITHM (SEE-SEE PARTRIDGE)

The basic idea of this optimization algorithm is taken from the behavior of the chicks of a type of bird called See-see partridge. The chicks of this type of bird are located in a regular queue at the time of danger to reach a safe place and they start to move behind their mother to reach a safe point. To simulate the behavior of the chicks of this bird in the form of an optimization algorithm, each chick is considered as a particle of the suboptimal problem. The state of each particle should be according to the behavior of this type of chicks in a regular queue that we know this queue takes us to the best optimal point and this does not mean that

Rohollah Omidvar and Behrouz Minaei Bidgoli

minimizing the search space, but also, it is converging particles after some searches in a regular queue to the best point answers (bird mother). According to Fig. (4), each chick in the search space seeks to find a chick with the priority of a unit higher than itself and it tries to adjust its motion equation based on this chick.

Fig. (4). Chicks motion in proposed algorithm.

The value of priority variable is a number that causes the particles move in a regular convergence line to the global optimum after some moving in the search space.

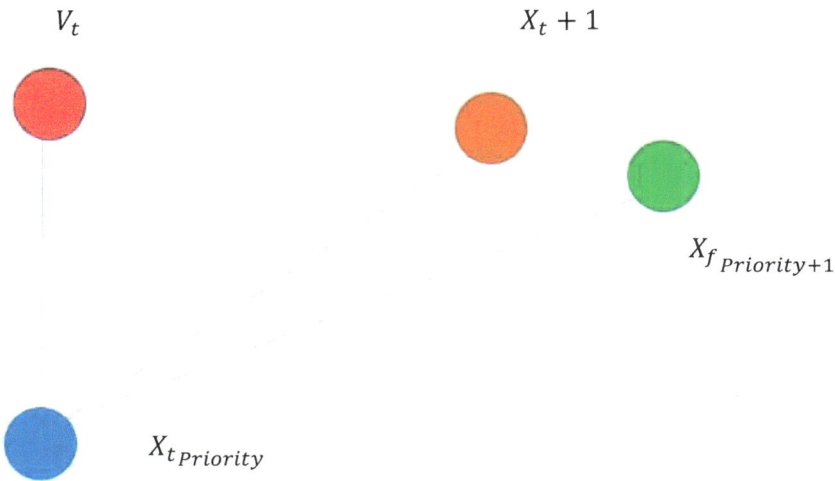

Fig. (5). Particles motion in proposed algorithm.

According to Fig. (5), particle t for going to new position, $X_t + 1$, its velocity equation according to your previous velocity, V_t, and position of particle f its priority valuable is one until more than that of the particle. In each iteration of the algorithm, the particle that has a higher priority is located to be the base of other particles and particles adjust their movement based on these particles with higher priority and this automatically causes that the particle with a good optimum has a higher priority in each iteration and finally, the particle which is at the beginning of the line to the optimum solution will be the mother bird which has the best cost for the algorithm. In fact, the particle that has the best cost is the mother bird. We consider a variable for each particle entitled as priority variable. For particle *i*, priority variable defined according to equation 1:

$$X_i.priority \qquad\qquad (1)$$

In every assessment, when a particle was better than the best personal experience or local optimum; a unit is added to the priority variable of that particle:

$$if \ \ X_i.cost > P_{best} \ \ \rightarrow \ P_{best} = X_i.position \ \ and \ \ X_i.priority = X_i.priority + 1 \qquad (2)$$

$X_i.cost$ The cost of each particle in the benchmark, P_{best} is the best personal experience of each particle, and $X_i.position$ is the location of each particle. In every time of assessment, if the local optimum is better than the global optimum and vice versa, the particle's priority variable goes higher and a unit is added to it:

$$if \quad P_{best} > G_{best} \quad \rightarrow G_{best} = P_{best} \ \ and \ \ X_i.priority = X_i.priority + 1 \qquad (3)$$

G_{best} is the global optimum. The motion equation of each particle is set almost similar to the particle swarm algorithm in the form of equation 4:

$$X_i.position = X_i.position + X_i.velocity \qquad\qquad (4)$$

$X_i.velocity$ is the velocity of each particle or chick. Then, Chickens sorted in array based on priority variable. Fig. (**6**) shows the sorting by priority.

Sort

chick   i=1   . . .   n

priority $i_{prioirity}$ . . . $n_{prioirity}$

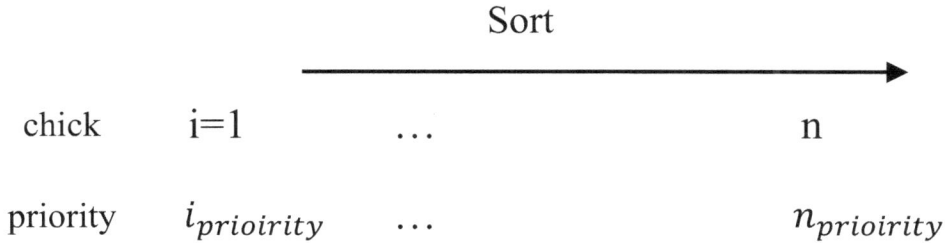

Fig. (6). Sorted array of chicks priority.

Now the particle velocity equation is calculated according to the Equation 5:

$$X_i.velocity = w * X_i.velocity + c * rand() * [position(X_{i+1}.priority)] - X_i.position \quad (5)$$

$X_i.velocity$ is the velocity of the particle, w is the coefficient impact of the previous velocity in the current velocity equation of particle, c is the coefficient impact of position of particle with upper priority in the current velocity equation of particle, $rand()$ is a random number between 0 and one to create a random movement for particles, $[position(X_{i+1}.priority)]$ is the location of the particle with one level higher priority than the current particle that the current particle tries to adjust its velocity according to the particle, $X_i.position$ is the current location of the particle. It can be seen that, according to Equation 5, each particle adjusts its movement based on a particle with one level higher priority. In this way, it does not matter the local and global optimums and at any point in time, it only moves to find a particle which is a unit ahead of that particle and for this reason, the calculation number, and time in this algorithm has a great benefit than the previous optimization algorithm. Fig. (**7**) shows the flowchart of the proposed method and Fig. (**8**) shows the pseudo-code of the proposed method.

3.2. SIMULATION RESULTS

The algorithms were simulated in MATLAB software based on the benchmark functions shown in Table **2** and in accordance with the parameters defined in Table **3**. The standard form of algorithms is used for compare. Comparison of the algorithm was done based on the best cost with the introduced algorithm in the previous works. The comparison of the proposed algorithm was done with 6 optimization algorithm on 14 static benchmarks and the results have been obtained out of 30 runs. To have accurate results and the random results do not have a negative impact on output, we run the algorithm 30 times and then, we select the average of these 30 runs as the final result. Adjusting the parameters of the algorithm was in such a way that the results should be done in an equal condition and no algorithm has any advantage than others in term of the parameter. The results were based on three criteria; first, the best cost of each algorithm to reach the best answer of the benchmark has been shown. This is the best cost in the 100th iteration of each algorithm. In the next step, the standard deviation of the particles' cost is shown in each iteration and finally, the standard deviation of 30 times running is shown that indicates the answers are much different in 30 runs of each algorithm. Variables and parameters are considered identical for algorithms. In the following, initially, the best cost diagram of each function is shown separately in 100 times running and then, the exact values have been shown in a table. Then, the standard deviation diagram of the cost of each algorithm is shown and finally, the analysis of the results is presented. The number of assessments for all algorithms is 100. The number of population is 100 and the number of variables is also 100.

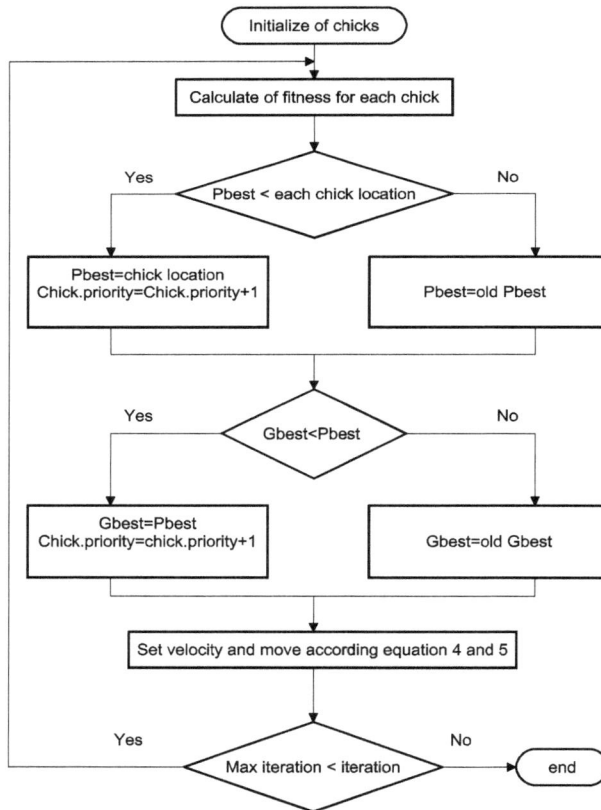

Fig. (7). Flowchart of proposed algorithm.

1. //initialize all chicken

2. Initialize

3. Repeat

4. For each chicken i

5. //update the chicken's best position and priority

6. If $f(x_i) > f(pb_i)$ then

7. $pb_i = x_i$

8. $prioirity_i = prioirity_i + 1$

9. End if

10. //update the global best position and priority

11. If $f(pb_i) > f(gb)$ then

12. $gb = pb_i$

13. $prioirity_i = prioirity_i + 1$

14. End if

15. End for

16. //update chicken's velocity and position

17. For each chicken i

18. For each dimension d

19. $v_{i,d} = v_{i,d} + C * Rand(0,1) * [position(priority_{i+1})] - x_{i,d}$

20. $x_{i,d} = x_{i,d} + v_{i,d}$

21. End for

22. End for

23. //advance iteration

24. $it = it + 1$

25. Until $it > MaxIterations$

Fig. (8). Pseudo-code of SSPCO algorithm.

Table 2. Functions introduced [19].

Field	F	Function	Dimension	Optima	Figure
Unimodal Functions	F1	**Shifted Sphere**	N	0	
	F2	**Shifted Schwefel's Problem 1.2**	N	0	
	F3	**Shifted Rotated High Conditioned Elliptic**	N	0	
	F4	**Shifted Schwefel's Problem 1.2**	N	0	
	F5	**Schwefel's Problem 2.6**	N	0	
Multimodal Functions	F6	**Shifted Rosenbrock's**	N	0	
	F7	**Shifted Rotated Griewank's**	N	0	
	F8	**Shifted Rotated Ackley's**	N	0	
	F9	**Shifted Rastrigin's**	N	0	
	F10	**Shifted Rotated Rastrigin's**	N	0	
	F11	**Shifted Rotated Weierstrass**	N	0	
	F12	**Schwefel's Problem 2.13**	N		

(Table 2) cont.....

Field	F	Function	Dimension	Optima	Figure
Expanded Functions	**F13**	**Expanded Extended Griewank's plus Rosenbrock's**	N	0	
	F14	**Shifted Rotated Expanded Scaffer's**	N	0	

Table 3. Parameter setting.

Value	Parameter	Item No.
100	*pop*	*1*
100	*var*	*2*
-10	*Xmin*	*3*
+10	*Xmax*	*4*
2	*c*	*5*
100	*Iteration*	*6*
0.5	*Percent of crossover*	*7*
0.01	*Percent of mutation*	*8*
10	*Harmony memory size*	*9*
100	*New harmony memory size*	*10*
0.75	*Harmony memory*	*11*
0.05	*Pitch adjustment rate*	*12*
0.1	*Fret width*	*13*
10	*Number imperialist*	*14*

We have achieved the results by the 4 components, Best Cost, mean (mean of cost), STD (Standard Deviation) and Run time. The best cost is the one that is achieved at the end of 100th assessments to obtain the solution in that specific problem of any given algorithm. The main evaluation of the algorithm will be based on the best cost. In all 14 functions, SSPCO has the lowest cost. In functions f2, f3, f4, f5, f9, f10 and f13 the difference between SSPCO algorithm cost and other algorithms has been dramatic. In general SSPCO algorithm has the best performance among the seven famous algorithms in terms of the cost. SSPCO algorithm has a good result in terms of standard deviation which indicates that besides the algorithm had the best performance to find the optimal solution it had a good diversity as well. Running time of the algorithm within 100 evaluations was always among 5 out of 14 superior algorithms. The results of SSPCO algorithm on the basis of dimensions and different variables are presented in Tables **4** and **5**. Table **4** shows the best cost for all algorithms. Moreover, Table **5** shows the average cost in different evaluations.

Table 4. Experimental results of PSO, GA, ABC, BA, HS, ICA and SSPCO over 30 independent runs on 14 test functions of 100 variables with 100 FES.

Function	Result	PSO	GA	ABC	BA	HS	ICA	SSPCO
F1	Best Cost	26.41‡	92.65‡	924.27‡	191.29‡	945.55‡	315.16‡	3.93e-05
	Mean	116.97	237.58	2658.62	3330.31	3333.38	1400.69	124.77
	STD	261.27	497.74	409.25	297.81	294.77	672.73	288.27
	Run Time	6.30	1.04	5.27	9.46	69.45	2.04	6.01
F2	Best Cost	205.85‡	219.31‡	4212.61‡	2166.27‡	5035.52‡	2498.66‡	1.19 e-05
	Mean	3610.68	5561.85	30033.16	158842.06	168897.98	3809.22	2627.30
	STD	16503.74	23646.75	16798.83	160117.37	178617.72	1303.33	5968.96
	Run Time	27.09	11.34	25.08	106.04	108.39	21.53	28.32
F3	Best Cost	229581‡	2887569‡	38653771‡	848514‡	7944091‡	1180717‡	1.20
	Mean	6254620	13233917	185444768	251509359	256545029	32391919	8834715
	STD	17179956	38497141	35902740	60397066	60758442	30608027	17044818
	Run Time	12.85	4.53	14.73	38.33	110.76	5.70	12.89
F4	Best Cost	473.13‡	160.38‡	8040.33‡	3221.37‡	4645.07‡	3728.49‡	5.33 e-05
	Mean	2967.37	6380.46	77228.14	216888.28	238289.25	6545.48	2703.78
	STD	10531.40	26471.95	40322.37	240474.74	279534.85	1016.66	6698.88
	Run Time	25.01	10.26	23.73	110.22	123.65	24.44	26.16
F5	Best Cost	1.89‡	2.14‡	9.17‡	7.50‡	7.69‡	8.59‡	0.00017
	Mean	2.60	2.92	9.89	9.89	9.90	9.07	1.39
	STD	1.22	1.82	0.10	0.11	0.08	0.20	1.95
	Run Time	7.40	1.71	6.53	17.83	82.57	3.26	6.74
	‡	5	5	5	5	5	5	
	†	0	0	0	0	0	0	
	§	0	0	0	0	0	0	

(Table 4) cont.....

F6	Best Cost	7312.05‡	28652.70‡	5780584.9‡	136091.47‡	2884928.2‡	409932.53‡	99.00
	Mean	173389.2	654985.6	14845029	20156460	20149319	6375948.3	221636.9
	STD	920134.0	2692011	3099406	2667490	2716132	3613297	980107.8
	Run Time	6.06	0.97	4.95	10.22	70.59	1.76	5.74
F7	Best Cost	0.41‡	0.63‡	1.30‡	1.05‡	1.24‡	1.08‡	6.68e-08
	Mean	0.66	0.90	1.66	1.83	1.83	1.35	0.43
	STD	0.27	0.17	0.09	0.07	0.07	0.16	0.48
	Run Time	7.43	1.20	5.68	12.63	76.04	2.46	6.52
F8	Best Cost	4.50‡	4.94‡	11.89‡	6.60‡	10.79‡	8.99‡	0.0017
	Mean	5.21	5.79	14.33	15.39	15.39	12.62	3.30
	STD	1.69	2.12	0.61	0.33	0.33	1.11	3.37
	Run Time	6.52	1.19	5.13	13.13	68.12	2.45	6.23
F9	Best Cost	535.85‡	621.44‡	2271.52‡	736.17‡	1820.48‡	1263.01‡	0.012
	Mean	1015.22	997.72	3503.70	4335.84	4329.21	2528.08	771.56
	STD	419.14	583.42	457.35	309.91	305.16	556.33	665.56
	Run Time	6.24	1.01	4.95	11.45	72.87	1.97	5.68
F10	Best Cost	477.59‡	622.81‡	2179.64‡	796.56‡	1886.28‡	1423.63‡	8.41e-05
	Mean	955.75	988.61	3496.23	4321.29	4324.2	2415.03	655.19
	STD	447.00	588.10	435.53	312.74	296.78	505.96	626.74
	Run Time	7.63	1.58	6.17	16.54	70.72	3.19	7.16
F11	Best Cost	0.48‡	0.59‡	1.34‡	1.03‡	1.20‡	1.07‡	6.44e-09
	Mean	0.70	0.85	1.63	1.83	1.83	1.30	0.45
	STD	0.24	0.19	0.10	0.07	0.07	0.17	0.49
	Run Time	9.04	2.58	8.98	29.38	78.26	6.19	10.36

(Table 4) cont.....

F12	Best Cost	18.00‡	34.53‡	22.54‡	9.19‡	29.11‡	14.85‡	5.15e-05
	Mean	30.01	42.11	39.48	49.13	48.75	26.85	36.92
	STD	13.48	3.17	6.96	3.25	2.80	7.30	27.23
	Run Time	42.64	19.10	40.91	192.98	141.16	37.46	42.64
	‡	7	7	7	7	7	7	
	†	0	0	0	0	0	0	
	§	0	0	0	0	0	0	
F13	Best Cost	855.62‡	10482‡	230902350‡	1082214‡	17143008‡	22333320‡	45.99
	Mean	10000343	64048235	1855030148	285121961	290002582	571645970	24690423
	STD	87680349	344360683	699959131	579378814	560805949	457465377	173990551
	Run Time	32.69	14.60	31.77	145.75	117.30	27.85	32.00
F14	Best Cost	0.0019‡	0.0097‡	0.0097‡	0.0023‡	0.0097‡	0.0097‡	8.37e-07
	Mean	0.36	0.04	0.45	0.48	0.48	0.01	0.40
	STD	0.33	0.096	0.29	0.31	0.31	0.0039	0.34
	Run Time	6.53	1.03	5.49	11.61	76.82	1.90	6.35
	‡	2	2	2	2	2	2	
	†	0	0	0	0	0	0	
	§	0	0	0	0	0	0	
	‡	14	14	14	14	14	14	
	†	0	0	0	0	0	0	
	§	0	0	0	0	0	0	

Fig. (**9**) shows the population distribution of the algorithms in different iterations.

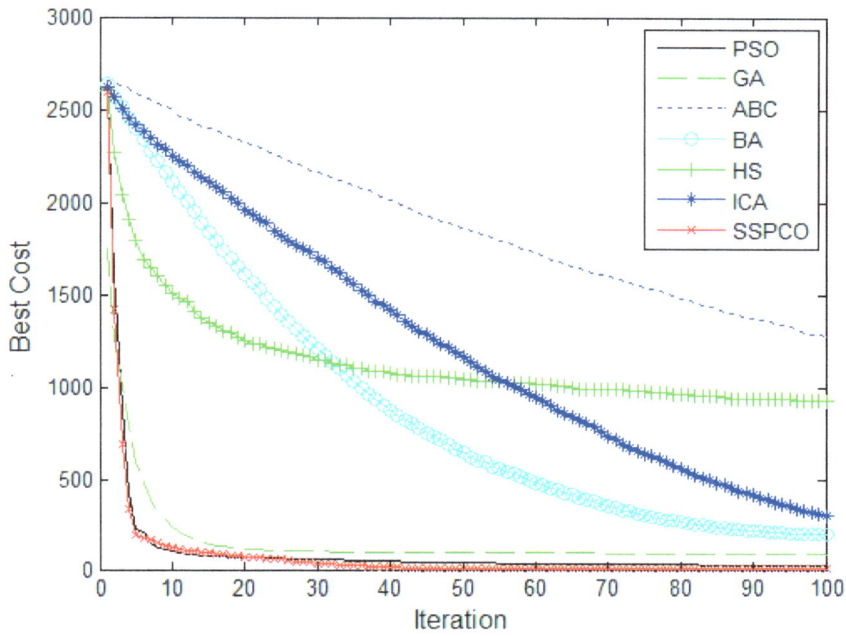

(a)

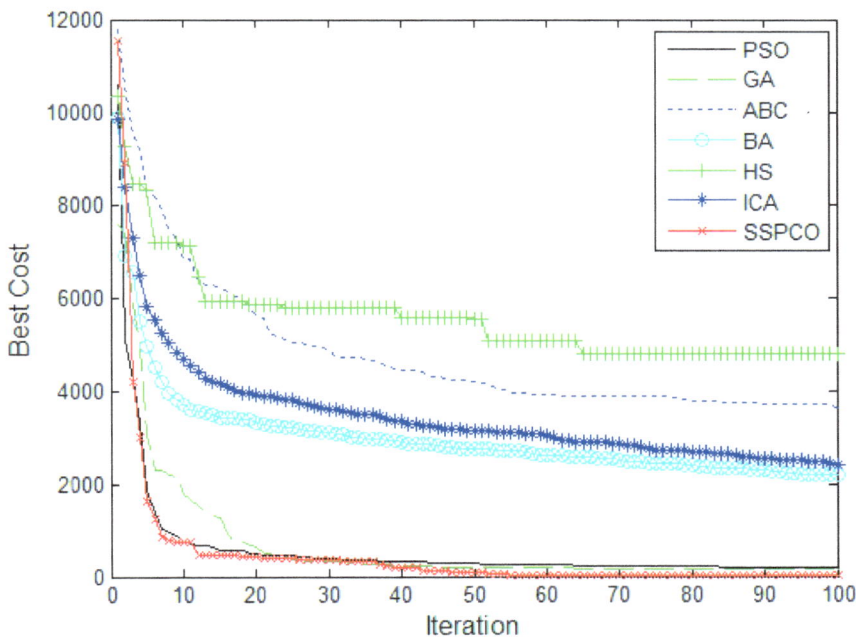

(b)

Fig. 9 cont.....

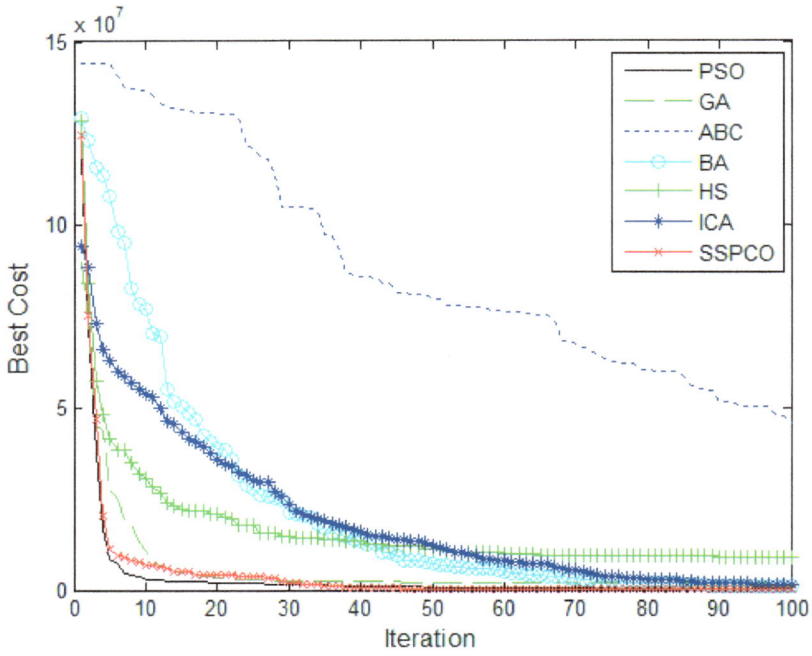

(c)

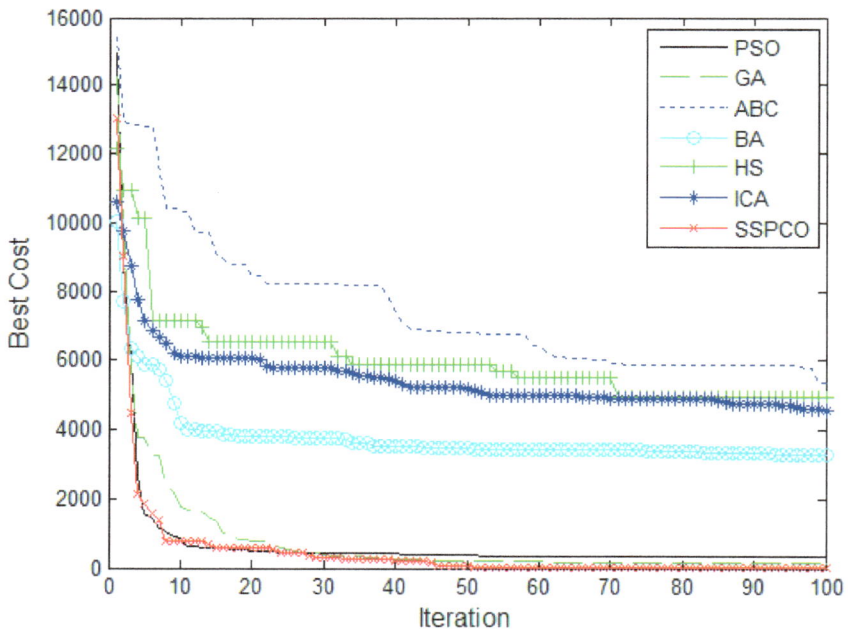

(d)

Fig. 9 cont.....

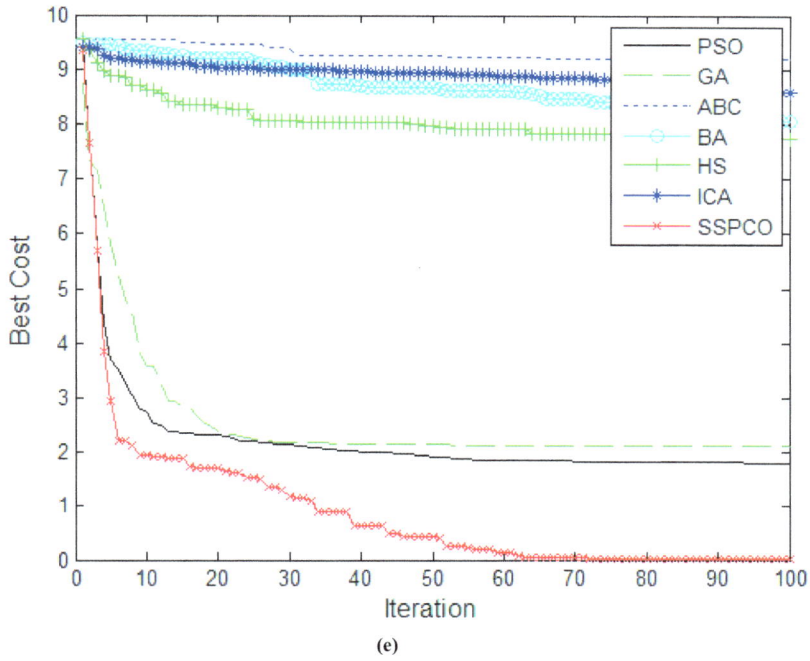

(e)

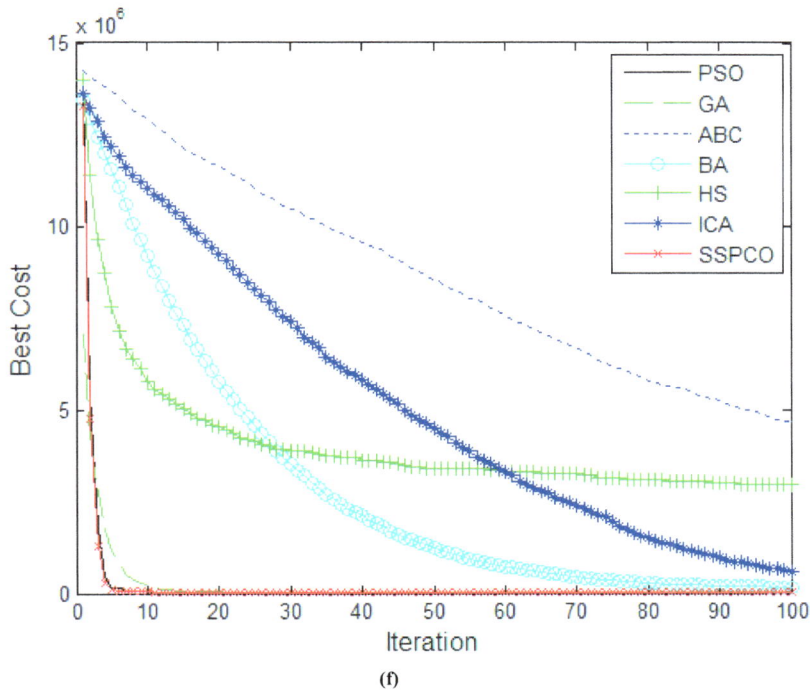

(f)

Fig. 9 cont.....

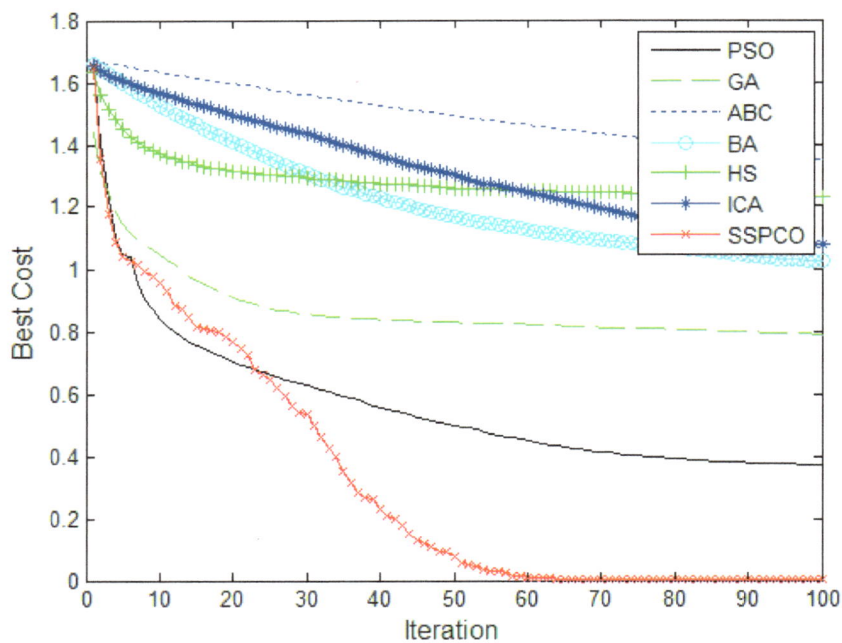

(g)

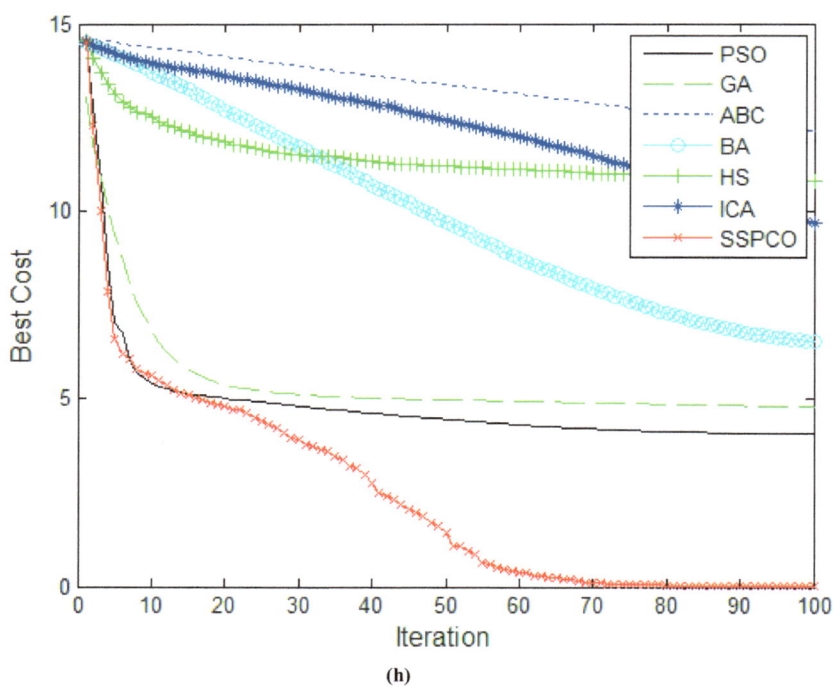

(h)

Fig. 9 cont.....

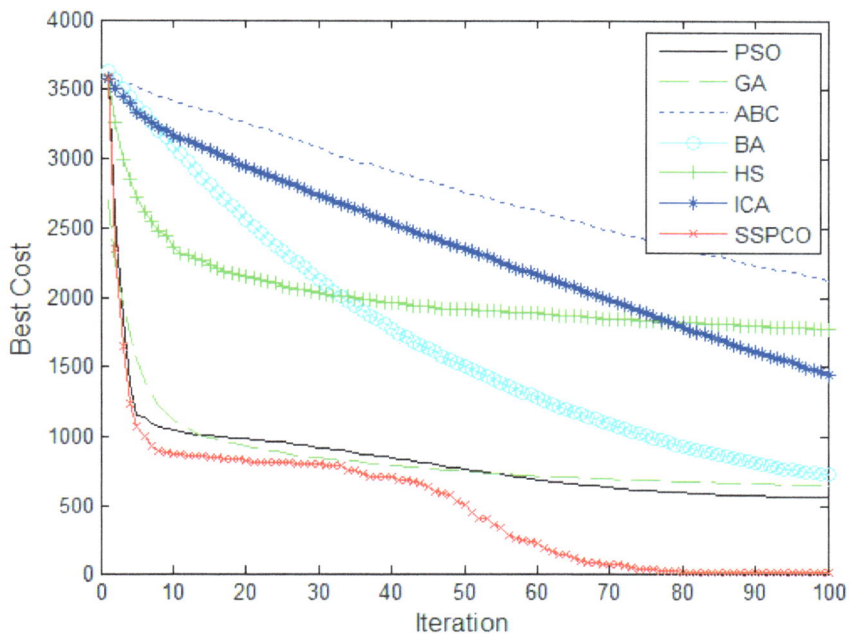

(i)

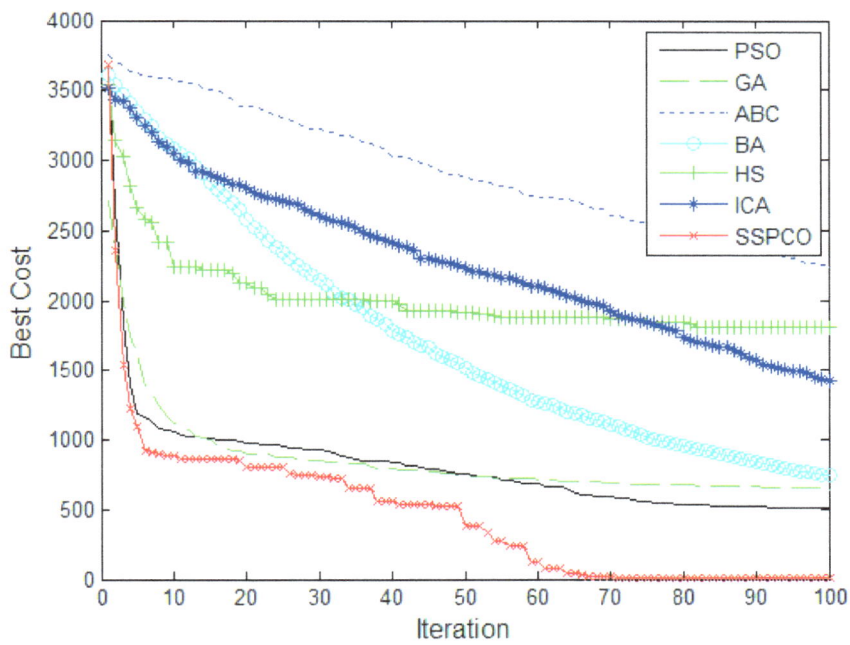

(j)

Fig. 9 cont.....

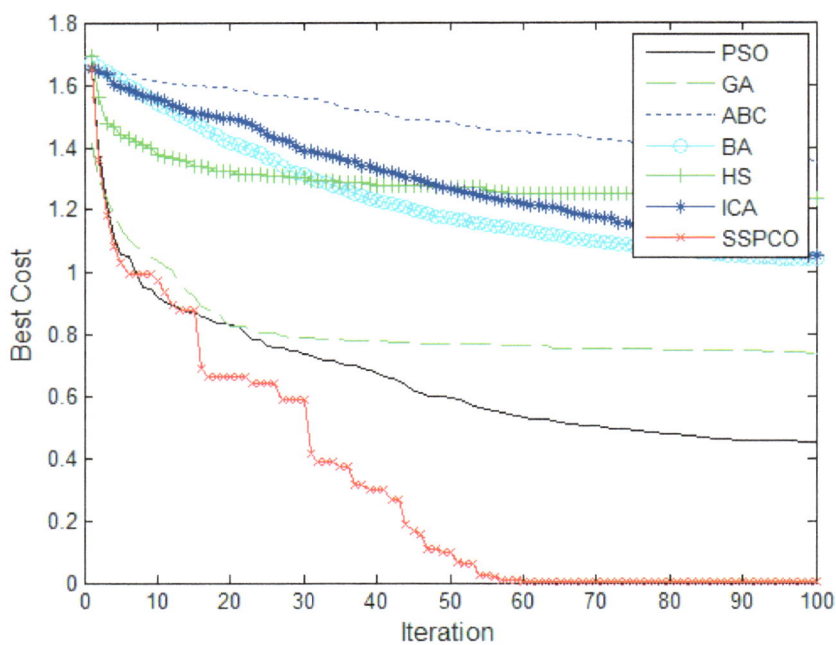

(k)

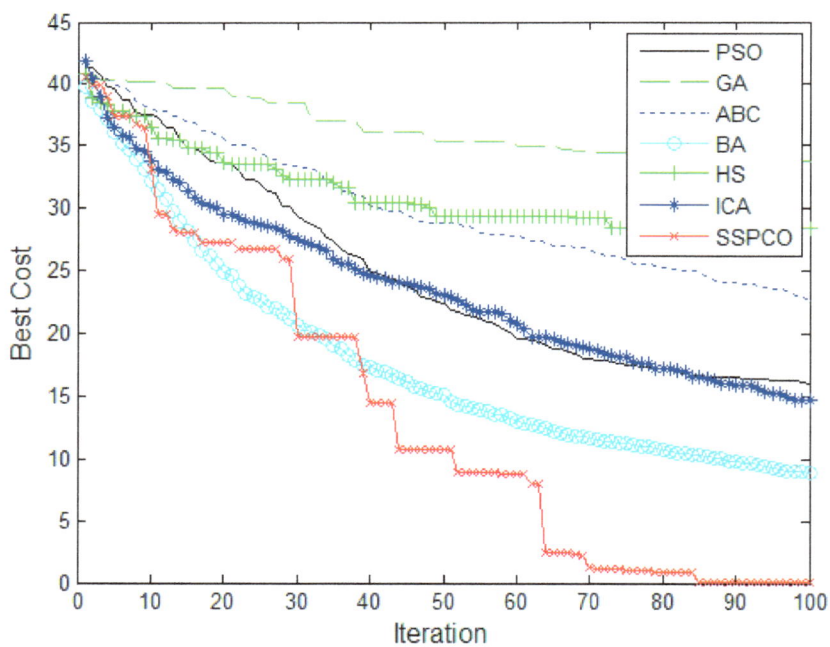

(l)

Fig. 9 cont.....

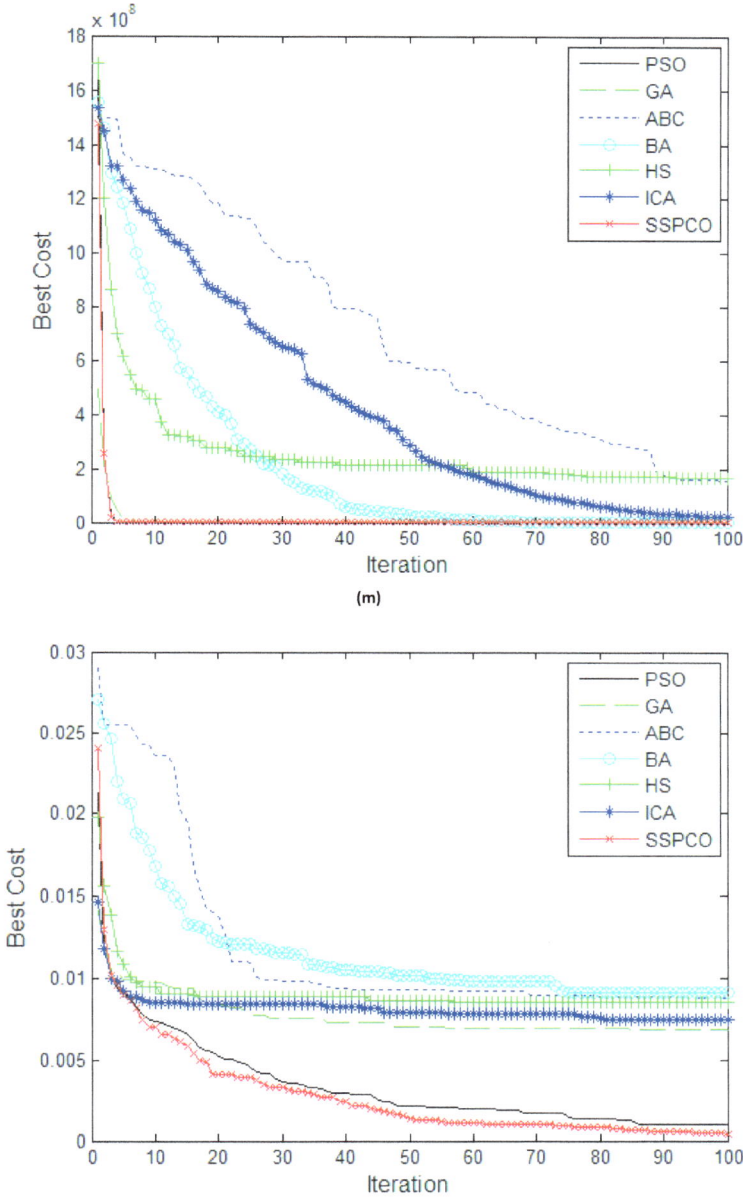

Fig. (9). Evolution of the mean function standard deviation derived from PSO, GA, ABC, BA, HS, ICA and SSPCO *versus* the number of FES on 14 test problems. (**a**) F1. (**b**) F2.(**c**) F3. (**d**) F4. (**e**) F5. (**f**) F6. (**g**) F7. (**h**) F8. (**i**) F9. (**j**) F10. (**k**) F11. (**l**) F12. (**m**) F13. (**n**) F14.

Fig. (**10**) shows the average of the best cost of populations in different iterations.

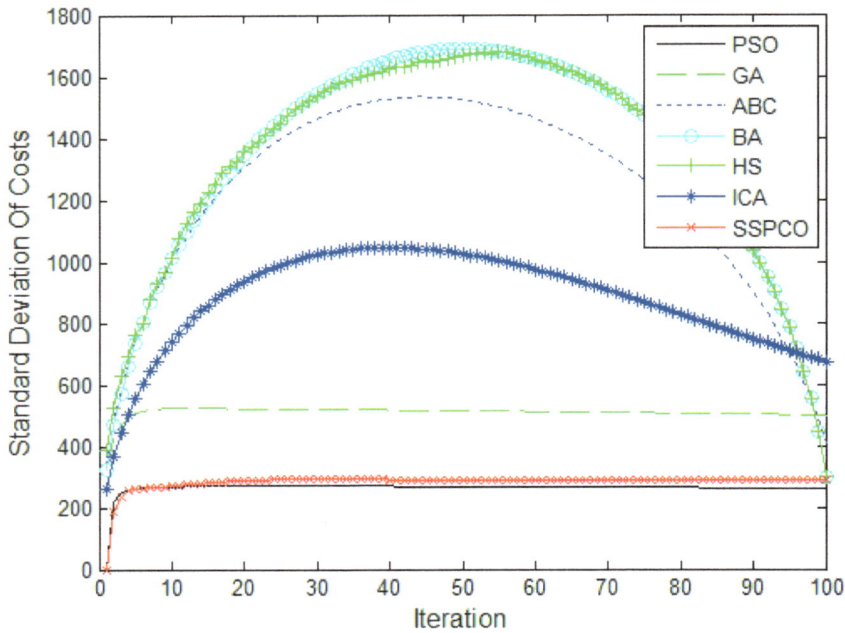

(a)

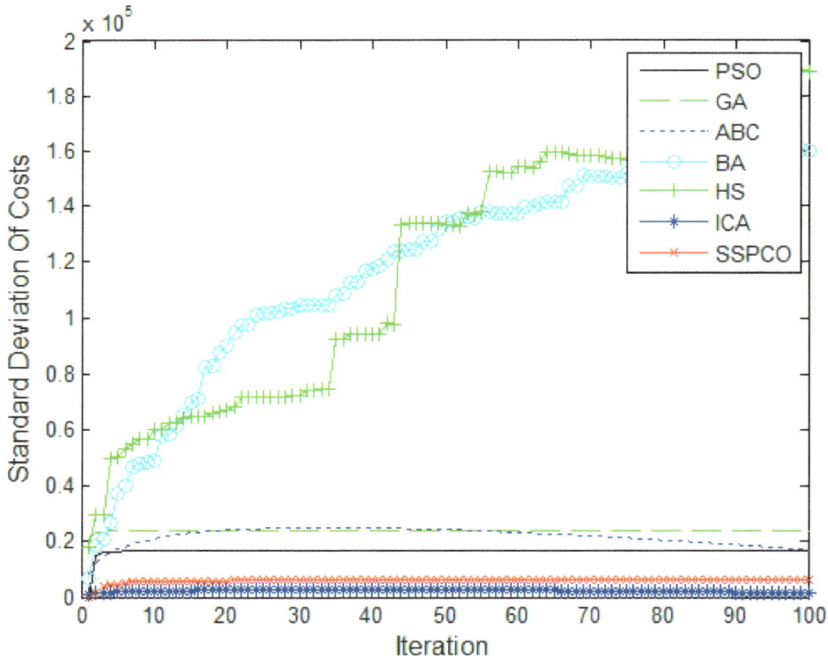

(b)

Fig. 10 cont.....

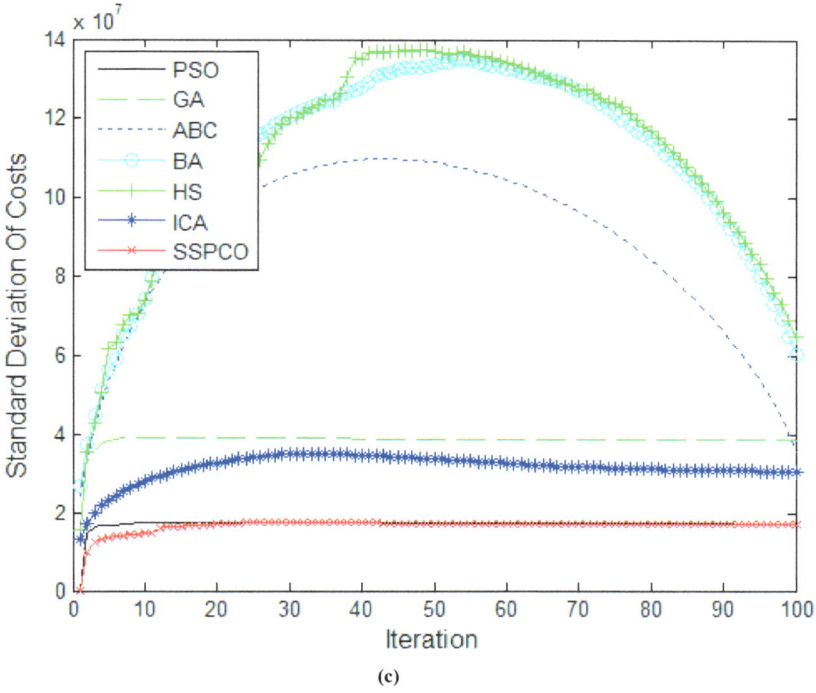

(c)

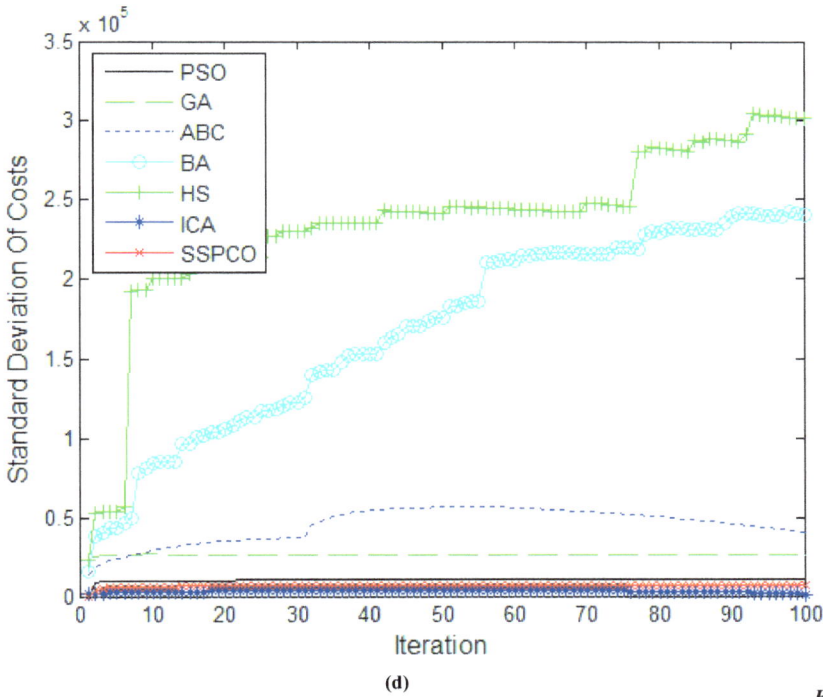

(d)

Fig. 10 cont.....

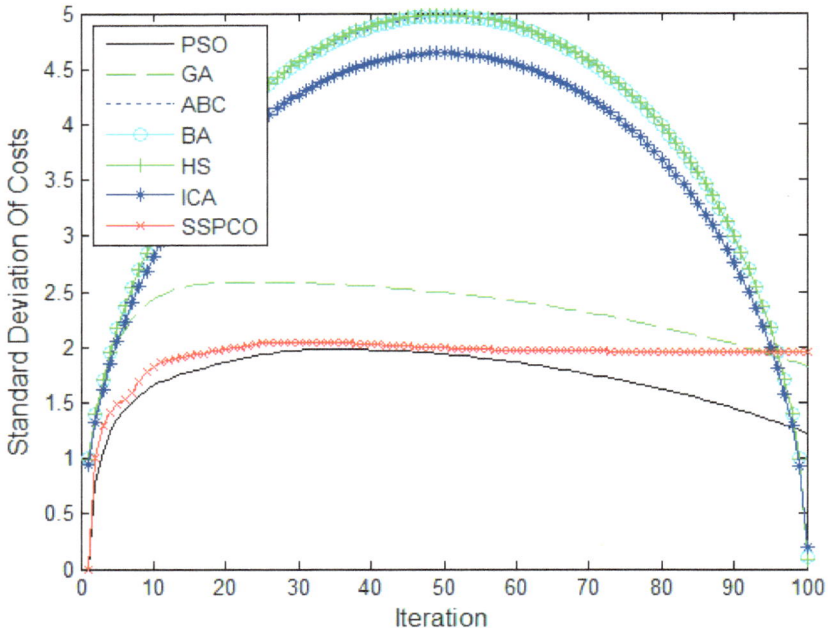

(e)

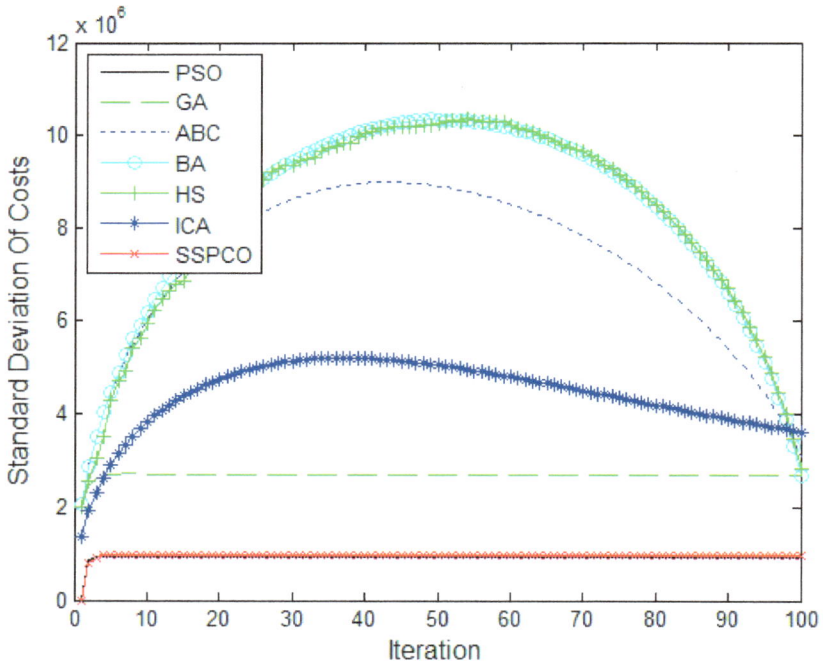

(f)

Fig. 10 cont.....

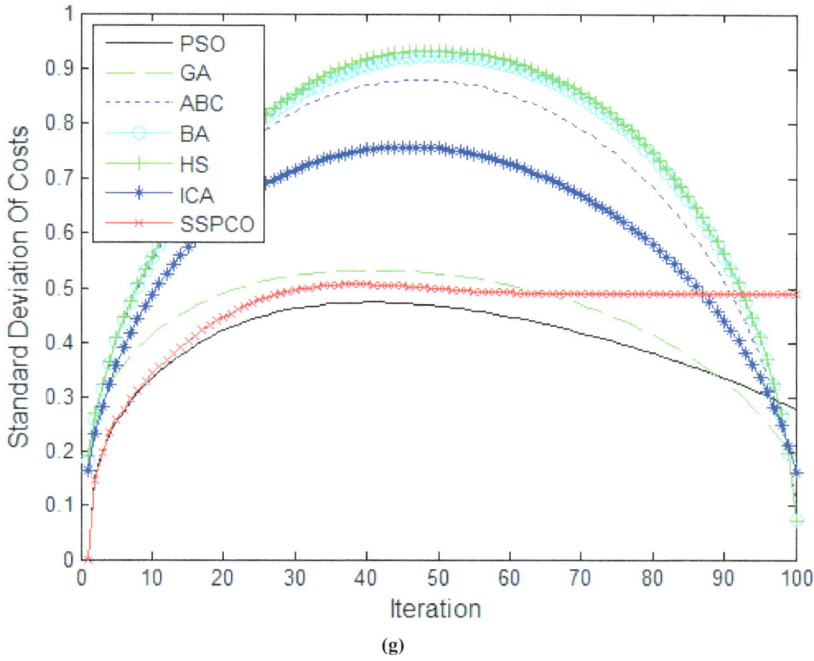

(g)

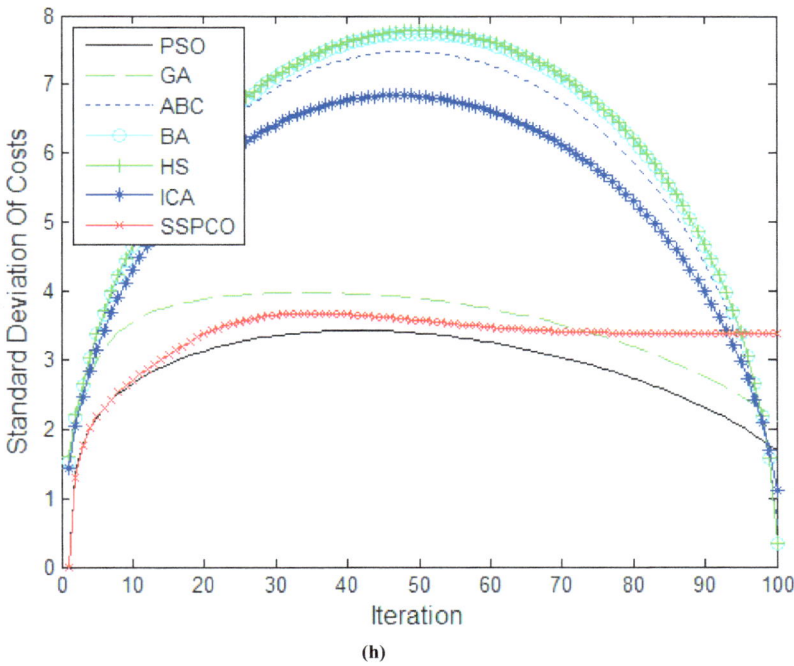

(h)

Fig. 10 cont.....

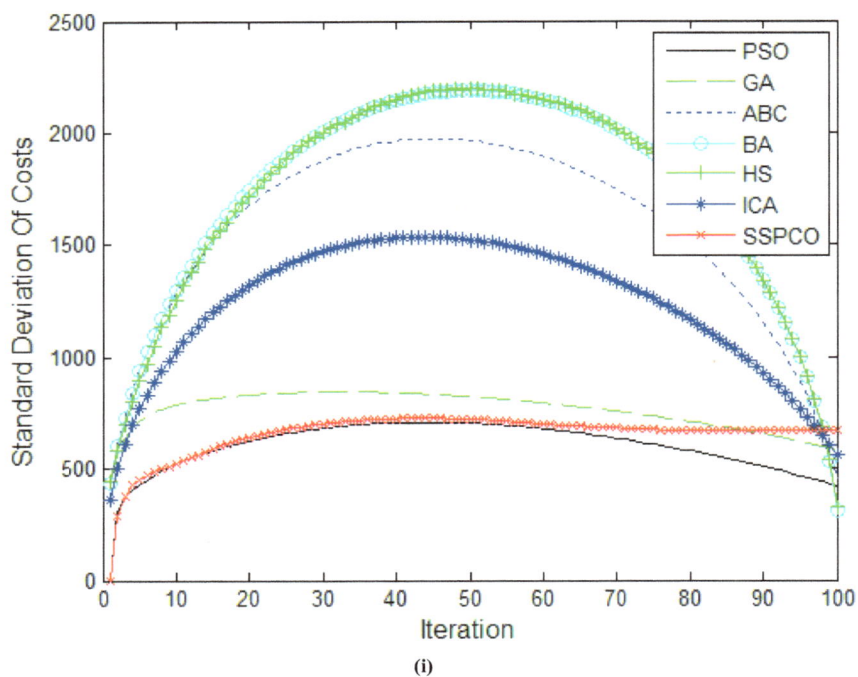

(i)

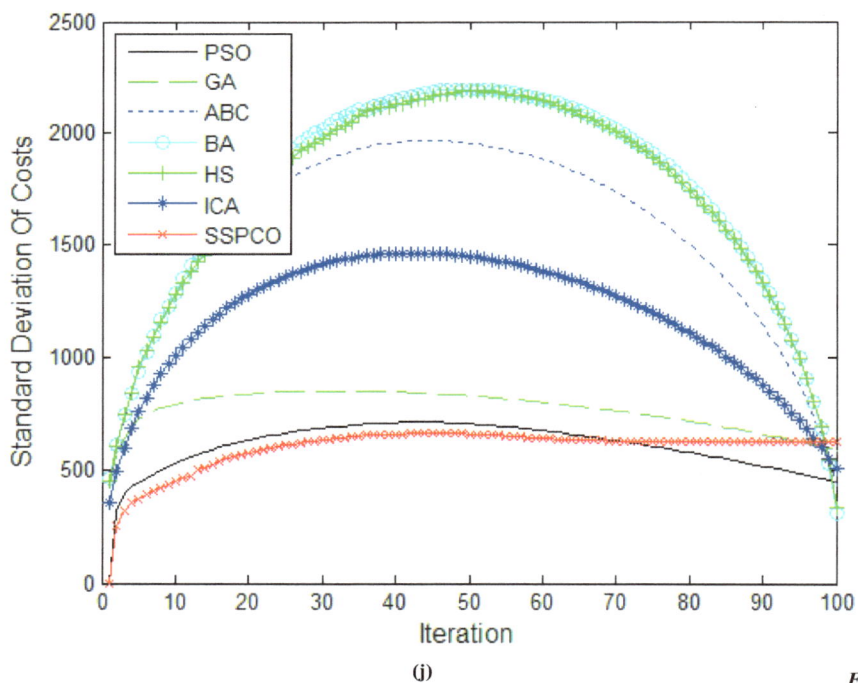

(j)

Fig. 10 cont.....

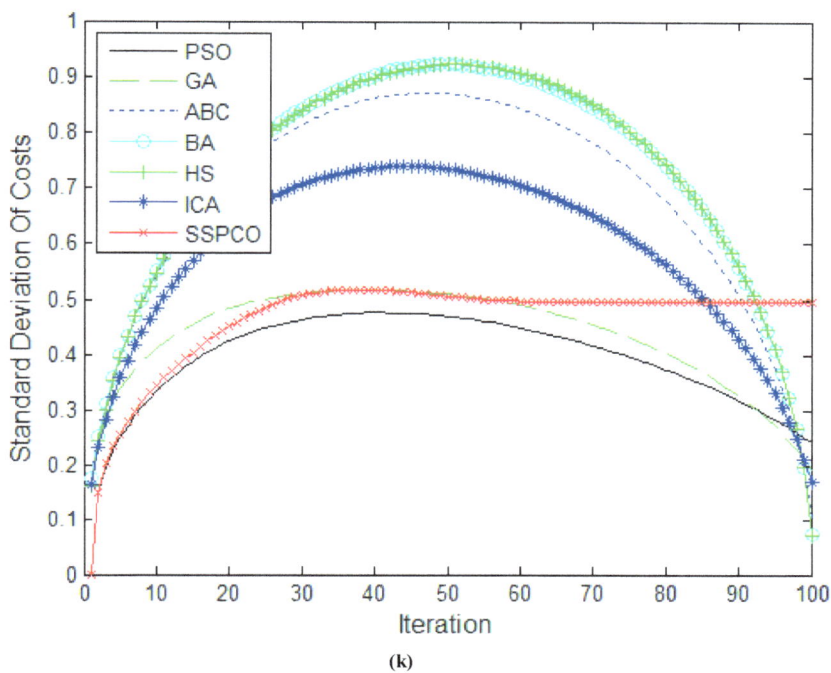

(k)

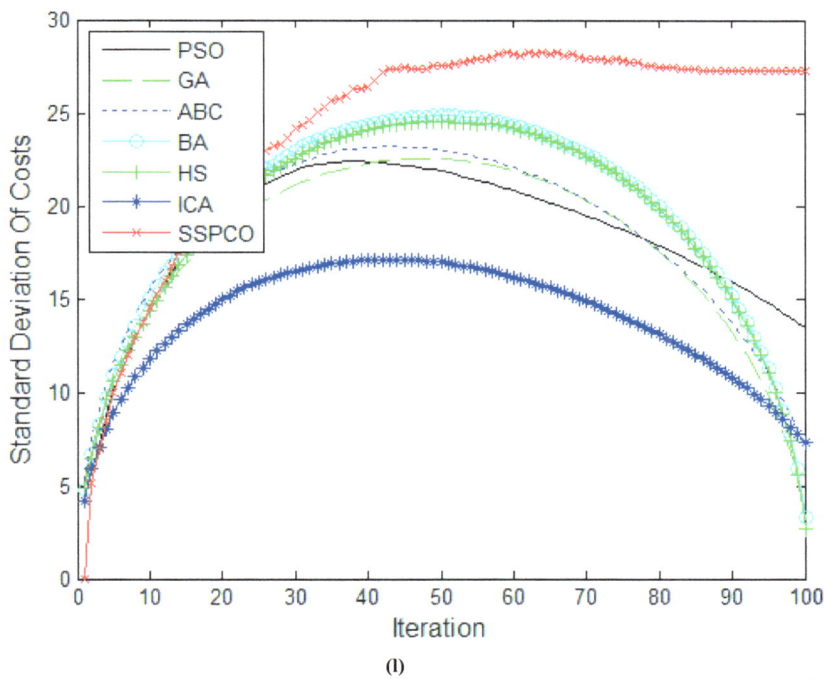

(l)

Fig. 10 cont.....

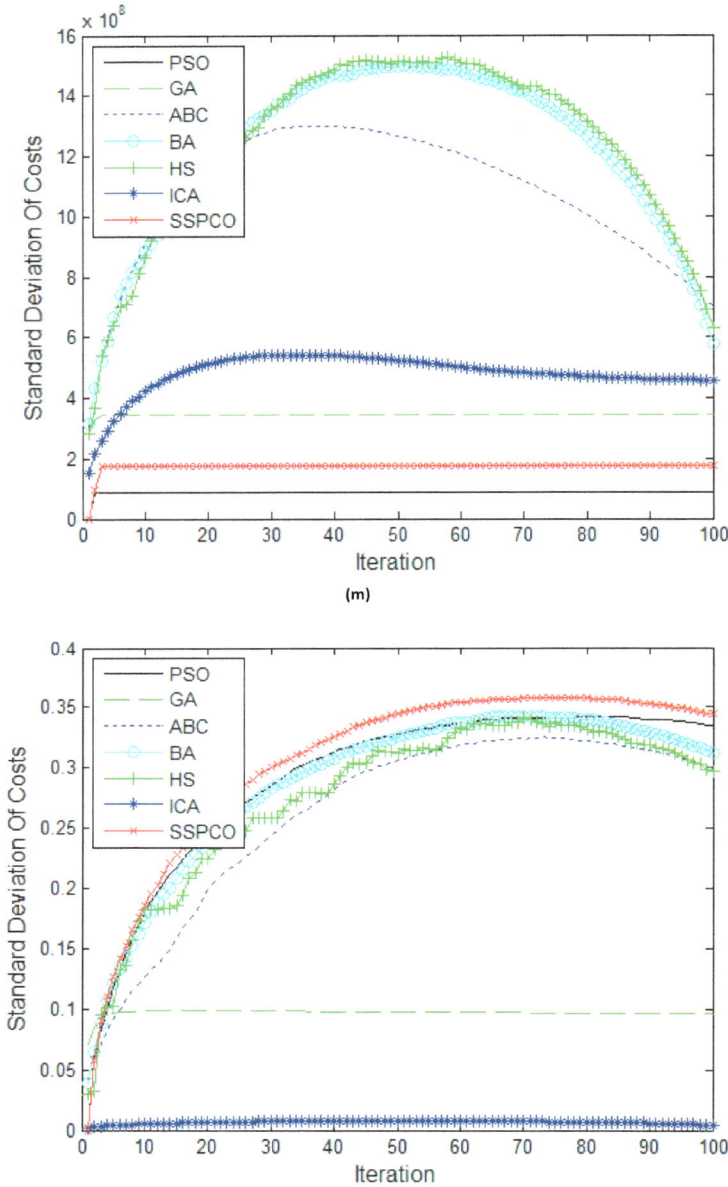

Fig. (10). Evolution of the mean function mean of cost derived from PSO, GA, ABC, BA, HS, ICA and SSPCO *versus* the number of FES on 14 test problems. (**a**) F1. (**b**) F2.(**c**) F3. (**d**) F4. (**e**) F5. (**f**) F6. (**g**) F7. (**h**) F8. (**i**) F9. (**j**) F10. (**k**) F11. (**l**) F12. (**m**) F13. (**n**) F14.

Fig. (**11**) shows the average of the best cost of populations in different iterations.

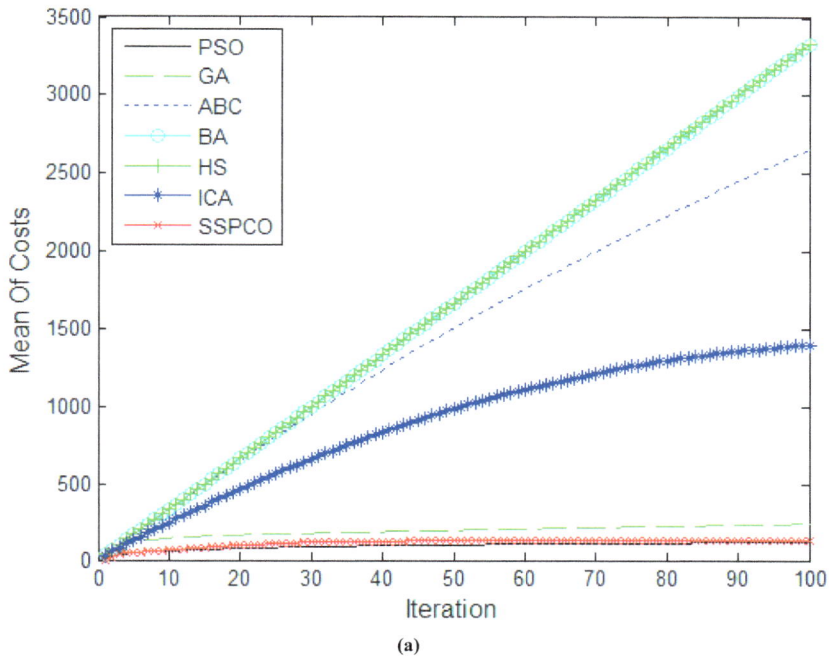

(a)

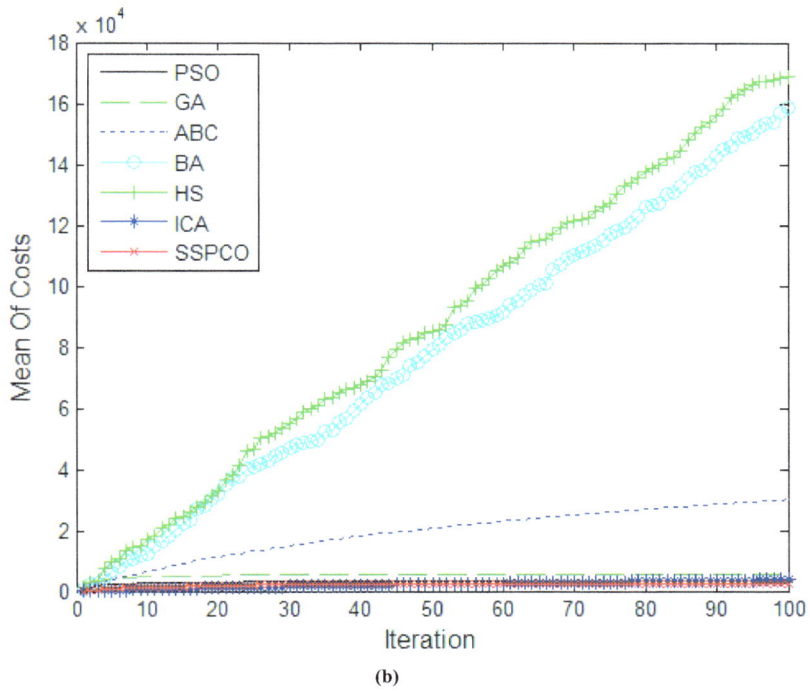

(b)

Fig. 11 cont.....

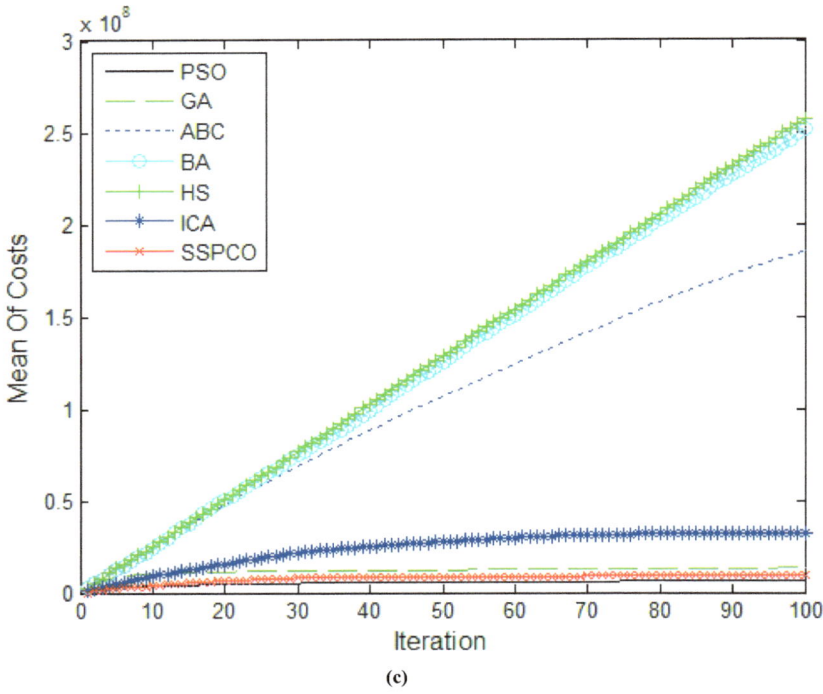

(c)

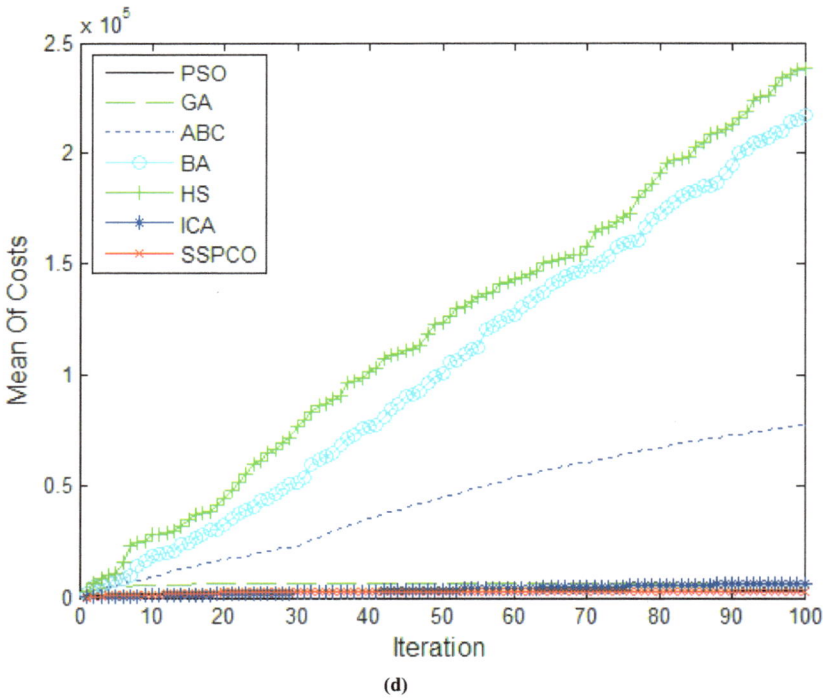

(d)

Fig. 11 cont.....

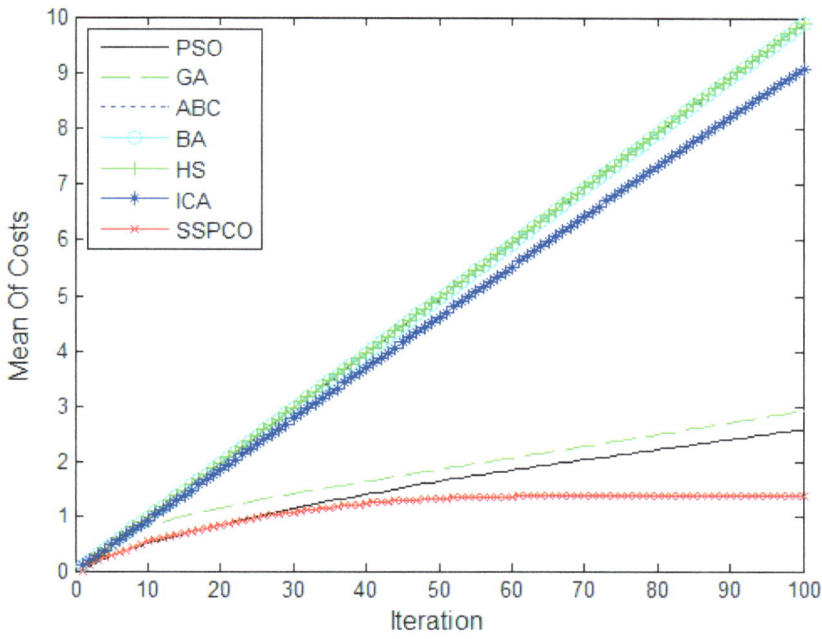

(e)

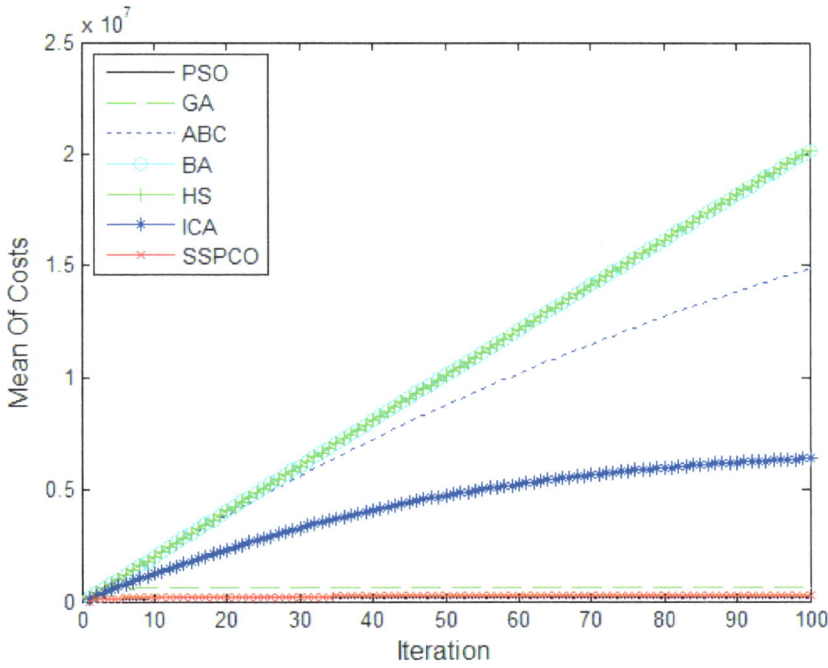

(f)

Fig. 11 cont.....

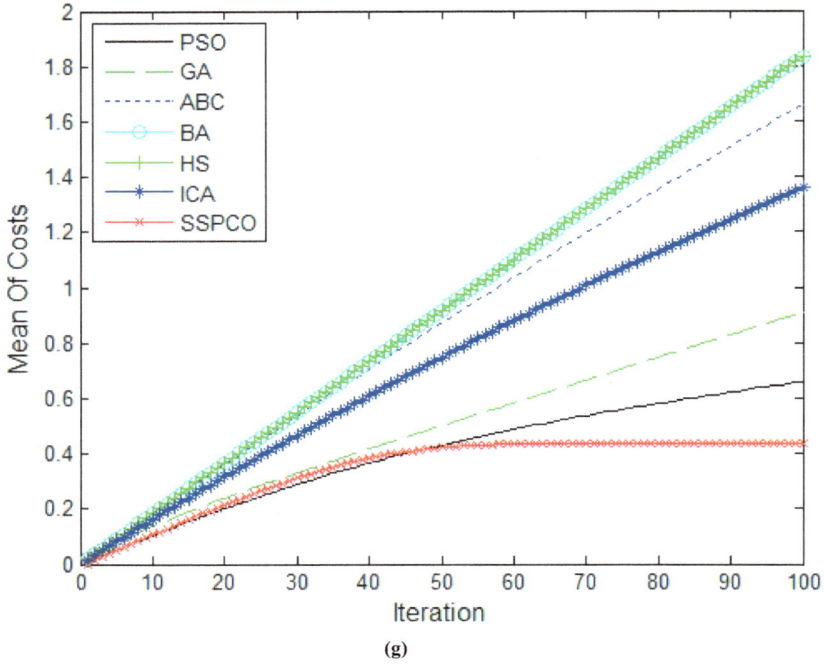

(g)

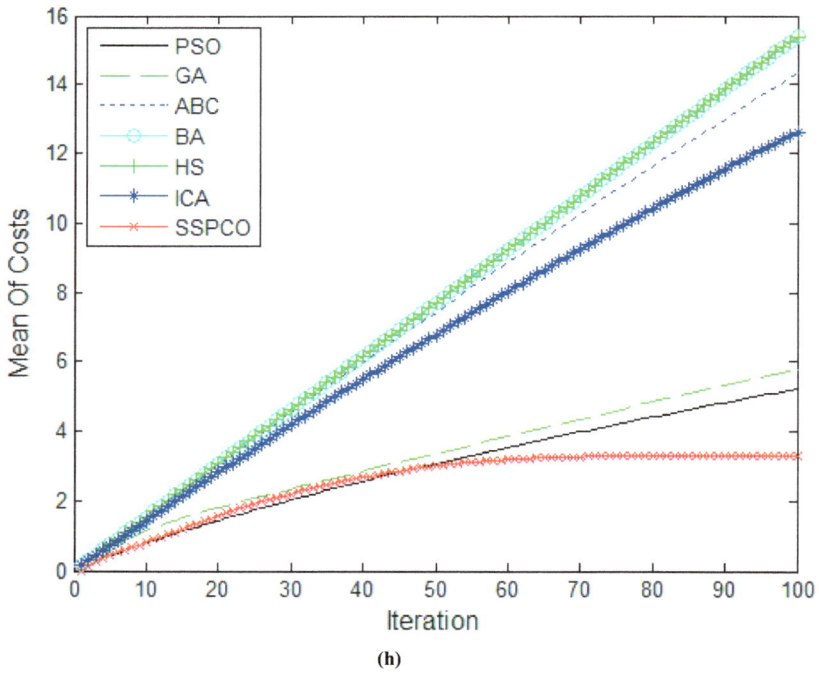

(h)

Fig. 11 cont.....

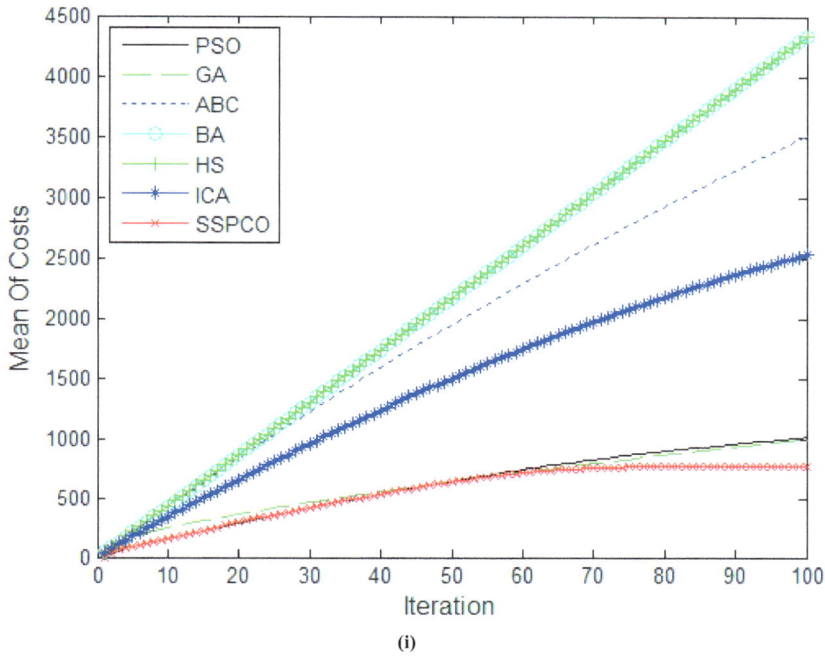

(i)

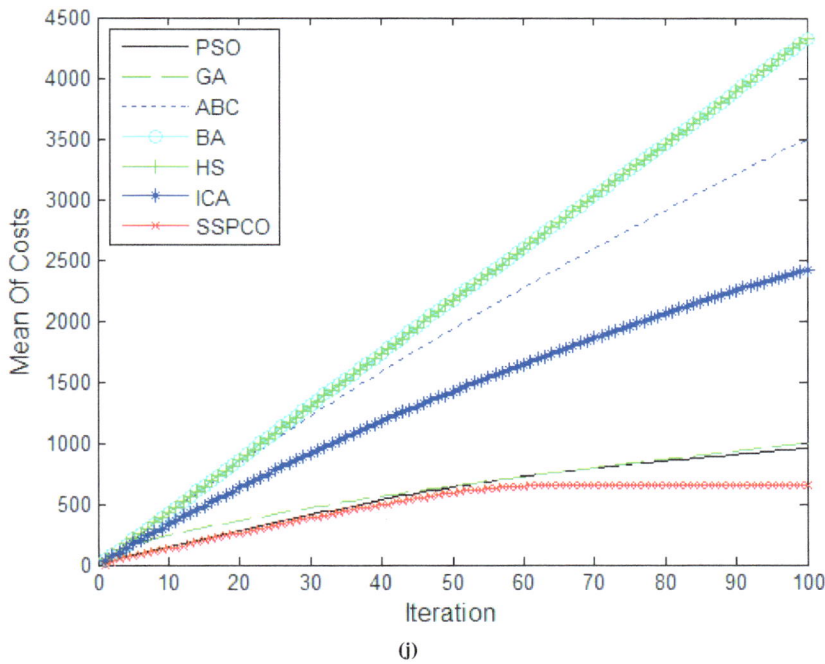

(j)

Fig. 11 cont.....

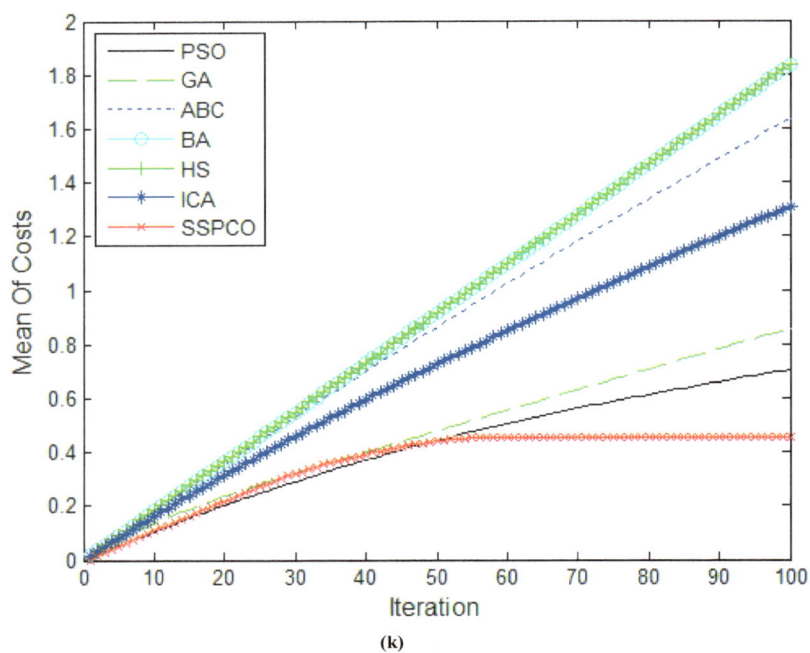

(k)

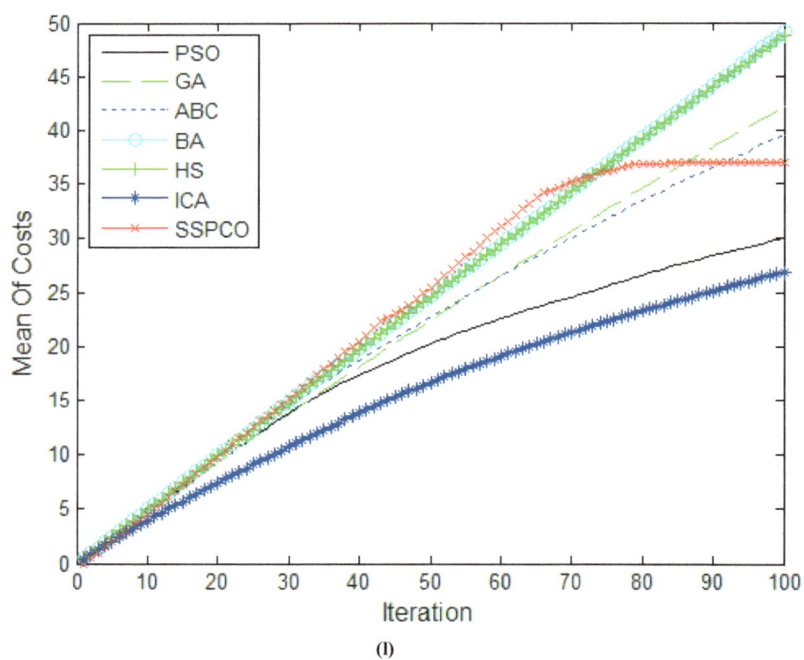

(l)

Fig. 11 cont.....

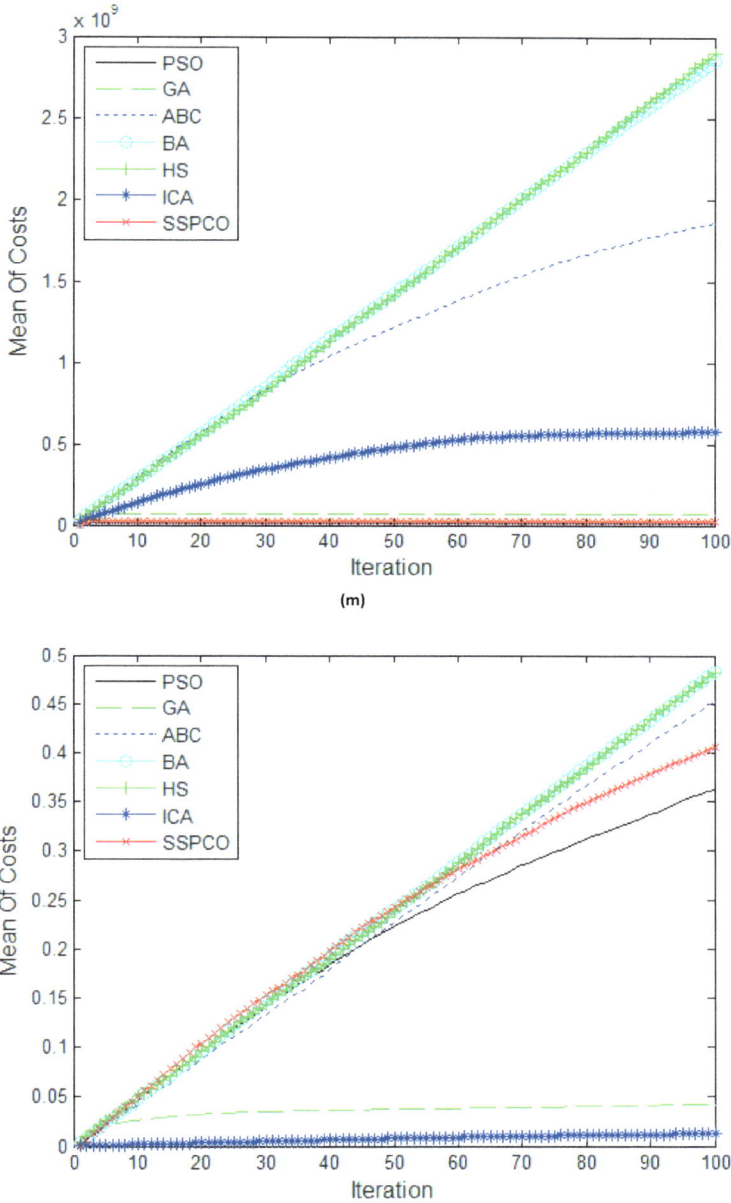

Fig. (11). Evolution of the mean function mean of cost derived from PSO, GA, ABC, BA, HS, ICA and SSPCO *versus* the number of FES on 14 test problems. (**a**) F1. (**b**) F2.(**c**) F3. (**d**) F4. (**e**) F5. (**f**) F6. (**g**) F7. (**h**) F8. (**i**) F9. (**j**) F10. (**k**) F11. (**l**) F12. (**m**) F13. (**n**) F14.

Fig. (**12**) shows the execution time of the algorithms in the specified iteration.

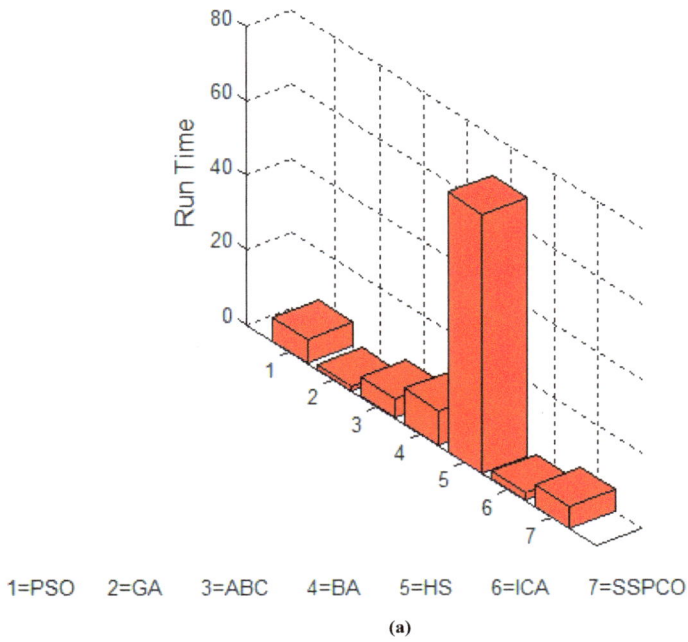

1=PSO   2=GA   3=ABC   4=BA   5=HS   6=ICA   7=SSPCO

(a)

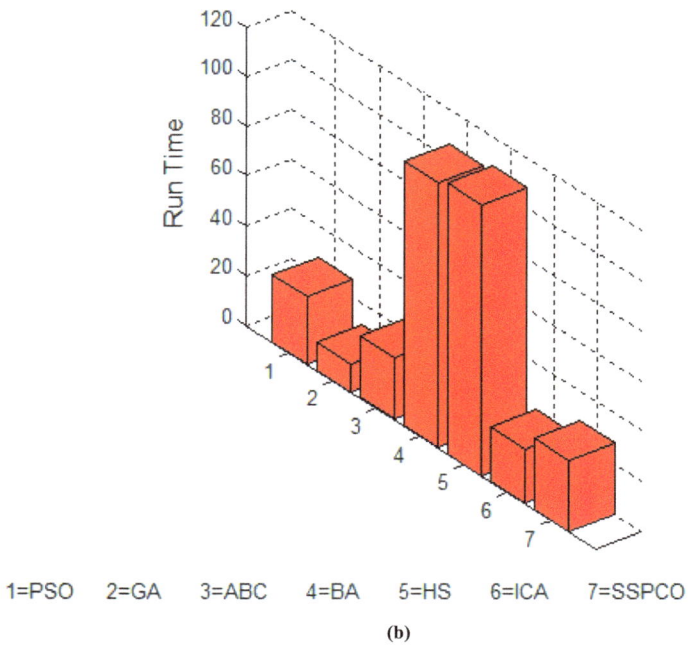

1=PSO   2=GA   3=ABC   4=BA   5=HS   6=ICA   7=SSPCO

(b)

Fig. 12 cont.....

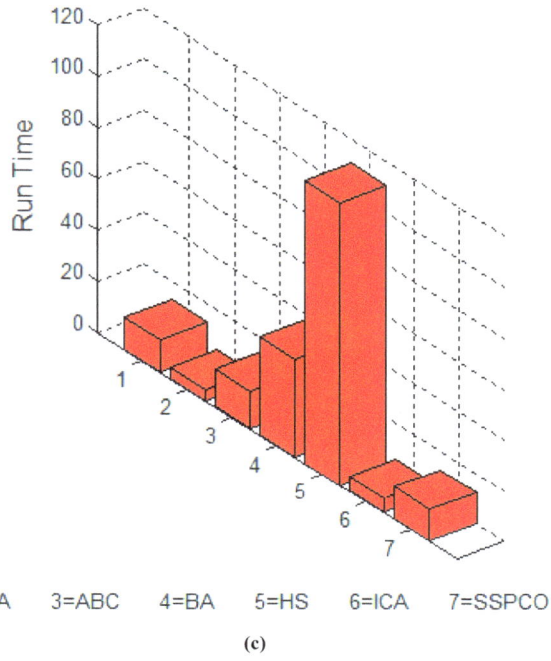

1=PSO   2=GA   3=ABC   4=BA   5=HS   6=ICA   7=SSPCO

(c)

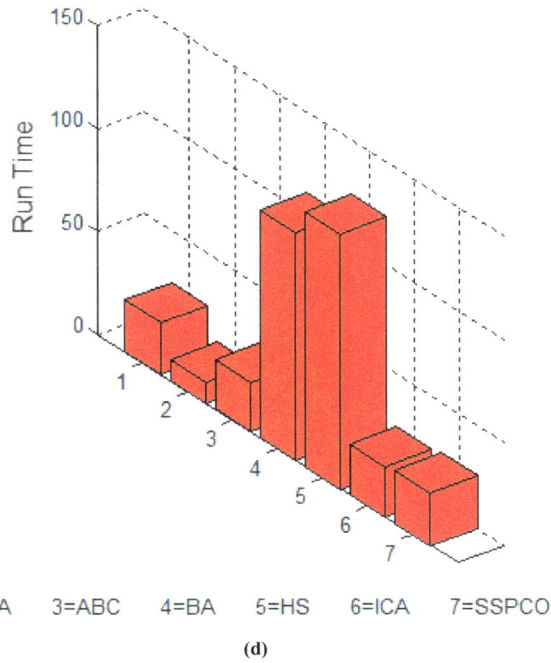

1=PSO   2=GA   3=ABC   4=BA   5=HS   6=ICA   7=SSPCO

(d)

Fig. 12 cont.....

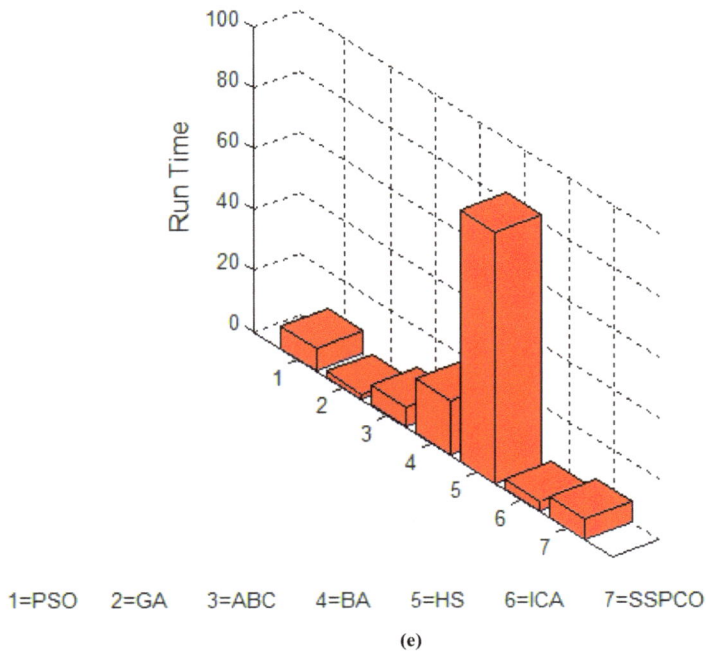

1=PSO   2=GA   3=ABC   4=BA   5=HS   6=ICA   7=SSPCO

(e)

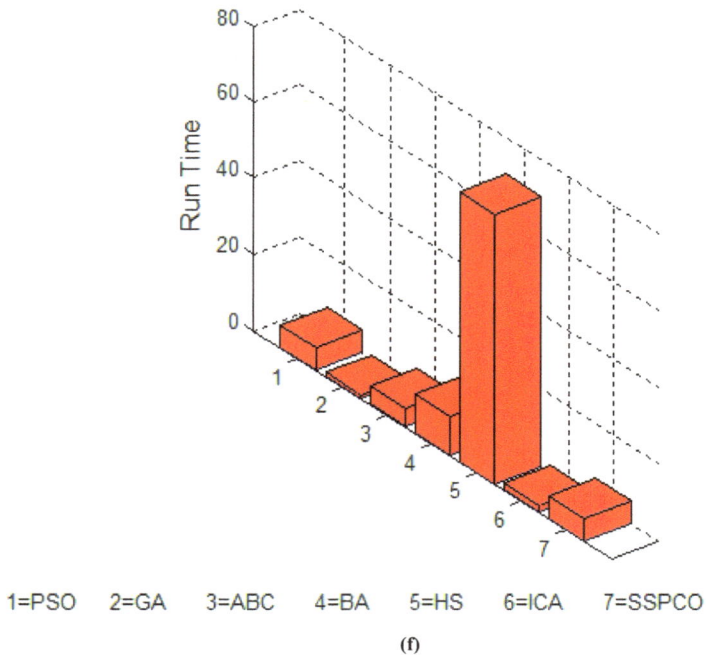

1=PSO   2=GA   3=ABC   4=BA   5=HS   6=ICA   7=SSPCO

(f)

Fig. 12 cont.....

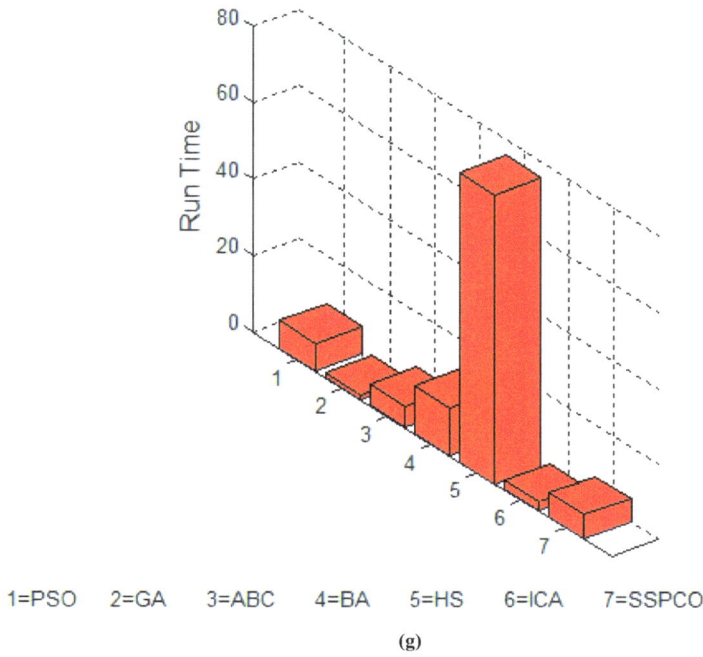

(g)

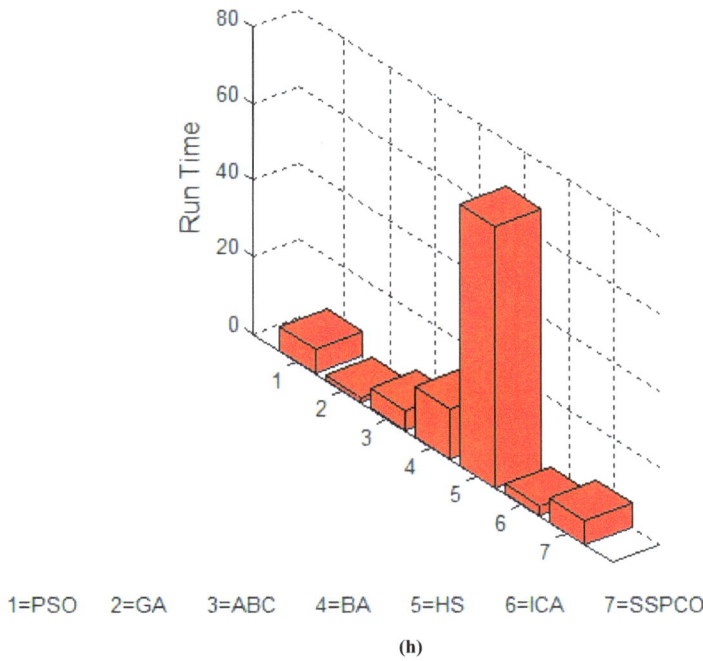

(h)

Fig. 12 cont.....

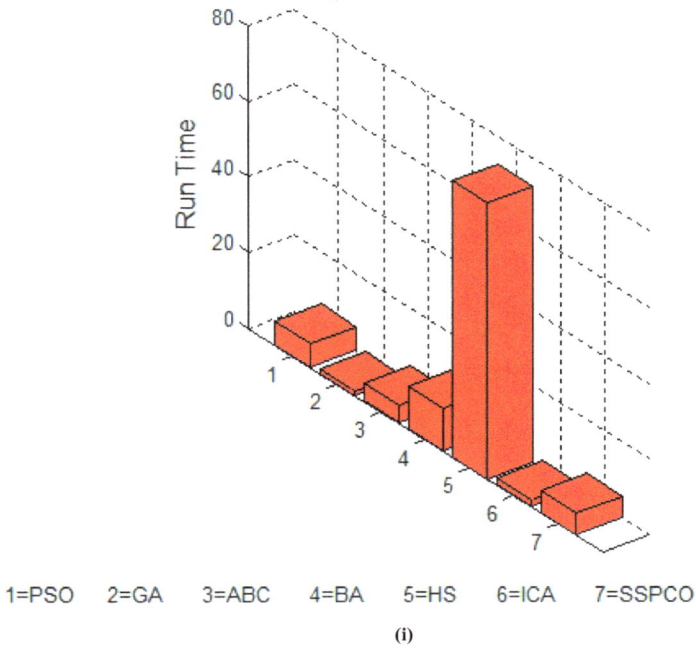

1=PSO   2=GA   3=ABC   4=BA   5=HS   6=ICA   7=SSPCO

(i)

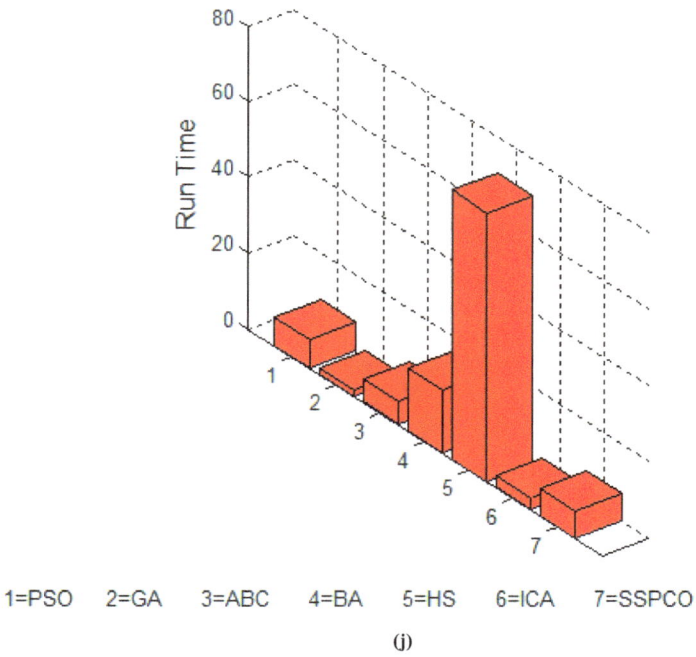

1=PSO   2=GA   3=ABC   4=BA   5=HS   6=ICA   7=SSPCO

(j)

Fig. 12 cont.....

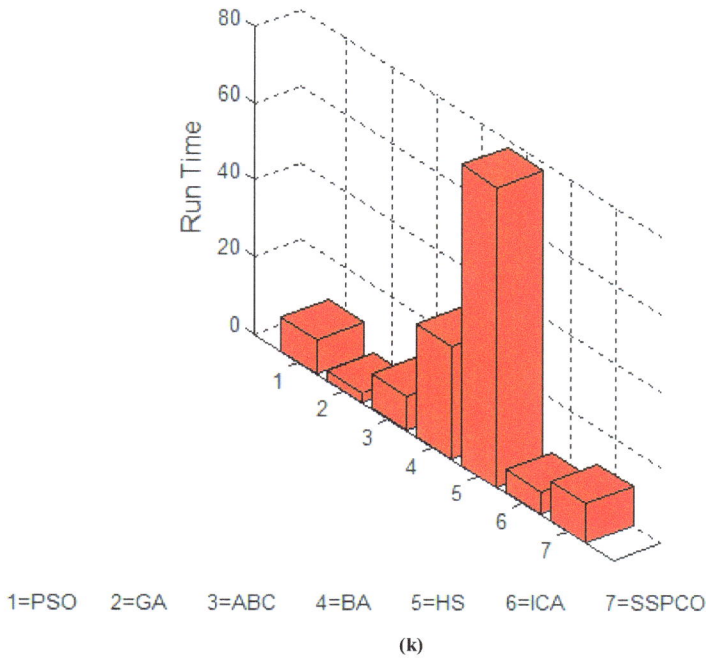

1=PSO   2=GA   3=ABC   4=BA   5=HS   6=ICA   7=SSPCO

(k)

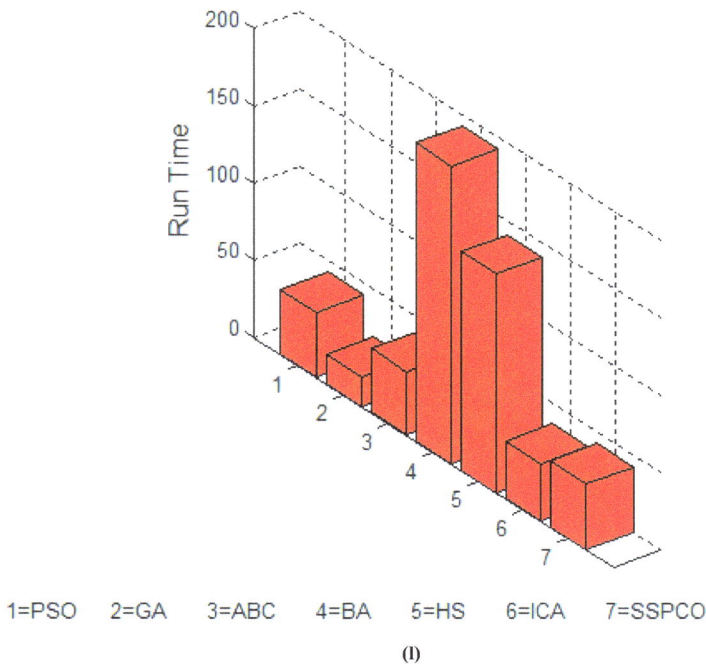

1=PSO   2=GA   3=ABC   4=BA   5=HS   6=ICA   7=SSPCO

(l)

Fig. 12 cont.....

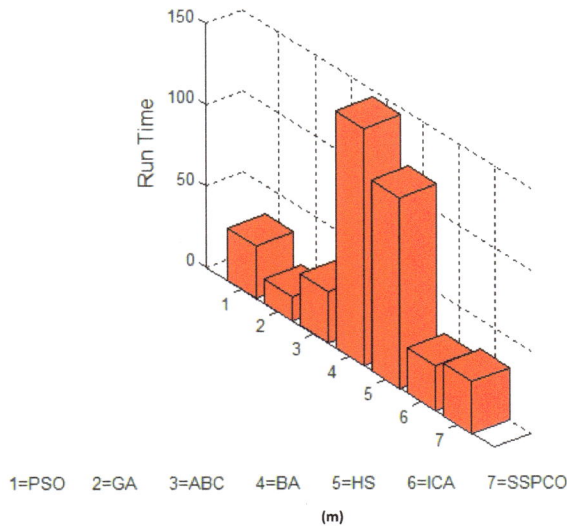

1=PSO   2=GA   3=ABC   4=BA   5=HS   6=ICA   7=SSPCO

(m)

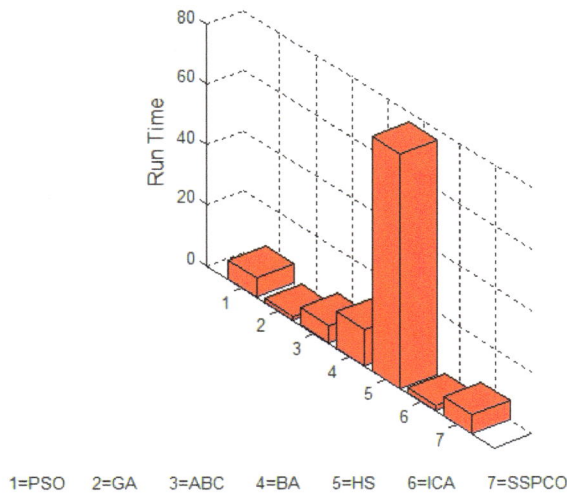

1=PSO   2=GA   3=ABC   4=BA   5=HS   6=ICA   7=SSPCO

Fig. (12). Evolution of the mean function run time derived from PSO, GA, ABC, BA, HS, ICA and SSPCO *versus* the number of FES on 14 test problems. (**a**) F1. (**b**) F2.(**c**) F3. (**d**) F4. (**e**) F5. (**f**) F6. (**g**) F7. (**h**) F8. (**i**) F9. (**j**) F10. (**k**) F11. (**l**) F12. (**m**) F13. (**n**) F14.

Fig. (**13**) represents the best population in the various evaluations. Fig. (**14**) also shows the best population in different dimensions.

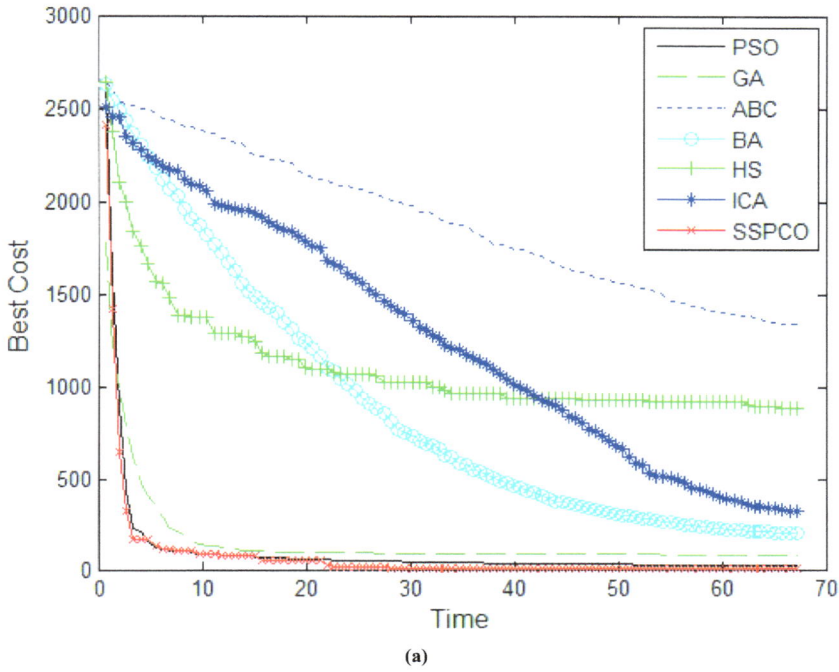

(a)

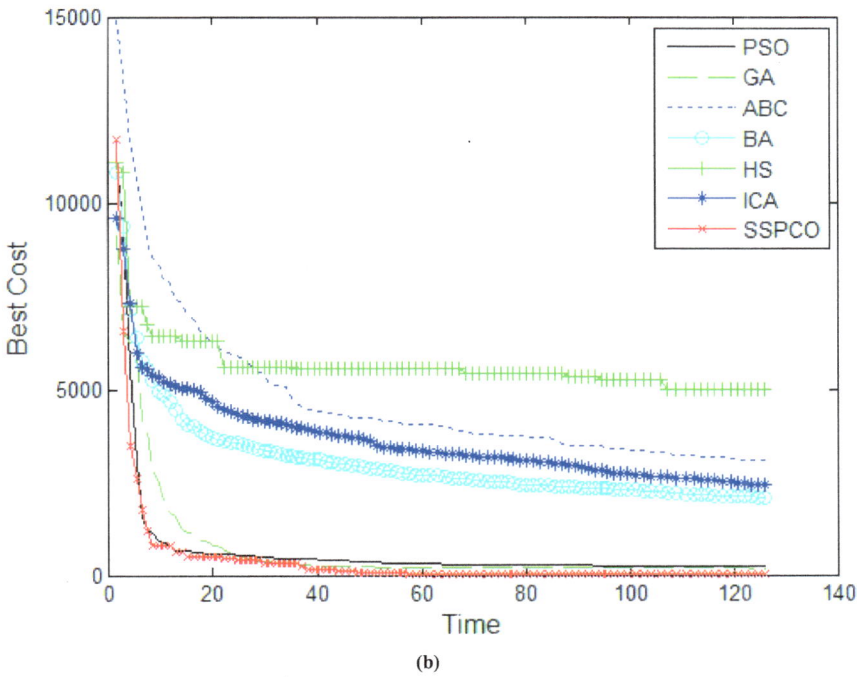

(b)

Fig. 13 cont.....

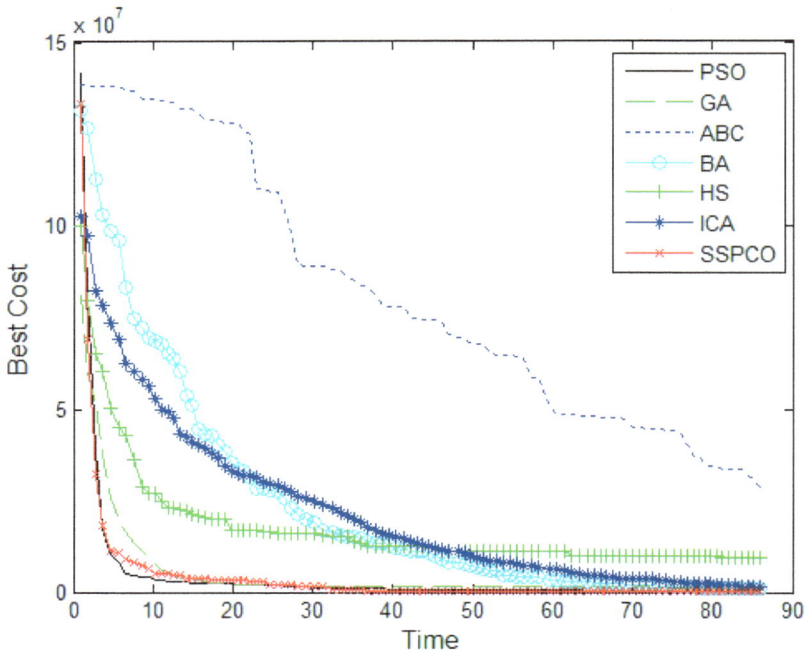

(c)

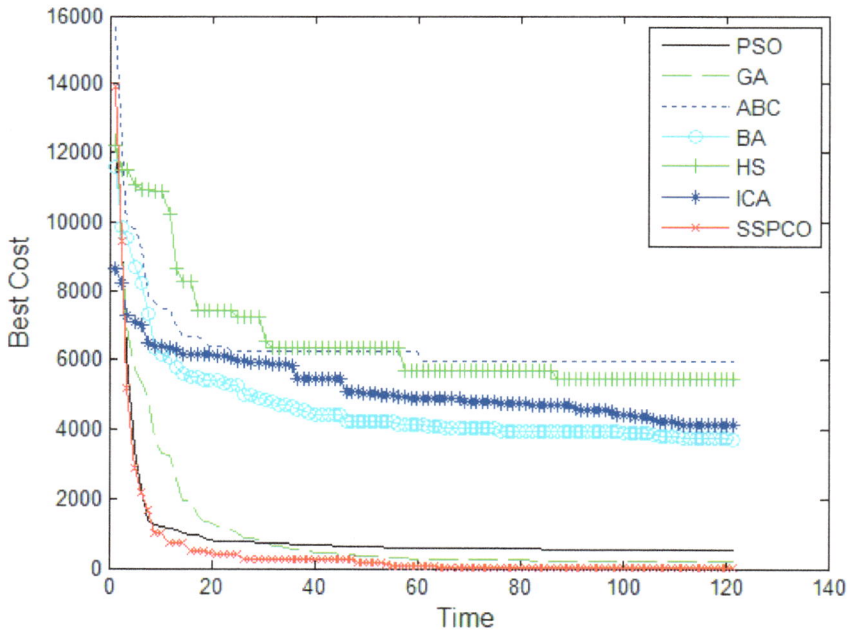

(d)

Fig. 13 cont.....

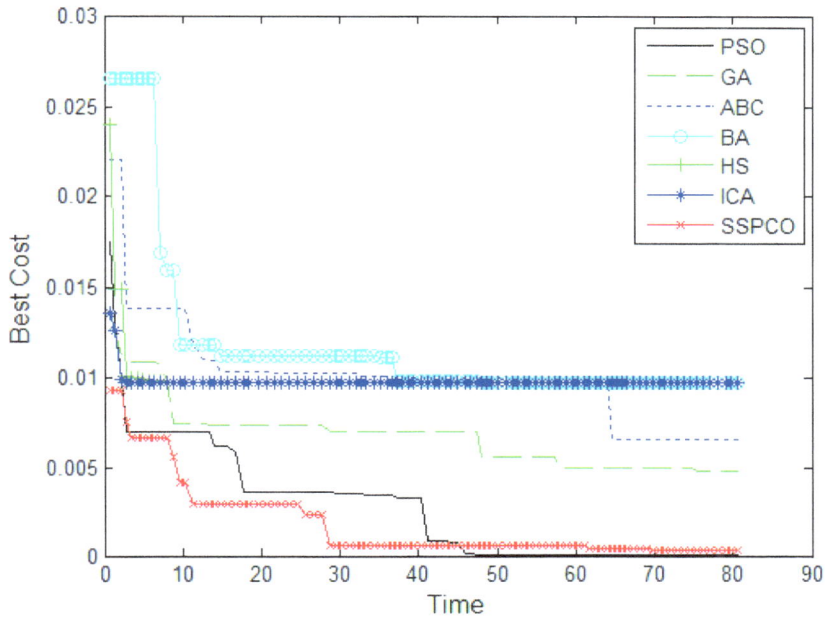

(e)

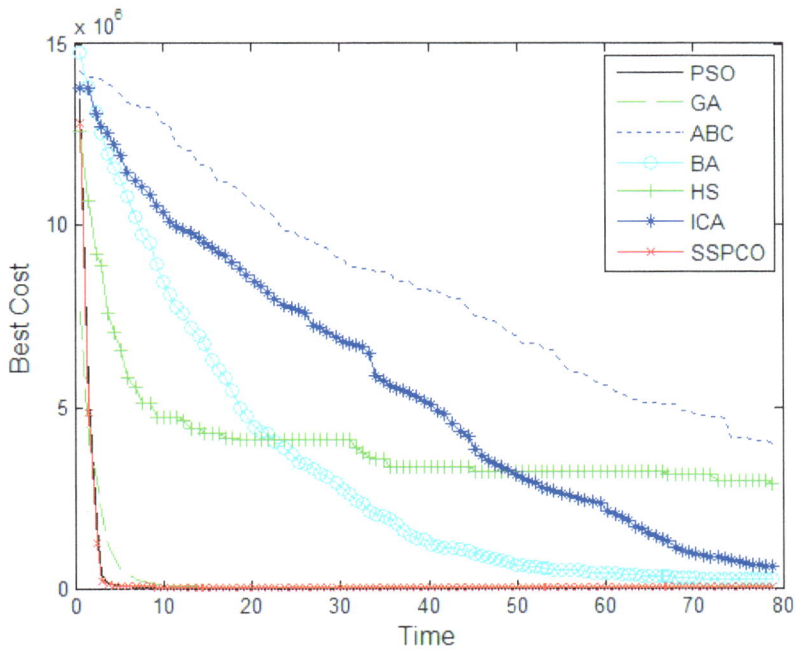

(f)

Fig. 13 cont.....

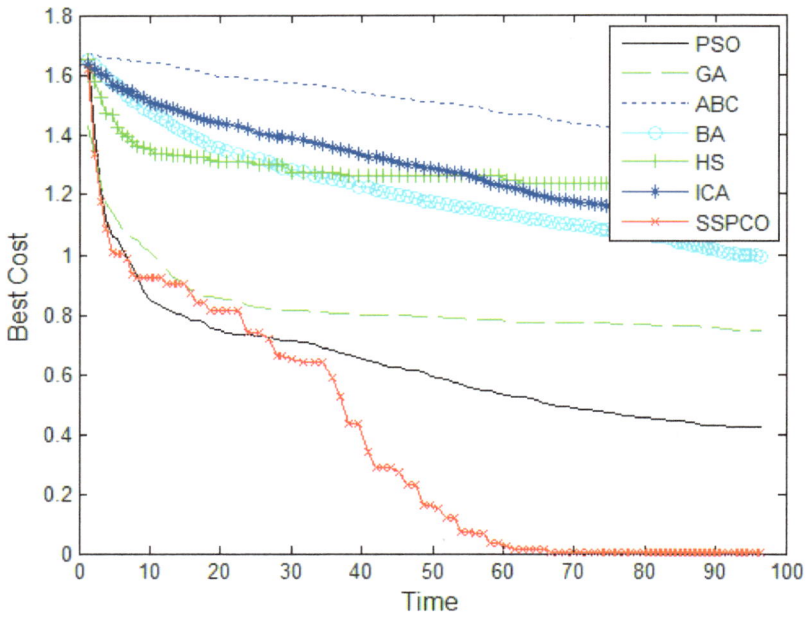

(g)

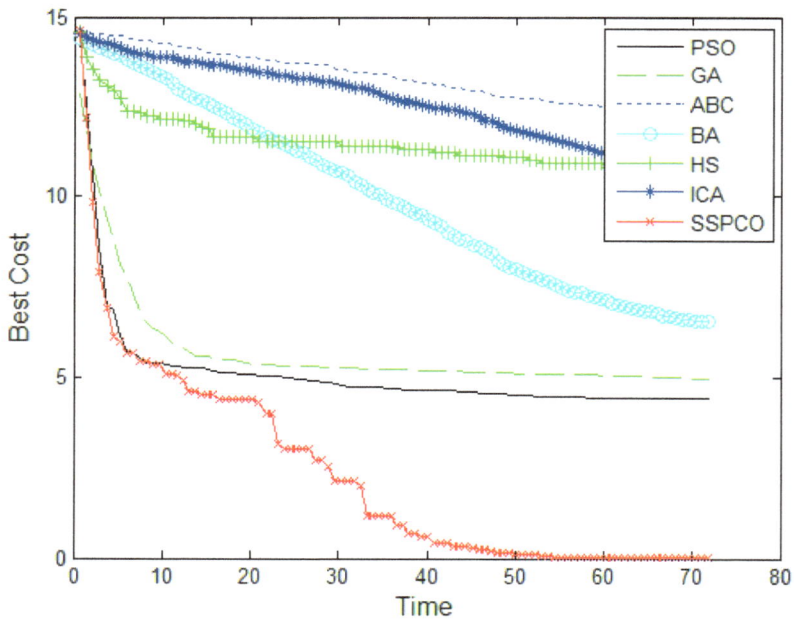

(h)

Fig. 13 cont.....

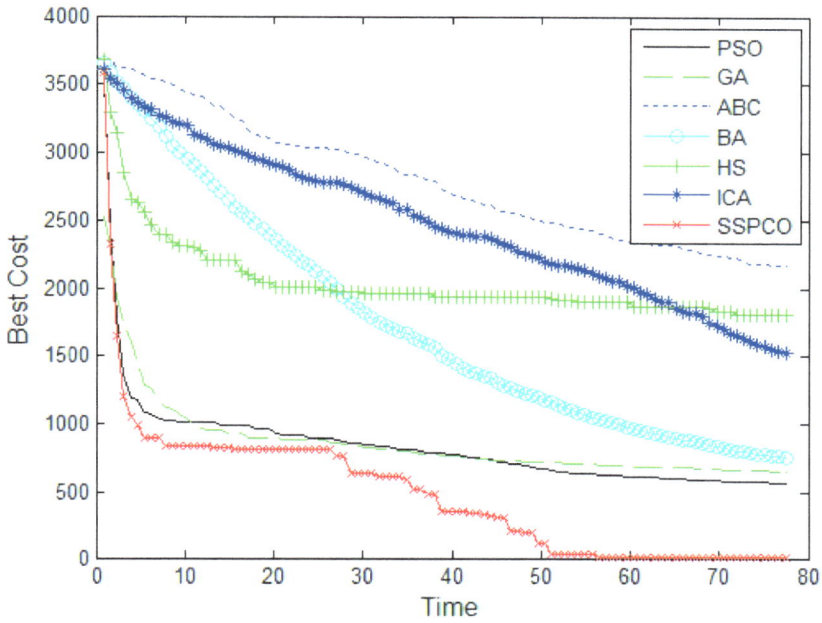

(i)

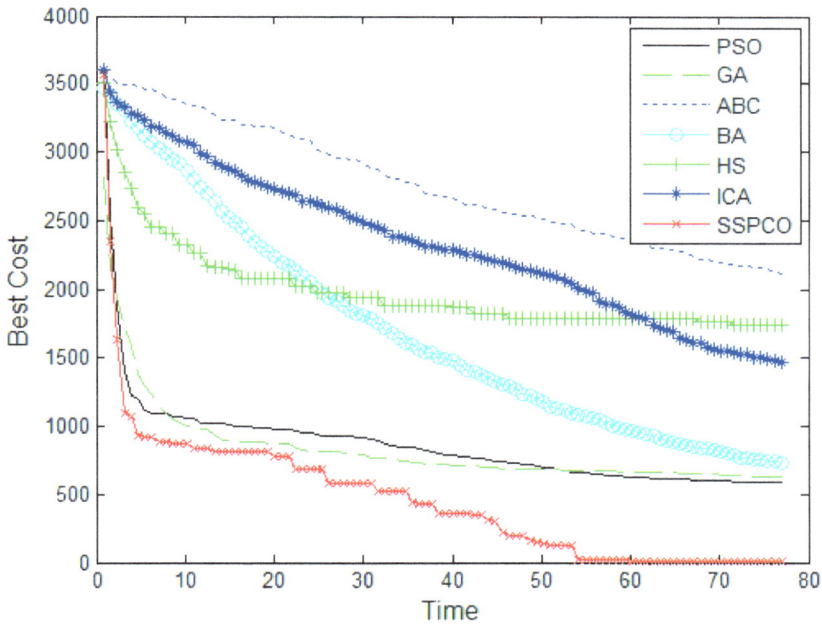

(j)

Fig. 13 cont.....

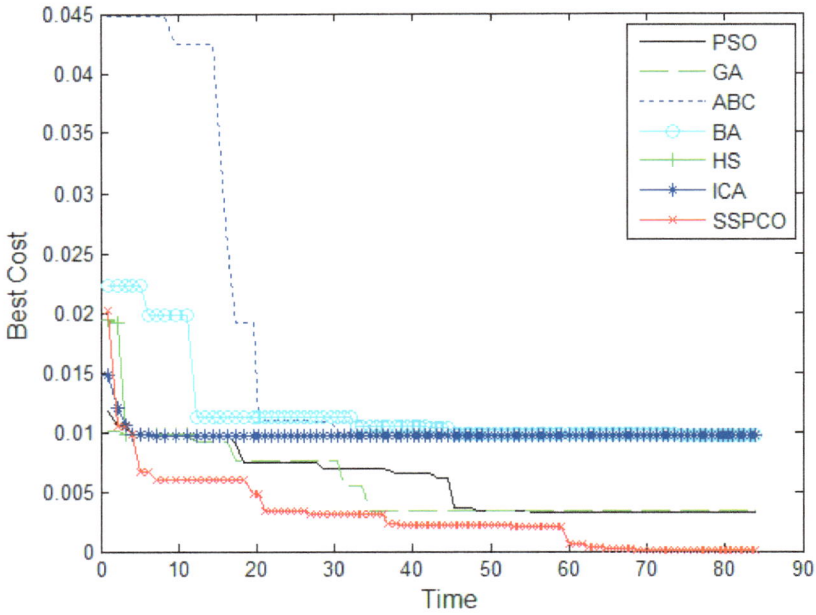

(k)

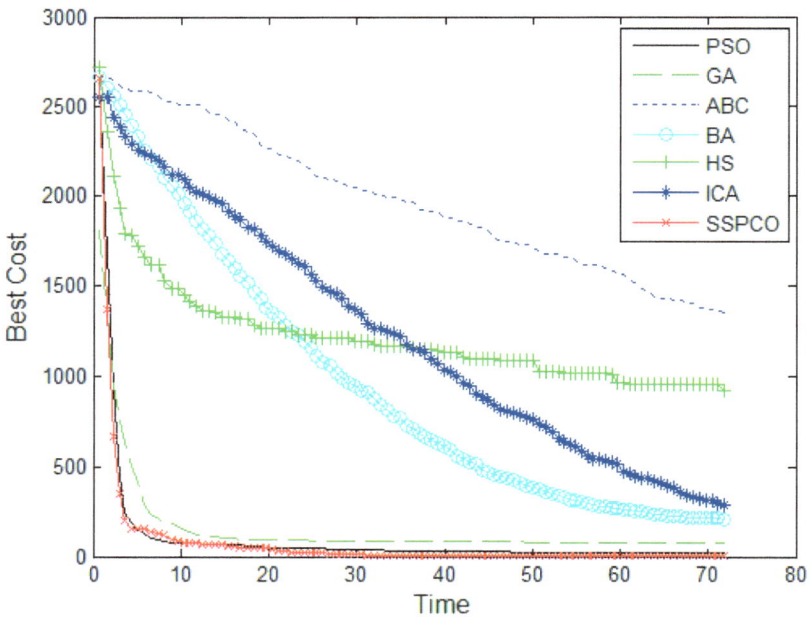

(l)

Fig. 13 cont.....

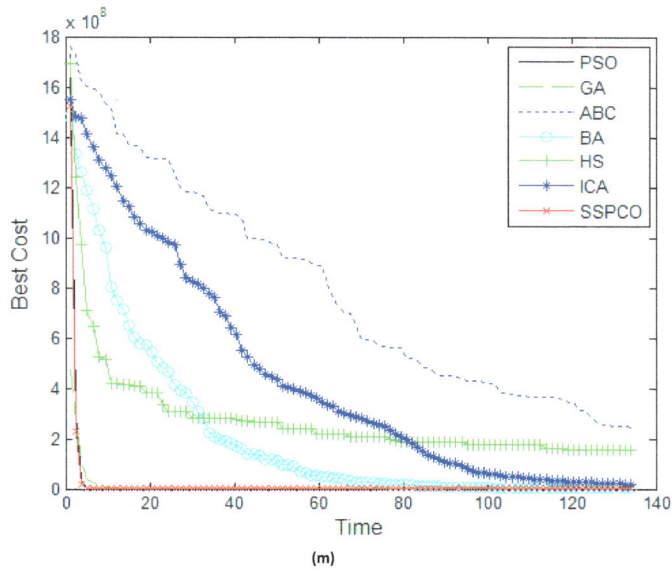

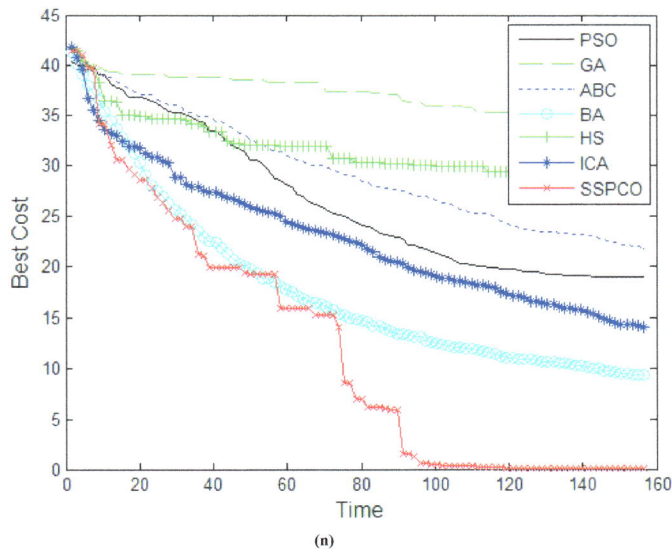

Fig. (13). Evolution of the mean function best cost according time derived from PSO, GA, ABC, BA, HS, ICA and SSPCO *versus* the number of FES on 14 test problems. (**a**) F1. (**b**) F2.(**c**) F3. (**d**) F4. (**e**) F5. (**f**) F6. (**g**) F7. (**h**) F8. (**i**) F9. (**j**) F10. (**k**) F11. (**l**) F12. (**m**) F13. (**n**) F14.

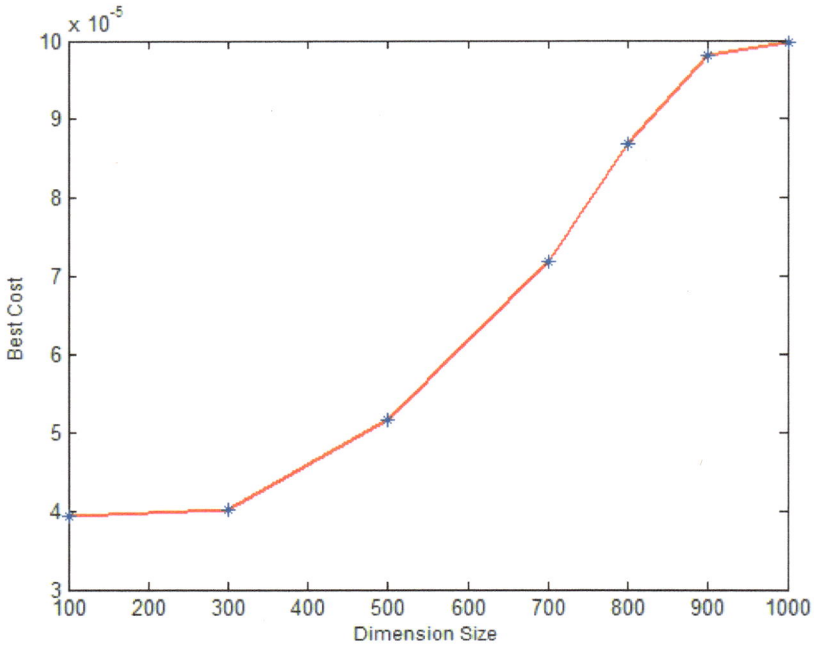

(a)

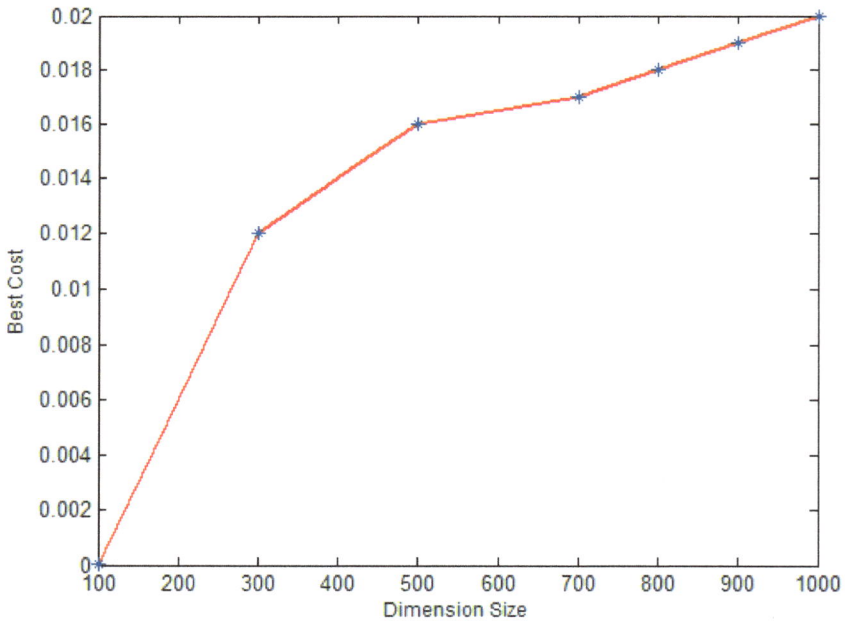

(b)

Fig. 14 cont.....

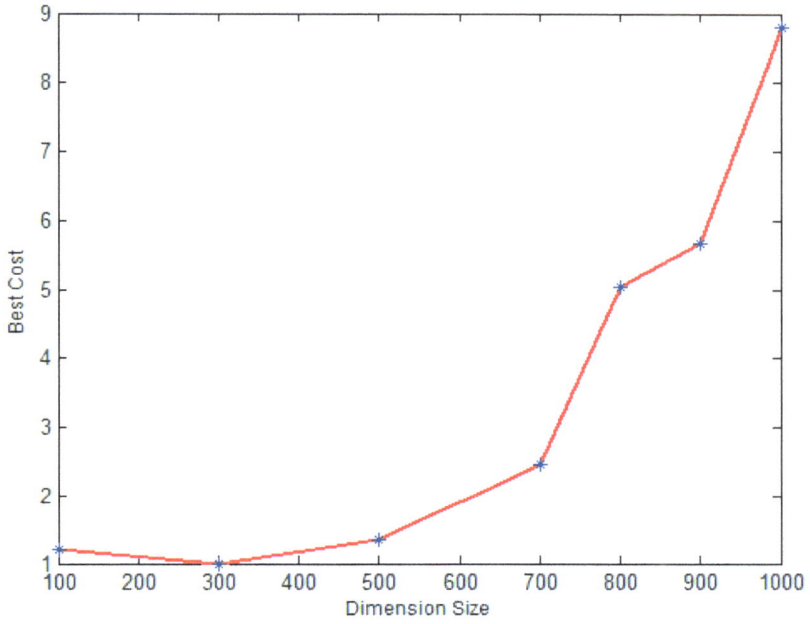

(c)

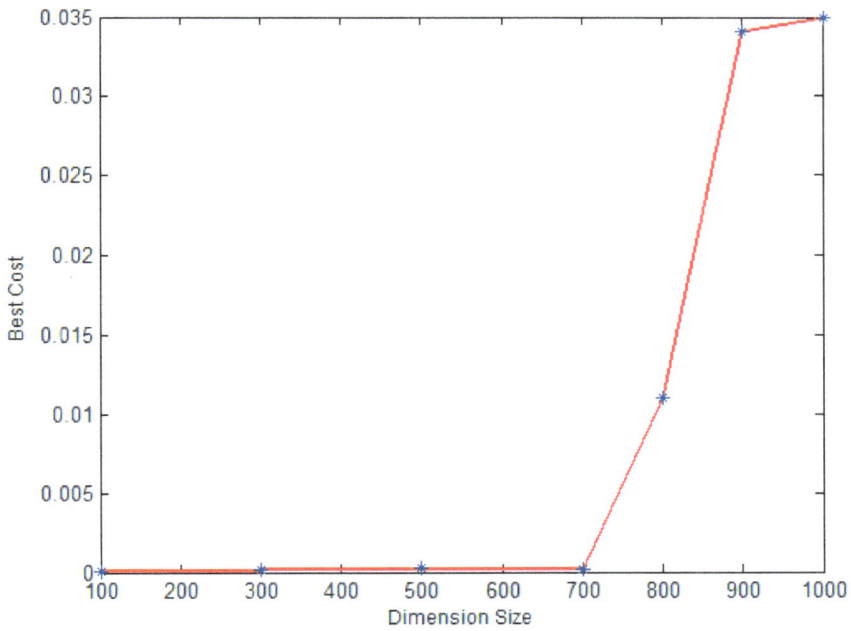

(d)

Fig. 14 cont.....

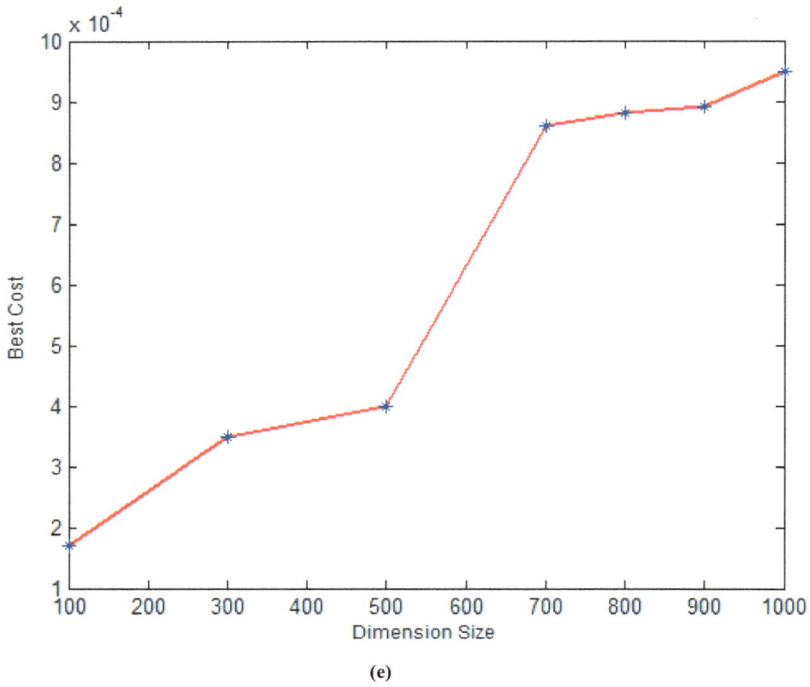

(e)

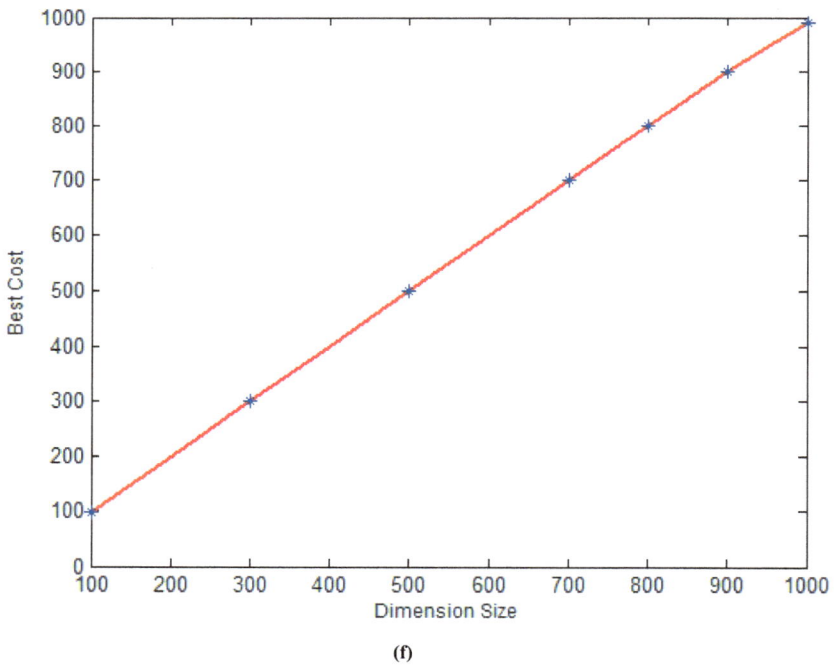

(f)

Fig. 14 cont.....

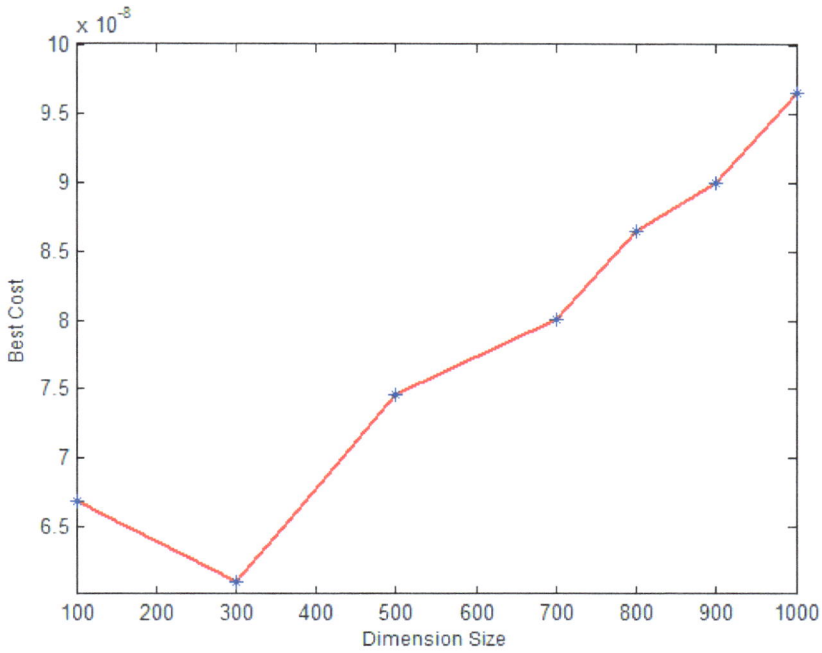

(g)

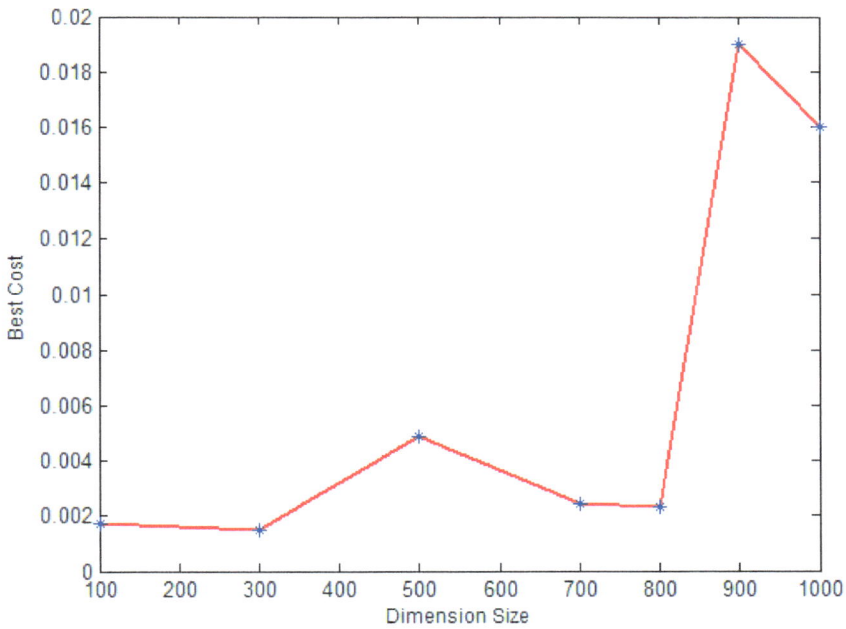

(h)

Fig. 14 cont.....

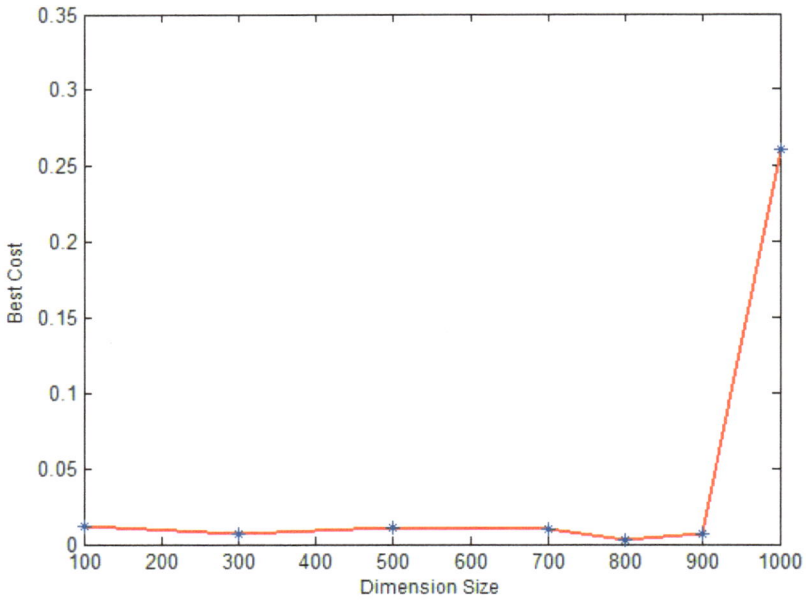

(i)

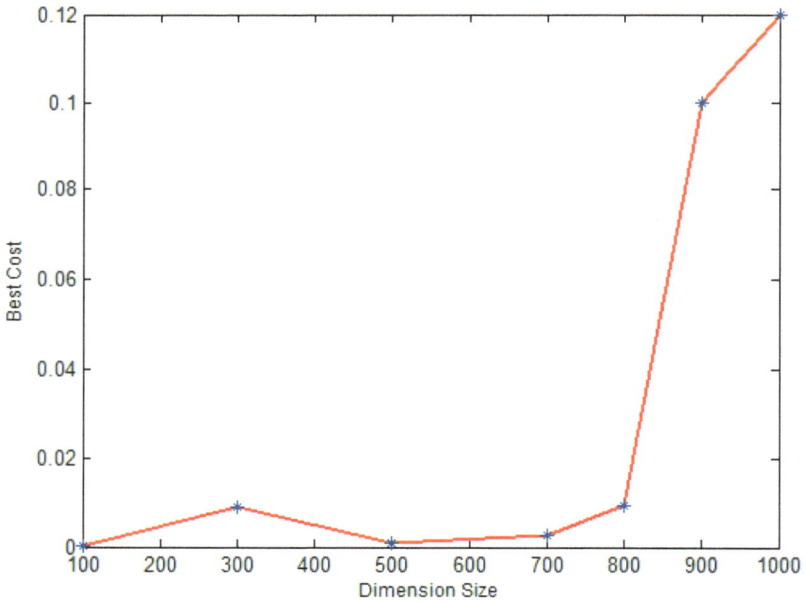

(j)

Fig. 14 cont.....

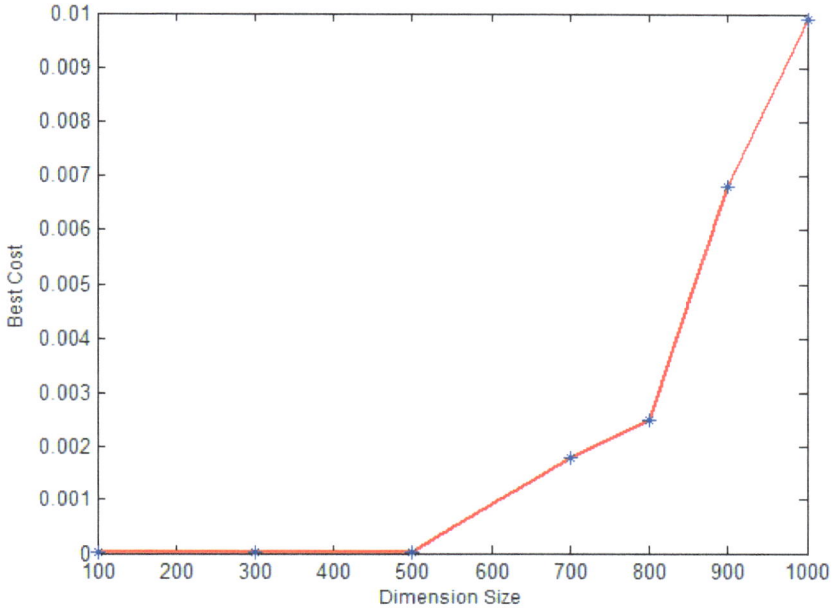

(k)

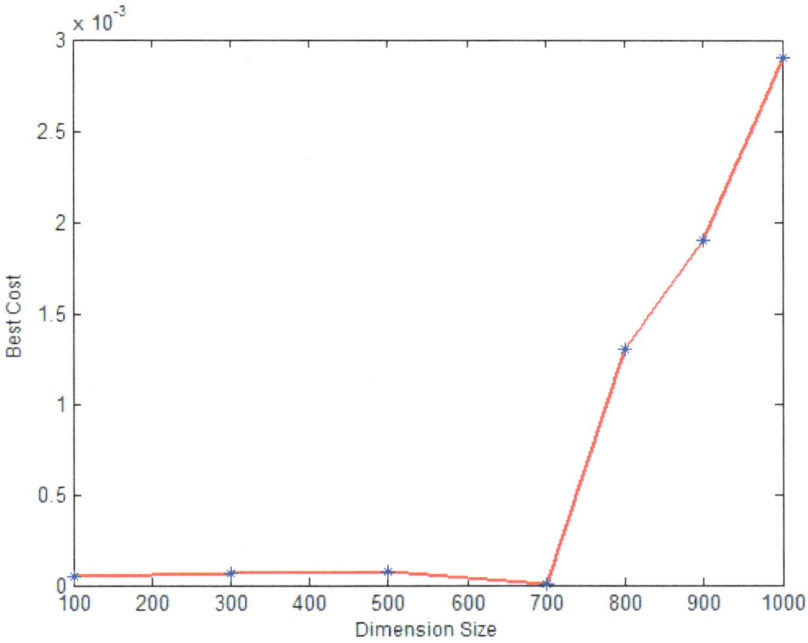

(l)

Fig. 14 cont.....

(m)

(n)

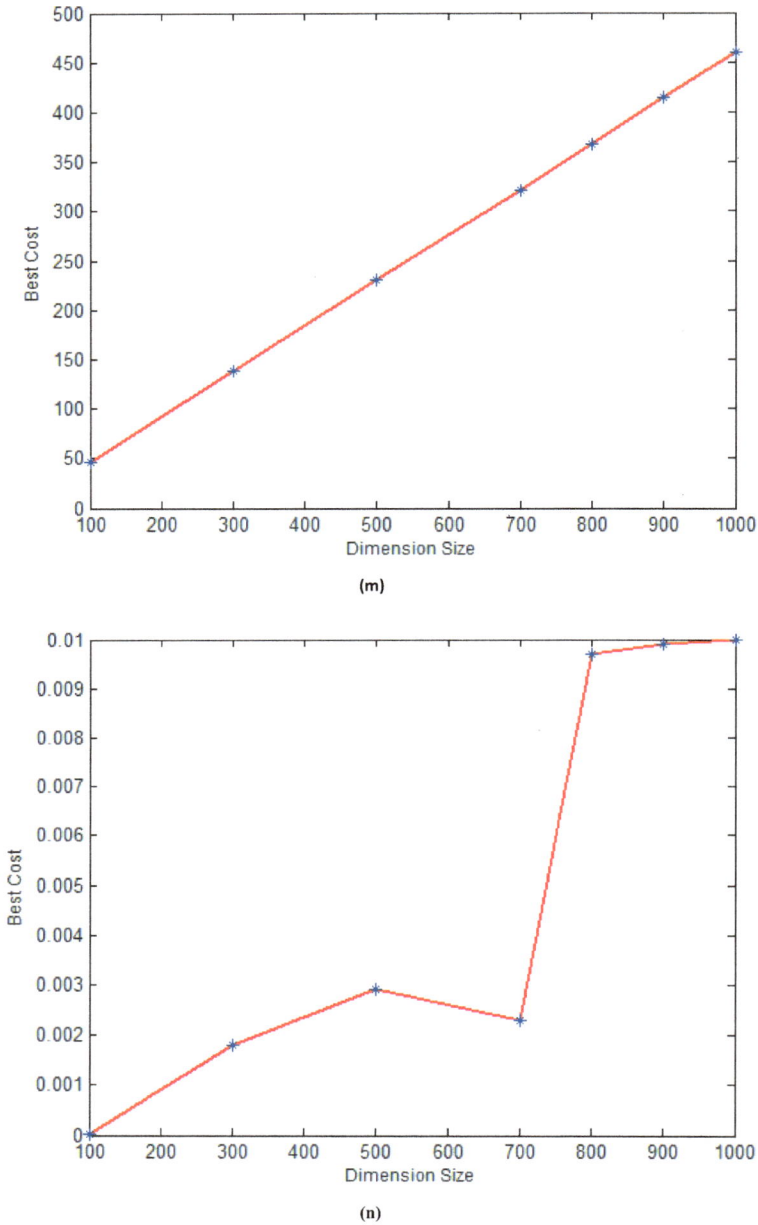

Fig. (14). Evolution of the mean function best cost derived from SSPCO based on different dimension size for 14 test problems. (**a**) F1. (**b**) F2.(**c**) F3. (**d**) F4. (**e**) F5. (**f**) F6. (**g**) F7. (**h**) F8. (**i**) F9. (**j**) F10. (**k**) F11. (**l**) F12. (**m**) F13. (**n**) F14.

Table 5. Experimental results of SSPCO over 30 independent runs on F1−F14 test functions based on different dimension sizes with 100 FES.

Function	Result	N=100	N=300	N=500	N=700	N=800	N=900	N=1000
F1	Best Cost	3.93e-05	4.02e-05‡	5.15e-05‡	7.19e-05‡	8.67e-05‡	9.81e-05‡	9.96e-05‡
	Mean	124.77	399.23	854.96	917.13	802.72	1.32e+03	1.37e+03
	STD	288.27	887.38	2.07e+03	1.98e+03	1.95e+03	2.78e+03	2.65e+03
	Run Time	6.01	6.33	6.35	6.22	6.27	6.50	6.76
F2	Best Cost	1.19 e-05	0.012‡	0.016‡	0.017‡	0.018‡	0.019‡	0.020‡
	Mean	2627.30	7.15e+03	6.41e+04	1.94e+05	2.49e+05	1.30e+05	2.73e+05
	STD	5968.96	1.46e+04	2.34e+05	4.64e+05	4.88e+05	2.43e+05	5.19e+05
	Run Time	28.32	75.96	143.59	230.82	268.47	324.98	378.18
F3	Best Cost	1.20	1.00†	1.33‡	2.46‡	5.04‡	5.67‡	8.79‡
	Mean	8834715	3.45e+07	5.58e+07	5.91e+07	7.05e+07	1.00e+08	8.90e+07
	STD	17044818	6.28e+07	1.23e+08	1.46e+08	1.58e+08	2.31e+08	1.81e+08
	Run Time	12.89	12.71	17.73	20.46	23.81	26.03	27.84
F4	Best Cost	5.33e-05	1.09e-04‡	2.66e-04‡	1.81e-04‡	0.011‡	0.034‡	0.035‡
	Mean	2703.78	1.48e+04	6.61e+04	1.24e+05	1.40e+05	2.22e+05	3.04e+05
	STD	6698.88	4.21e+04	1.91e+05	2.29e+05	3.19e+05	4.66e+05	4.49+05
	Run Time	26.16	69.83	169.55	225.31	268.56	313.04	372.35
F5	Best Cost	0.00017	0.00035‡	0.00040‡	0.00086‡	0.00088‡	0.00089‡	0.00095‡
	Mean	1.39	2.92	2.89	9.89	9.90	9.07	1.39
	STD	1.95	1.82	2.10	1.11	2.08	1.20	1.95
	Run Time	6.74	6.71	6.53	5.83	9.57	6.26	6.74
F6	Best Cost	99.00	298.98‡	498.95‡	698.97‡	798.99‡	898.99‡	989.99‡
	Mean	221636.9	8.15e+05	8.86e+05	2.81e+06	1.51e+06	1.98e+06	2.29e+06
	STD	980107.8	3.97e+06	4.25e+06	1.13e+07	7.60e+06	9.45e+06	8.46e+06
	Run Time	5.74	9.29	9.23	10.57	10.49	9.89	10.34
F7	Best Cost	6.68e-08	6.09e-08†	7.46e-08‡	8.01e-08‡	8.65e-08‡	9.00e-08‡	9.66e-08‡
	Mean	0.43	0.52	0.54	0.63	0.61	0.73	0.74
	STD	0.48	0.64	0.69	0.83	0.96	1.04	1.14
	Run Time	6.52	12.66	17.07	20.22	23.99	24.30	26.17
F8	Best Cost	0.0017	0.0015‡	0.0049‡	0.0024‡	0.0023‡	0.019‡	0.016‡
	Mean	3.30	3.61	3.75	3.47	3.59	3.61	3.87
	STD	3.37	3.50	3.43	3.33	3.45	3.31	2.80
	Run Time	6.23	8.49	9.25	9.41	9.51	10.41	10.77

(Table 5) cont.....

F9	Best Cost	0.012	0.0067†	0.011†	0.0094†	0.0024†	0.0064†	0.26‡
	Mean	771.56	2.17e+03	4.38e+03	5.66e+03	5.91e+03	5.86e+03	8.23e+03
	STD	665.56	1.92e+03	3.57e+03	4.70e+03	5.83e+03	5.96e+03	6.80e+03
	Run Time	5.48	8.49	8.96	8.94	9.08	10.03	10.04
F10	Best Cost	8.41e-05	0.009‡	0.0010‡	0.0027‡	0.0093‡	0.10‡	0. 12‡
	Mean	655.19	2.85e+03	3.97e+03	4.70e+03	6.78e+03	6.26e+03	7.24e+03
	STD	626.74	2.02e+03	2.94e+03	4.68e+03	6.00e+03	6.01e+03	6.90e+03
	Run Time	7.16	9.07	8.45	8.98	9.61	9.74	9.43
F11	Best Cost	6.44e-09	6.99e-09‡	7.24e-09‡	0.0018‡	0.0025‡	0.0068‡	0.0099‡
	Mean	0.45	0.55	0.36	0.40	0.65	0. 73	0.75
	STD	0.49	0.41	0.53	0.69	0.43	0.51	0.39
	Run Time	10.36	12.36	12.45	12.66	13.38	14.00	16.26
F12	Best Cost	5.15e-05	6.17e-05‡	7.13e-05‡	7.15e-06†	0.0013‡	0.0019‡	0.0029‡
	Mean	36.92	56.12	46.62	38.02	66.88	45.32	32.33
	STD	27.23	54.21	57.73	71.24	34.71	63.35	55.20
	Run Time	42.24	44.25	48.64	54.88	66.87	69.36	70.00
F13	Best Cost	45.99	137.97‡	229.96‡	321.49‡	367.93‡	413.98‡	459.91‡
	Mean	24690423	5.35e+07	2.36e+07	5.56e+07	1.17e+08	2.89e+08	2.46e+08
	STD	173990551	3.70e+08	1.58e+08	4.95e+08	1.11e+09	1.96e+09	1.83e+09
	Run Time	32.00	90.75	139.97	194.18	217.71	260.66	277.59
F14	Best Cost	8.37e-07	0.0018‡	0.0029‡	0.0023‡	0.0097‡	0.0099‡	0.01‡
	Mean	0.40	150.61	165.19	174.12	145.65	144.02	166.00
	STD	0.34	91.51	141.63	152.00	162.32	169.35	198.32
	Run Time	6.35	121.45	177.80	178.98	189.36	192.25	199.35
	‡		11	13	12	13	13	14
	†		3	1	2	1	1	0
	§		0	0	0	0	0	0

Proposed algorithm to conduct the mother particle to the best answer and this increases the diversity and the proposed algorithm has a higher standard deviation than the other algorithms and the answer has a high variation in these algorithms while it can achieve the best answer in less time than other algorithms. For example, in the results in F1 function show the high performance of the algorithm in finding the best answer in shortest possible time and the algorithm in the 100th iteration has the best cost of 3.93e-05 while, the best next algorithm in the 100th iteration has the best cost of 26.41. The algorithm has a great distance with other algorithms in finding the best answer and it could reach a good answer after the

80th iteration. In the F2 function, the results of the algorithms in achieving the best answer are similar to each other but the particle swarm algorithm and the proposed algorithm are better than others especially, the proposed algorithm which has the best possible cost in the 100th iteration. In F5 function, the algorithms almost have similar results and the proposed algorithm has a much better cost in the 100th iteration than the other algorithms and in the 100th iteration, it has the cost of 0.00017 while other algorithms have the best cost in the range of 1.89 to 9.17. In the standard deviation, the particles' cost of the proposed algorithm has a good convergence and has a standard deviation almost similar to the other algorithms. The results show that in the mentioned function, the proposed algorithm has the best cost than other algorithms in the 100th iteration and the algorithm has a high velocity to achieve the answer and almost, it has a very good cost than other algorithms from the 30th iteration onwards. In the section of the standard deviation, the algorithm has a high standard deviation that reflects the mission of the algorithm which shows all particles are in the service of this issue. For the test of the dependence of results to parameter, in Tables **5** and **6** measured the best cost in all functions with different population and dimension parameter values.

Table 6. Experimental results of SSPCO based on different populations over 30 independent runs on F1−F14 test functions of 100 variables (N) with 100 FES.

Function	Result	N=100	N=300	N=500	N=700	N=800	N=900	N=1000
F1	Best Cost	3.93e-05	1.44e-05†	9.42e-06†	2.05e-05†	6.14e-05‡	8.74e-07†	8.30e-06†
	Mean	124.77	107.23	124.86	104.74	148.40	146.16	113.30
	STD	288.27	214.87	277.69	253.11	353.26	334.78	244.29
	Run Time	6.01	19.86	30.60	45.63	51.62	56.52	62.63
F2	Best Cost	1.19 e-05	3.66e-07†	0.0018‡	2.08e-05‡	1.76e-06†	1.22e-05‡	7.82e-06†
	Mean	2627.30	1.24e+03	1.82e+03	1.95e+03	1.95e+03	1.84e+03	2.35e+03
	STD	5968.96	2.48e+03	3.34e+03	3.78e+03	4.20e+03	4.46e+03	6.58e+03
	Run Time	28.32	83.82	129.21	170.05	198.26	213.58	231.94
F3	Best Cost	1.20	5.87‡	3.75‡	1.40‡	0.49†	0.35†	0.27‡
	Mean	8834715	9.15e+06	7.52e+06	7.70e+06	7.99e+06	1.09e+07	7.84e+06
	STD	17044818	1.95e+07	1.39e+07	1.38e+07	1.44e+07	1.84e+07	1.54e+07
	Run Time	12.89	26.36	44.62	60.76	72.41	78.03	88.17
F4	Best Cost	5.33e-05	0.0014‡	3.39e-04‡	1.12e-05†	1.41e-05†	2.06e-05†	4.65e-05†
	Mean	2703.78	2.31e+03	2.94e+03	2.82e+03	1.60e+03	1.55e+03	1.98e+03
	STD	6698.88	8.67e+03	6.00e+03	5.59e+03	4.12e+03	2.88e+03	4.22e+03
	Run Time	26.16	91.19	170.18	181.22	238.13	226.68	326.23

(Table 6) cont.....

Function	Result	N=100	N=300	N=500	N=700	N=800	N=900	N=1000
F5	Best Cost	0.00017	0.00015†	0.00010†	0.0008†	0.0007†	0.0003†	0.0001†
	Mean	1.39	2.12	2.80	9.89	8.00	8.67	1.39
	STD	1.95	2.82	1.10	2.19	2.08	2.60	2.65
	Run Time	6.74	7.71	8.13	11.53	15.37	22.06	26.14
F6	Best Cost	99.00	98.99‡	98.96‡	98.98‡	98.98‡	98.99‡	98.99‡
	Mean	221636.9	1.98e+05	1.03e+05	3.24e+05	1.98e+05	2.25e+05	1.65e+05
	STD	980107.8	1.12e+06	4.44e+05	1.80e+06	5.31e+05	1.07e+06	4.96e+05
	Run Time	5.74	20.95	35.15	67.65	51.58	65.26	73.33
F7	Best Cost	6.68e-08	2.26e-06‡	5.87e-08†	8.01e-08‡	8.65e-08‡	9.00e-08‡	9.66e-08‡
	Mean	0.43	0.45	0.45	0.63	0.61	0.73	0.74
	STD	0.48	0.49	0.50	0.83	0.96	1.04	1.14
	Run Time	6.52	28.37	25.07	20.22	23.99	24.30	26.17
F8	Best Cost	0.0017	8.59e-05†	0.0025‡	0.0021‡	7.69e-07†	5.62e-04†	1.33e-04†
	Mean	3.30	3.21	3.29	3.50	3.26	3.57	2.99
	STD	3.37	3.54	3.21	3.49	3.50	3.31	3.32
	Run Time	6.23	22.61	35.48	51.49	70.37	91.28	84.73
F9	Best Cost	0.012	0.0076†	0.0019†	1.98e-04†	6.04e-04†	1.94e-04†	2.98e-04†
	Mean	771.56	752.34	757.41	660.89	822.03	692.79	725.54
	STD	665.56	670.48	671.78	656.55	712.96	646.25	675.33
	Run Time	5.48	20.11	36.17	47.25	74.10	75.41	67.06
F10	Best Cost	8.41e-05	0.024‡	0.0050‡	1.22e-04‡	4.91e-04‡	0.0043‡	0.0019‡
	Mean	655.19	927.00	816.92	752.87	760.03	720.48	804.29
	STD	626.74	636.94	650.93	729.52	685.21	683.17	620.34
	Run Time	7.16	21.58	35.21	52.02	57.80	68.73	70.87
F11	Best Cost	6.44e-09	5.99e-09†	4.24e-09†	4.44e-09§	6.24e-09†	4.33e-09†	3.24e-09†
	Mean	0.45	0.55	0.66	0.60	0.46	0.73	0.75
	STD	0.49	0.41	0.43	0.59	0.53	0.69	0.39
	Run Time	10.36	12.36	15.39	19.65	25.03	39.00	42.08
F12	Best Cost	5.15e-05	4.17e-05†	2.01e-05†	3.19e-06‡	4.21e-05†	6.81e-05‡	5.01e-05†
	Mean	36.92	56.12	46.62	38.02	66.88	55.32	32.33
	STD	27.23	54.21	67.83	81.64	64.79	66.35	45.80
	Run Time	42.24	48.25	49.64	64.88	76.87	99.36	80.10

(Table 6) cont.....

Function	Result	N=100	N=300	N=500	N=700	N=800	N=900	N=1000
F13	Best Cost	45.99	45.99§	45.97†	45.97†	45.97†	45.99§	45.98†
	Mean	24690423	3.16e+06	1.06e+07	1.49e+07	2.09e+07	1.17e+07	5.02e+06
	STD	173990551	2.43e+07	7.70e+07	9.03e+07	1.45e+08	9.25e+07	2.99e+07
	Run Time	32.00	126.79	170.96	251.43	265.89	339.43	380.86
F14	Best Cost	8.37e-07	0.0038‡	2.92e-04‡	0.046‡	0.0060‡	1.12e-06‡	0.017‡
	Mean	0.40	38.86	33.61	43.12	44.70	27.50	42.01
	STD	0.34	27.13	25.66	20.40	29.76	27.23	21.14
	Run Time	6.35	147.18	227.73	317.77	339.18	370.03	406.90
	‡		6	7	8	5	6	5
	†		7	7	5	9	7	9
	§		1	0	1	0	1	0

"‡", "†", and "§" denote that the performance of SSPCO is better than, worse than, and similar to that of the.

In next section of simulation, SSPCO is compared with JADE [36], CMA-ES [37], SSA [38], EPSDE [39], GL-25 [40], jDE [41], MRPSO [42] and SaDE [43] on $F_1 - F_{14}$ in order to save runtime. In the experiments, the parameter settings of eight algorithms keep the same as in their original papers. The statistical results, in terms of F-mean and SD obtained in 25 independent runs under the same termination criterion by each algorithm, are reported in Table **7**. The last three rows of Table **7** summarize the experimental results. From the last three rows of Table **7**, we can see that SSPCO performs significantly better than other eight algorithms in 12 functions. While SSPCO algorithm significantly outperforms other eight algorithms, it has drawbacks in two functions comparing with other algorithms. Its first drawback is in function f6 and the second drawback is in the function f13.

Table 7. Experimental results of JADE, CMA-ES, CLPSO, EPSDE, GL-25, jDE, MRPSO, SaDE, and SSPCO over 25 independent runs on $F_1 - F_{14}$ test functions of 30 variables with 300,000 FES.

Function	Result	JADE	CMA-ES	SSA	EPSDE	GL-25	jDE	MRPSO	SaDE	SSPCO
F1	F_{mean}	0.00E+00§	1.43E-25‡	0.00E+00§	2.02E-30‡	1.87E-27‡	0.00E+00§	2.31E-27‡	0.00E+00§	0.00E+00
	SD	0.00E+00	3.66E-26	0.00E+00	1.01E-29	4.16E-27	0.00E+00	3.41E-28	0.00E+00	0.00E+00
F2	F_{mean}	2.41E-28‡	6.27E-25‡	7.01E+02‡	5.59E-26‡	6.25E+01‡	5.06E-08‡	4.99E-10‡	3.72E-05‡	0.00E+00
	SD	1.61E-28	1.50E-25	1.18E+02	1.06E-25	1.10E+02	6.18E-08	7.72E-10	1.40E-04	0.00E+00
F3	F_{mean}	7.68E+03‡	4.91E-21‡	1.37E+07‡	5.14E+06‡	1.93E+06‡	1.88E+05‡	4.82E+05‡	4.90+05‡	1.08E-260
	SD	5.43E+03	1.06E-21	4.37E+06	2.07E+07	7.48E+05	1.54E+05	2.01E+05	1.83E+05	1.24E+06
F4	F_{mean}	1.62E-13‡	7.07E+04‡	6.01E+03‡	2.48E+00‡	8.59E+02‡	2.67E-02‡	1.25E+03‡	1.09E+02‡	5.54E-266
	SD	4.13E-13	2.01E+05	1.26E+03	7.60E+00	6.14E+02	4.14E-02	9.00E+02	1.08E+02	134.35

(Table 7) cont.....

Function	Result	JADE	CMA-ES	SSA	EPSDE	GL-25	jDE	MRPSO	SaDE	SSPCO
F5	F_{mean}	3.84E-07‡	3.54E-10‡	3.97E+03‡	1.52E+03‡	2.49E+03‡	1.66E+02‡	8.43E+03‡	3.33E+03‡	6.67E-19
	SD	8.28E-07	8.35E-11	4.88E+02	1.03E+03	1.86E+02	2.12E+02	1.98E+03	4.54E+02	9.68E-18
F6	F_{mean}	7.88E+00†	6.38E-01†	3.34E+00†	9.57E-01†	2.16E+01†	1.62E+01†	3.03E+01†	5.38E+01†	28.98
	SD	2.29E+01	1.49E+00	5.01E+00	1.74E+00	1.95E+00	2.29E+01	7.38E+01	3.22E+01	3.44E+04
F7	F_{mean}	5.12E-03‡	6.80E-03‡	4.40E-01‡	1.68E-02‡	1.48E-02‡	1.10E-02‡	2.31E-02‡	1.58E-02‡	0.00E+00
	SD	6.92E-03	7.29E-03	6.99E-02	1.40E-02	8.72E-03	8.81E-03	2.01E-02	1.08E-02	0.00E+00
F8	F_{mean}	2.07E+01‡	2.07E+01‡	2.09E+01‡	2.09E+01‡	2.10E+01‡	2.09E+01‡	2.09E+01‡	2.10E+01‡	0.00E+00
	SD	3.16E-01	4.77E-01	6.14E-02	4.54E-02	3.87E-02	5.69E-02	5.19E-02	4.81E-02	0.00E+00
F9	F_{mean}	0.00E+00§	4.32E+02‡	0.00E+00§	0.00E+00§	2.75E+01‡	0.00E+00§	1.17E+01‡	1.19E-01‡	0.00E+00
	SD	0.00E+00	1.13E+02	0.00E+00	0.00E+00	7.93E+00	0.00E+00	4.28E+00	3.30E-01	0.00E+00
F10	F_{mean}	3.73E+01‡	4.78E+01‡	9.40E+01‡	4.65E+01‡	1.46E+02‡	8.01E+01‡	1.13E+02‡	4.76E+01‡	0.00E+00
	SD	8.32E+00	1.54E+01	1.50E+01	9.44E+00	7.02E+01	1.03E+01	3.04E+01	1.34E+01	0.00E+00
F11	F_{mean}	2.37E+01‡	6.24E+00‡	2.55E+01‡	3.42E+01‡	3.27E+01‡	3.12E+01‡	1.64E+01‡	1.68E+01‡	0.00E+00
	SD	3.86E+00	2.47E+00	1.14E+00	3.48E+00	7.79E+00	1.26E+00	2.90E+00	2.08E+00	0.00E+00
F12	F_{mean}	1.20E+04‡	7.90E+03‡	1.42E+04‡	3.53E+04‡	6.53E+04‡	2.00E+04‡	5.79E+03‡	2.87E+03‡	0.00E+00
	SD	4.69E+03	8.13E+03	3.67E+03	6.95E+03	4.69E+04	1.23E+04	5.60E+03	3.26E+03	0.00E+00
F13	F_{mean}	1.87E+00†	3.11E+00†	1.97E+00†	1.87E+00†	6.97E+00†	2.38E+00†	2.32E+00†	3.98E+00†	7.63
	SD	2.60E-01	9.04E-01	2.01E-01	1.83E-01	5.62E+00	1.85E-01	7.61E-01	4.18E-01	1.25E-01
F14	F_{mean}	1.31E+01‡	1.47E+01‡	1.26E+01‡	1.34E+01‡	1.32E+01‡	1.32E+01‡	1.19E+01‡	1.30E+01‡	0.00E+00
	SD	2.43E-01	3.11E-01	2.04E-01	3.16E-01	2.02E-01	3.35E-01	4.82E-01	3.06E-01	0.00E+00
	‡	10	12	10	11	12	10	12	11	
	†	2	2	2	2	2	2	2	2	
	§	2	0	2	1	0	2	0	1	

"‡", "†", and "§" denote that the performance of SRA is better than, worse than, and similar to that of the corresponding algorithm, respectively.

We compared proposed algorithm in Table **8** with sinDE [44], JOA [45], NPSO [46] and D-PSO-C [47]. This comparison is done with D=30, pop size=40, iteration=10000*d in mean of 51 run for 28 test benchmark of CEC 2013 [48].

Table 8. Comparison among seven algorithms on CEC 2010 test functions.

Function	SinDE		JOA		D-PSO-C		NPSO		SSPCO	
	Mean	Std	Mean	Std	Mean	Std	Mean	Std	Mean	Std
1	2.23E−14	6.83E−14	1.78E−14	3.33E−14	2.44E−14	4.13E−11	2.52E−14	2.77E−12	**0.00E+00**	0.00E+00
2	2.16E+06	6.15E+05	2.09E+06	4.36E+05	2.76E+06	1.10E+05	2.22E+06	1.32E+05	**0.00E+00**	0.00E+00
3	8.49E+04	2.11E+05	8.19E+04	4.31E+05	9.11E+04	1.62E+05	8.57E+04	3.65E+05	**8.03E+04**	1.31E+05

(Table 6) cont.....

Function	SinDE		JOA		D-PSO-C		NPSO		SSPCO	
	Mean	Std	Mean	Std	Mean	Std	Mean	Std	Mean	Std
4	6.38E+03	2.00E+03	5.82E+03	1.80E+03	6.50E+03	3.49E+03	6.47E+03	3.09E+03	**0.00E+00**	0.00E+00
5	1.14E−13	7.65E−29	1.11E−13	5.14E−29	2.74E−13	4.15E−29	1.22E−13	1.85E−29	**0.00E+00**	0.00E+00
6	1.46E+01	2.42E+00	1.52E+01	4.38E+00	3.54E+01	3.52E+00	1.76E+01	1.72E+00	**1.32E+01**	1.00E+00
7	1.21E−01	1.57E−01	**1.09E−01**	2.18E−01	1.81E−01	4.28E−01	1.34E−01	2.17E−01	1.11E−01	1.12E−01
8	2.09E+01	4.96E−02	1.78E+01	3.54E−02	2.67E+01	3.77E−02	2.13E+01	6.06E−02	**1.47E+01**	2.14E−02
9	1.52E+01	3.05E+00	1.48E+01	2.31E+00	1.78E+01	2.13E+00	1.50E+01	2.87E+00	**1.33E+01**	1.09E+00
10	2.04E−02	1.30E−02	1.66E−02	2.19E−02	2.65E−02	3.25E−02	2.19E−02	2.43E−02	**1.52E−02**	1.22E−02
11	1.95E−02	1.39E−01	1.98E−02	2.55E−01	2.34E−02	2.44E−01	2.00E−02	4.35E−01	**0.00E+00**	0.00E+00
12	3.02E+01	8.65E+00	2.87E+01	3.44E+00	3.66E+01	4.33E+00	3.18E+01	4.22E+00	**2.54E+01**	2.75E+00
13	7.33E+01	2.07E+01	7.14E+01	1.87E+01	7.76E+01	4.47E+01	7.40E+01	3.27E+01	**7.02E+01**	2.09E+01
14	5.04E+01	1.92E+01	5.00E+01	3.52E+01	5.78E+01	5.02E+01	5.16E+01	6.48E+01	**4.78E+01**	2.02E+01
15	2.95E+03	4.86E+02	2.82E+03	3.21E+02	3.13E+03	3.22E+02	2.97E+03	4.86E+02	**2.48E+03**	2.00E+02
16	1.74E+00	2.52E−01	1.59E+00	1.45E−01	1.87E+00	3.55E−01	1.75E+00	3.28E−01	**1.46E+00**	1.50E−01
17	3.37E+01	7.97E−01	3.22E+01	5.79E−01	4.09E+01	3.23E−01	3.59E+01	4.55E−01	**3.08E+01**	2.10E−01
18	7.86E+01	1.42E+01	7.48E+01	3.56E+01	7.89E+01	3.45E+01	7.55E+01	4.44E+01	**7.16E+01**	2.33E+01
19	2.24E+00	3.79E−01	2.64E+00	2.12E−01	3.75E+00	2.73E−01	2.33E+00	2.28E−01	**2.06E+00**	1.23E+00
20	9.99E+00	5.50E−01	9.75E+00	3.22E−01	9.83E+00	4.82E−01	9.81E+00	4.88E−01	**9.34E+00**	2.71E−01
21	2.87E+02	6.40E+01	2.81E+02	3.91E+01	2.99E+02	6.40E+01	2.91E+02	3.91E+01	**2.77E+02**	2.38E+01
22	1.49E+02	1.76E+01	1.32E+02	2.90E+01	1.55E+02	4.75E+01	1.57E+02	3.22E+01	**1.20E+02**	3.09E+01
23	3.14E+03	5.31E+02	3.28E+03	3.22E+02	3.83E+03	4.11E+02	3.20E+03	2.39E+02	**3.12E+03**	2.88E+02
24	2.00E+02	7.16E−03	2.11E+02	3.44E−03	2.67E+02	4.46E−03	2.52E+02	6.86E−03	**1.89E+02**	4.79E−03
25	2.49E+02	6.85E+00	2.37E+02	3.63E+00	2.74E+02	3.05E+00	2.51E+02	5.73E+00	**2.08E+02**	3.66E+00
26	2.02E+02	1.40E+01	1.88E+02	4.43E+01	2.37E+02	5.65E+01	2.12E+02	4.47E+01	**1.79E+02**	2.72E+01
27	3.01E+02	2.36E+00	3.09E+02	4.65E+00	3.45E+02	7.66E+00	3.20E+02	6.47E+00	**2.81E+02**	3.31E+00
28	3.00E+02	0.00E+00	**0.00E+00**	0.00E+00	3.23E+02	2.00E+00	3.54E+02	3.39E+00	**0.00E+00**	0.00E+00

In the end of results section, we compare time complexity of proposed algorithm and PSO algorithm. First, in Table **9**, shows the best cost and run time for 14 tests with the time complexity. For proposed algorithm n based on populations and log n for iterations, that it can be said time complexity of proposed algorithm is n log n.

Table 9. Comparison of Time Complexity among PSO and SSPCO.

Algorithm	Mean of Best Cost	Mean of Run Time	Time Complexity
PSO	17106.62728	14.53071429	O(N Log N)
SSPCO	1.46E+02	14.48571429	O(N Log N)

3.3. CHAOTIC SSPCO ALGORITHM

SSPCO algorithm is simulated based on the behavior of partridge chicks [49]. Feeling risk, the chicks of this bird begin to move in an orderly queue behind the mother to come away from the danger zone. This behave is arises from the good experience of the chick in the front of desired queue. A priority variable is considered for each particle, in this algorithm. The priority variable is valued at zero at first, and any time that the position of particle is more appropriate than the best public or personal experience, one unit is added to the priority variable. In any iteration, the value of the priority variable of particles is sorted in an elite array. To go to the next position, each particle sets its movement based on the particle that its priority value is an index higher than the given particle in the elite array. In other words, any particle tries to reach to the position of the particle that its priority variable is an index higher than the given particle.

According to Fig. (15), chick X adjusts its speed equation based on the position of chick Y that its priority variable is an index higher in the arranged priority array of particles. Now, we combine this algorithm with chaos theory based on two methods. Chaos is a branch of the research areas of the nonlinear dynamics that has been widely studied. There are many applications in the actual systems using of modern methods in nonlinear field, whether man-made or natural that seem apparently random. However, this random apparent has no accidental origin, and generally is a result of a definite/deterministic and defined process. It is for more than a hundred years that biologists have been examined the samples of the populations of various species. Recently, scientists have been able to implement chaotic models in certain populations. For example, the study of the Canadian Lynx showed that there is also a chaotic behavior in the population growth [50]. For this reason, we have made a change in the population based algorithm and combined the chaos theory with the evolutionary algorithms to use the chaotic generators for producing/generating the populations of algorithms.

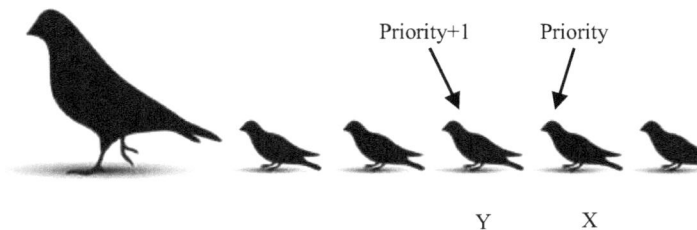

Fig. (15). Movement of chicks in algorithm.

3.4. THE FIRST METHOD: CHAOTIC SSPCO ALGORITHM

According to chaos theory, the initial population will be generated. In the first approach, we generate the initial population based on the chaos function known as Logestic [51]. The equation of Logistic function is as follow:

$$x_{n+1} = \mu . x_n (1 - x_n), \quad 0 \le x_0 \le 1, \tag{6}$$

Where μ is the control parameter, x is a variable and $n = 1,2,3,\dots$. Therefore, the chaos process of the local search can be defined based on the following equation:

$$cx_i^{(k+1)} = 4cx_i^{(k)} \left(1 - cx_i^{(k)}\right), \qquad i = 1,2,\dots,n, \tag{7}$$

We have been populated the SSPCO algorithm according to equation (7). Now, the cost function is applied to the generated population by chaos theory and the value of any population is determined according to the fitness of the cost function. In each iteration, if the position of any particle is better than its best personal experience, a unit will be added to its priority variable.

$$if \ \ X_i.cost > P_{best} \ \rightarrow \ P_{best}$$
$$= X_i.position \ \ and \ \ X_i.priority$$
$$= X_i.priority + 1 \tag{8}$$

If the estimated value of the fitness(the estimated fitness value) in the cost function of each particle is better than the best public experience, the position of that particle will be introduced as the best new public experience and a unit is added to its priority variable (of it).

$$if \ \ P_{best} > G_{best} \ \ \rightarrow G_{best} = P_{best} \ \ and \ \ X_i.priority \tag{9}$$
$$= X_i.priority + 1$$

Sort

| Chick | $i=1$ | ... | n |

| Priority | $i_{prioirity}$ | ... | $n_{prioirity}$ |

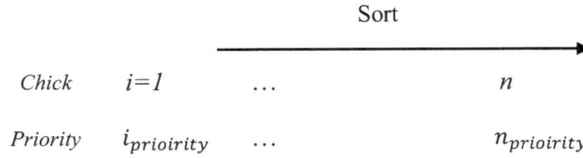

Fig. (16). Sorted array based on priority parameter of chicks.

Now in each iteration we arrange particles based on the value of their priority variables (Fig. **15**). Suppose, we call this array, the equation of the speed of particles will be as follows:

$$X_i.\,velocity = w * X_i.\,velocity + c * rand(\ ) * (PArray_{i+1}.\,psition) - X_i.\,position \tag{10}$$

Where w is the weight of /the/ inertia that determines the amount of effectiveness of the current speed in the speed equation of the next step (next speed equation), $X_i.velocity$ is the current speed of the particle, c is the social coefficient which is a constant number, $rand()$ is a random number between zero and one. Also, $PArray_{i+1}.psition$ is the position/location of the particle that the given particle tries to pursue//follow it, which in fact is the position of the particle that is an index higher than the given particle in the arranged array of priorities and $X_i.position$ is the current position of the particle. By obtaining the velocity equation of particles, the equation of motion is formed as follows:

$$X_i.\,Newposition = X_i.\,position + X_i.\,velocity \tag{11}$$

Where, $X_i.position$ is the current location of the particle and $X_i.velocity$ is the velocity of the particle that is calculated by equation (11). It is worthy to note that the similarity between this algorithm and PSO algorithm is exactly in equation (11). Fig. (**17**) shows the pseudo-code of the first proposed method. Fig. (**16**) shows the pseudo-code of the second proposed method.

initialize all chicken according: $4u(1 - u)$

Repeat

For each chicken i

update the chicken's best position and priority

If $f(x_i) > f(pb_i)$ *then*

$$pb_i = x_i$$

$$prioirity_i = prioirity_i + 1$$

End if

update the global best position and priority

If $f(pb_i) > f(gb)$ *then*

$$gb = pb_i$$

$$prioirity_i = prioirity_i + 1$$

End if

End for

update chicken's velocity and position

For each chicken i

For each dimension d

$$v_{i,d} = v_{i,d} + C * Rand(0,1) * [PArray_{i+1}.psition] - x_{i,d}$$

$$x_{i,d} = x_{i,d} + v_{i,d}$$

End for

End for

advance iteration

$$it = it + 1$$

Until it > MaxIterations

Fig. (17). Pseudo-code of proposed algorithm 1.

3.5. THE SECOND EQUATION: CHAOTIC SSPCO

In the second proposed method, we implement the populating based on another one of functions of chaos theory [52]. This equation is presented based on nonlinear dynamics. This pseudo random number generator is the first user of the non-linear dynamics in a network with the continuous statement for each node. This generator is discrete in time and space, but is continuous in state (in this generator, time and space are discrete, but the state is continuous), unlike the cellular machines that Wolfram used to generate random numbers. In the second proposed method, we generate the population based on this function and according to equation (12):

$$f(x) = 1 - 2 \times abs\left(u - \frac{1}{2}\right) \tag{12}$$

Where u is a random number in range [0, 1]. After producing the population with the help of equation (12), the particles are put in the cost function and their fitness (the fitness of them) is determined. According to the first method, in the case of fitness of particles, the priority values of them are added.

$$if \ \ X_i.cost > P_{best} \ \rightarrow \ P_{best} \\ = X_i.position \ \ and \ \ X_i.priority \\ = X_i.priority + 1 \tag{13}$$

$$if \ \ P_{best} > G_{best} \ \ \rightarrow G_{best} = P_{best} \ and \ \ X_i.priority \\ = X_i.priority + 1 \tag{14}$$

The speed and motion equations of particles in this method are initialized same as the first method.

$$X_i.velocity = w * X_i.velocity + c * rand() * \\ (PArray_{i+1}.psition) - X_i.position \tag{15}$$

$$X_i.Newposition = X_i.position + X_i.velocity \tag{16}$$

Fig. (**18**) shows the pseudo-code of the second proposed method.

initialize all chicken according: $1 - 2 \times abs\left(u - \frac{1}{2}\right)$

Repeat

For each chicken i

update the chicken's best position and priority

If $f(x_i) > f(pb_i)$ then

$$pb_i = x_i$$

$$prioirity_i = prioirity_i + 1$$

 End if

update the global best position and priority

If $f(pb_i) > f(gb)$ then

$$gb = pb_i$$

$$prioirity_i = prioirity_i + 1$$

End if

End for

update chicken's velocity and position

For each chicken i

For each dimension d

$$v_{i,d} = v_{i,d} + C * Rand(0,1) * [PArray_{i+1}.psition] - x_{i,d}$$

$$x_{i,d} = x_{i,d} + v_{i,d}$$

End for

End for

advance iteration

$$it = it + 1$$

Until it > MaxIterations

Fig. (18). Pseudo-code of proposed algorithm 2.

3.6. SIMULATION AND RESULTS

The simulations of two proposed methods have been done in MATLAB software and have been compared in two result parts with chaotic algorithms and other optimization algorithms which have been proposed in recent years.

First, we see the figure of particle motions on a cost function in two proposed chaotic methods. Fig. (**19**) shows the procedure of the particle motions over a cost function to achieve a general optimum in a chaotic manner based on the first function.

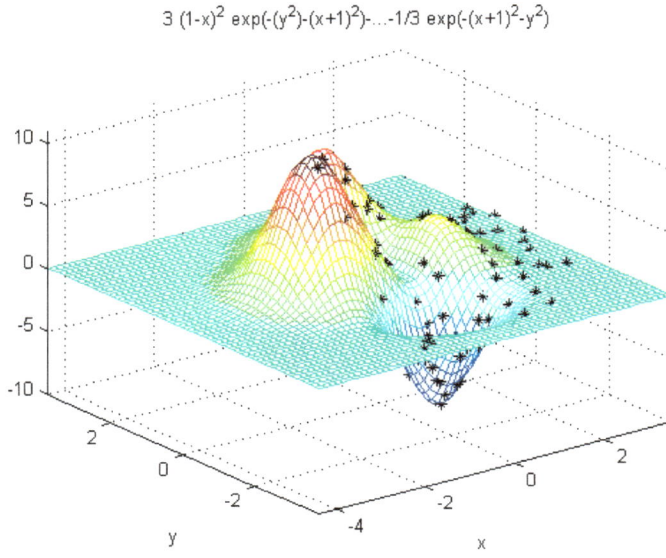

(a)

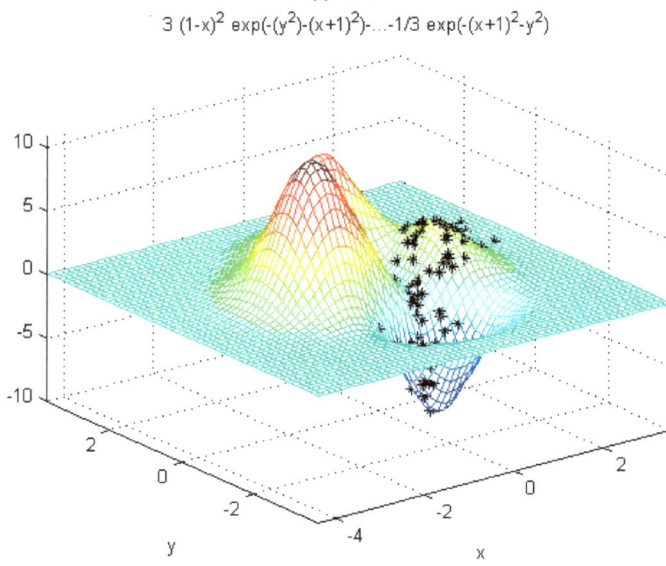

(b)

Fig. 19 cont.....

$3 (1-x)^2 \exp(-(y^2)-(x+1)^2)-\ldots-1/3 \exp(-(x+1)^2-y^2)$

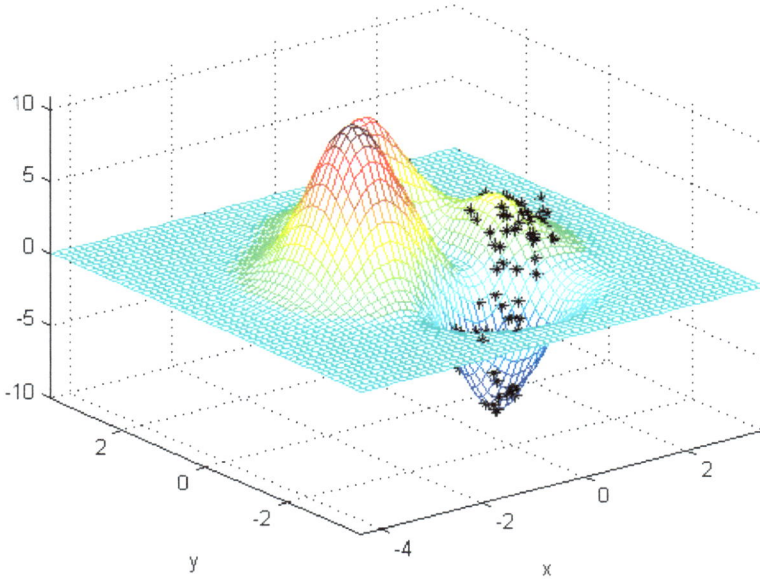

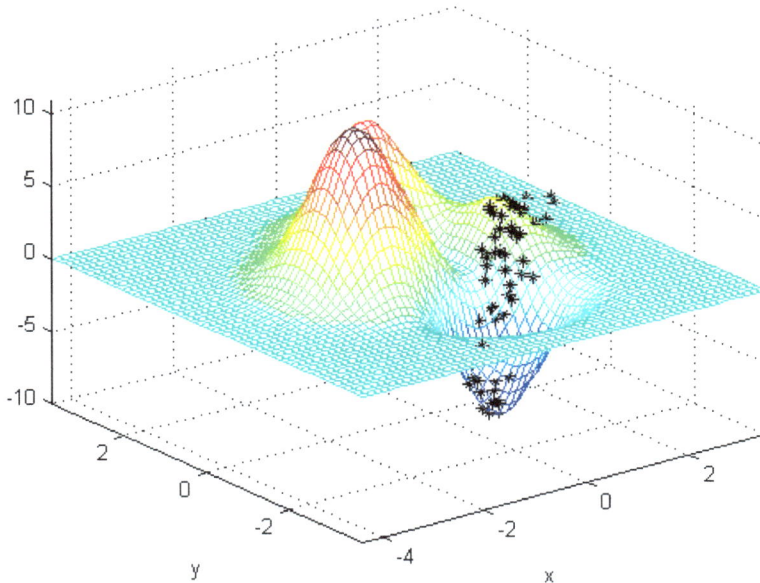

(c)

$3 (1-x)^2 \exp(-(y^2)-(x+1)^2)-\ldots-1/3 \exp(-(x+1)^2-y^2)$

(d)

Fig. 19 cont.....

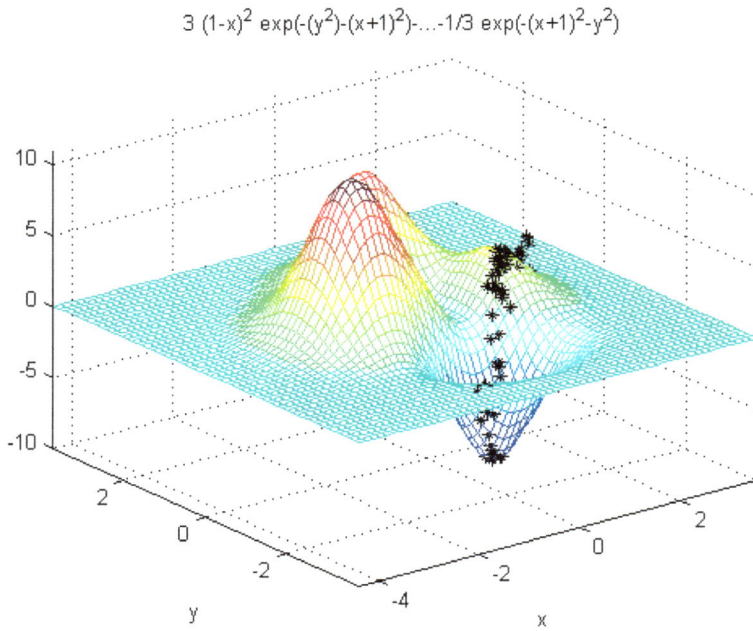

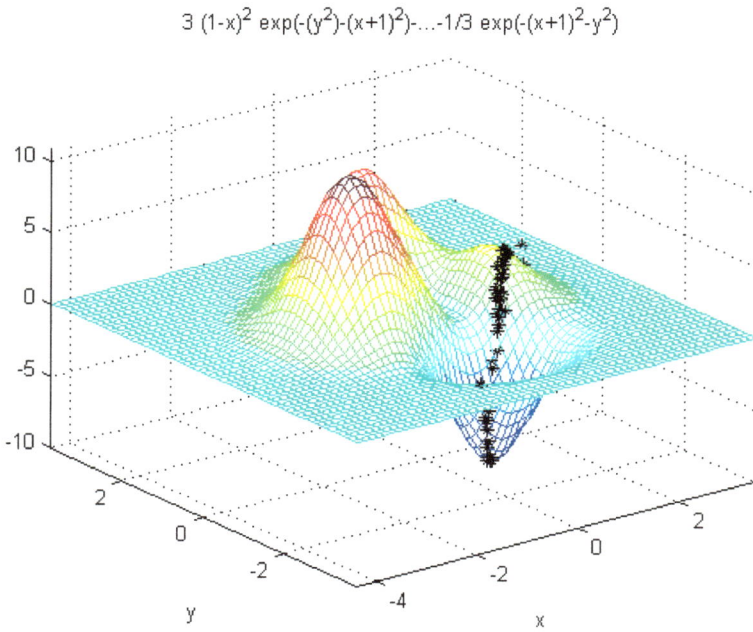

$$3 (1-x)^2 \exp(-(y^2)-(x+1)^2)-\ldots-1/3 \exp(-(x+1)^2-y^2)$$

(e)

$$3 (1-x)^2 \exp(-(y^2)-(x+1)^2)-\ldots-1/3 \exp(-(x+1)^2-y^2)$$

(f)

Fig. 19 cont.....

$3 \ (1-x)^2 \ \exp(-(y^2)-(x+1)^2)-...-1/3 \ \exp(-(x+1)^2-y^2)$

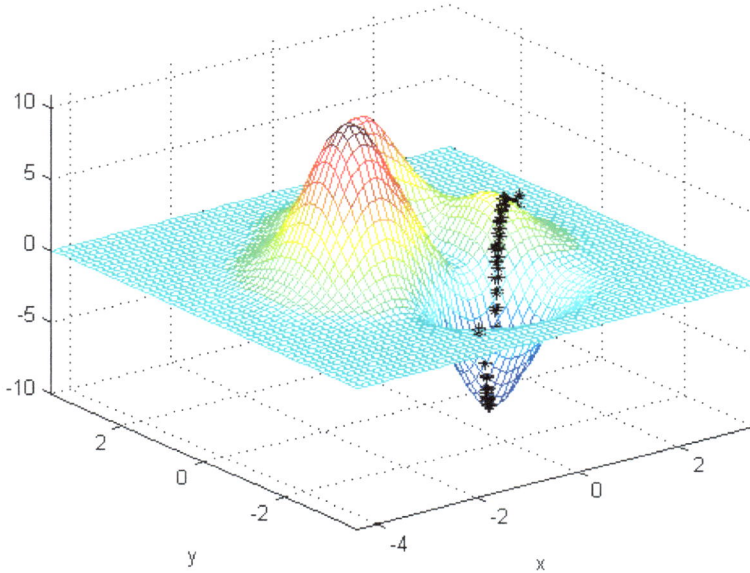

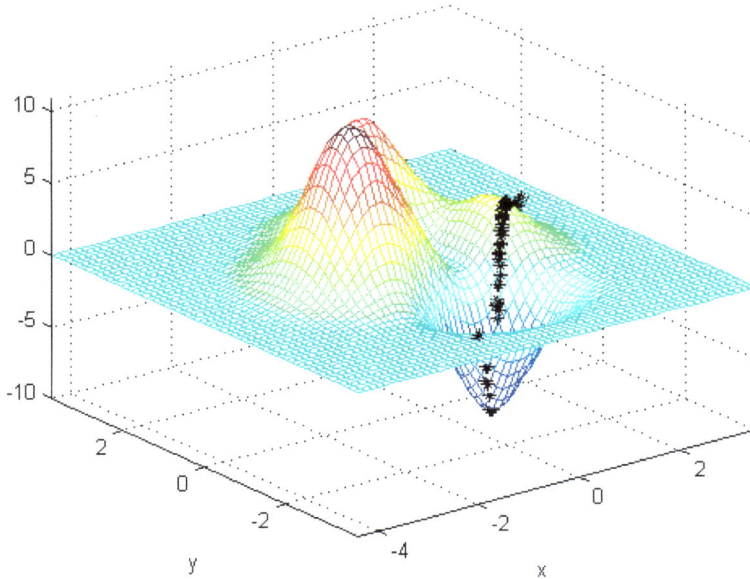

(g)

$3 \ (1-x)^2 \ \exp(-(y^2)-(x+1)^2)-...-1/3 \ \exp(-(x+1)^2-y^2)$

(h)

Fig. 19 cont.....

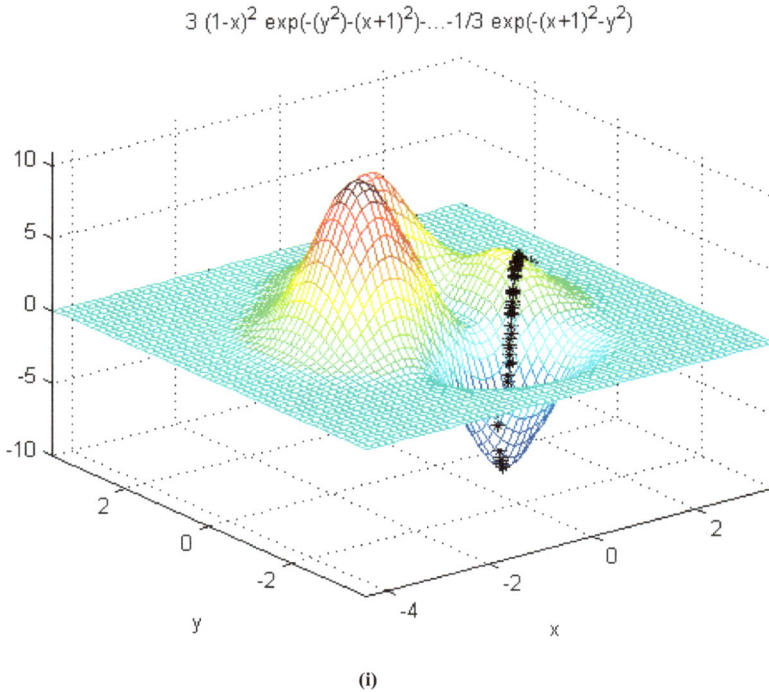

$$3 (1-x)^2 \exp(-(y^2)-(x+1)^2)-\ldots-1/3 \exp(-(x+1)^2-y^2)$$

(i)

Fig. (19). Movement of chicks in proposed algorithm 1 on a fitness function and in different iterations.

The first picture on the left side in above shows haw was been the procedure of generating the population for the first method in space of the problem. The images have been simulated from 9 different iterations of 100 iterations. The number of particles in the population of this simulation has been 100 and we can observe in the following that particles are moving in a queue towards the optimal solution, according to the general framework of SSPCO algorithm. According to the procedure of optimization algorithm SSPCO, a particle or chick adjusts its next move based on the chicks that the value of its priority variable is a unit greater than the given particle; it causes to form a queue-like situation towards the optimum solution. Also in Fig. (**20**), the procedure of particles moving towards the global optimum on the same cost function has been showed. Also, in the first image of Fig. (**20**), the procedure of chaotic populating is observed. This Figure shows that in the second function, the manner of populating is more appropriate for the cost function.

$3 (1-x)^2 \exp(-(y^2)-(x+1)^2)-...-1/3 \exp(-(x+1)^2-y^2)$

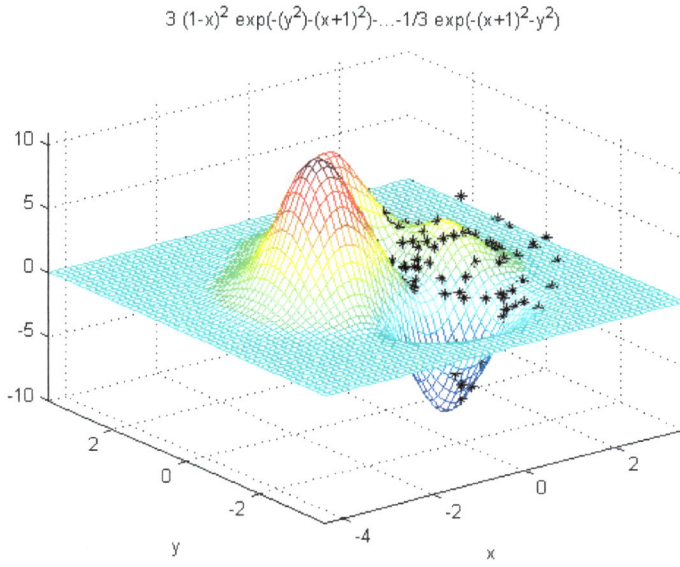

(a)

$3 (1-x)^2 \exp(-(y^2)-(x+1)^2)-...-1/3 \exp(-(x+1)^2-y^2)$

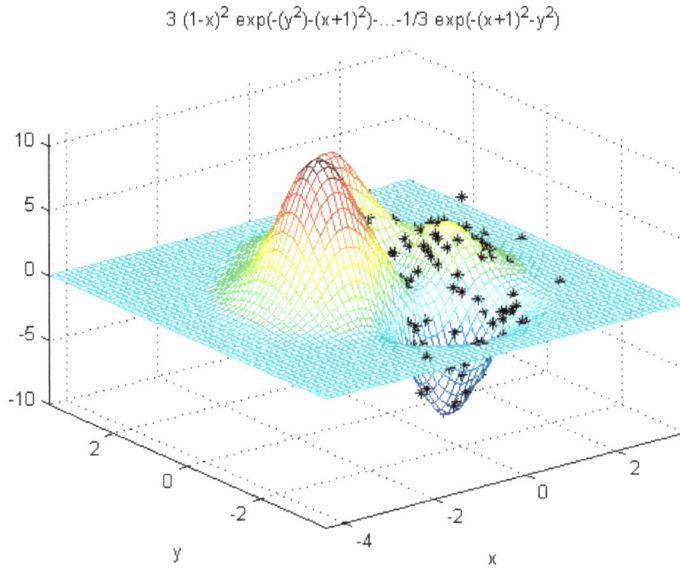

(b)

Fig. 20 cont.....

$3 (1-x)^2 \exp(-(y^2)-(x+1)^2)-...-1/3 \exp(-(x+1)^2-y^2)$

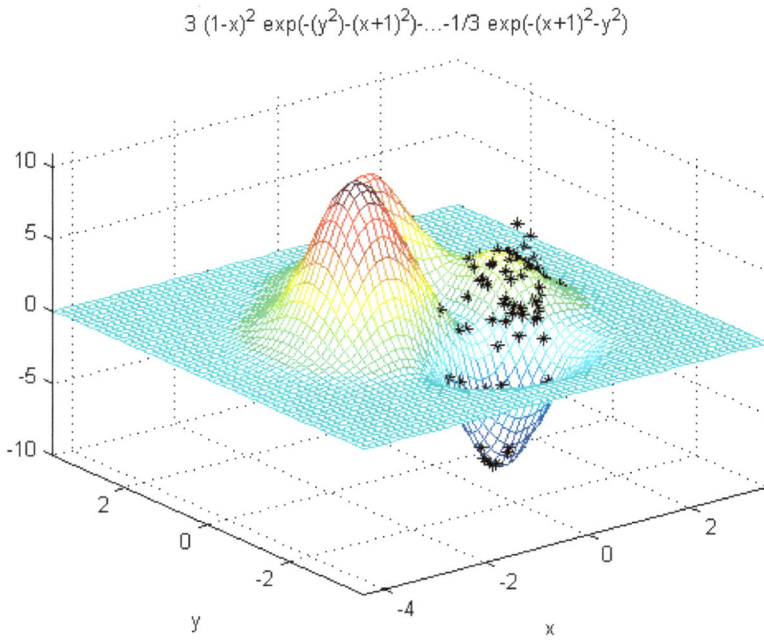

(c)

$3 (1-x)^2 \exp(-(y^2)-(x+1)^2)-...-1/3 \exp(-(x+1)^2-y^2)$

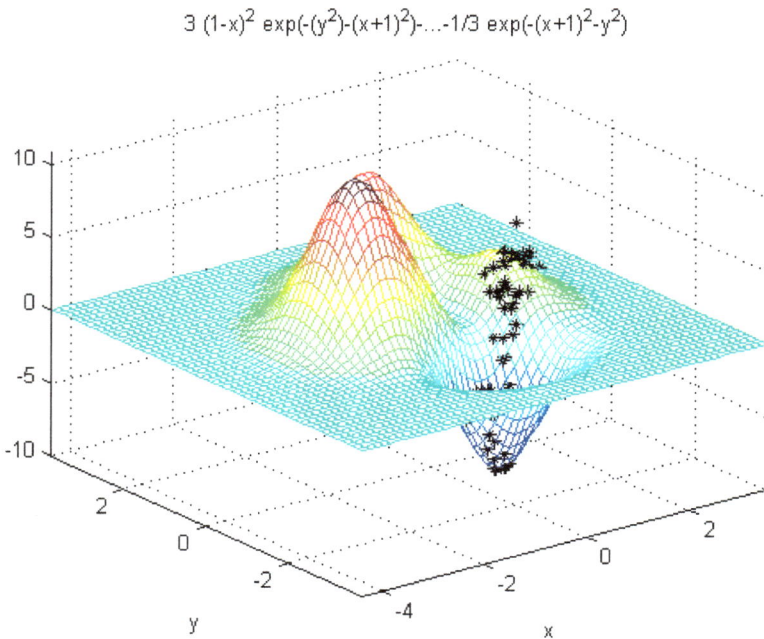

(d)

Fig. 20 cont.....

$$3 (1-x)^2 \exp(-(y^2)-(x+1)^2)-...-1/3 \exp(-(x+1)^2-y^2)$$

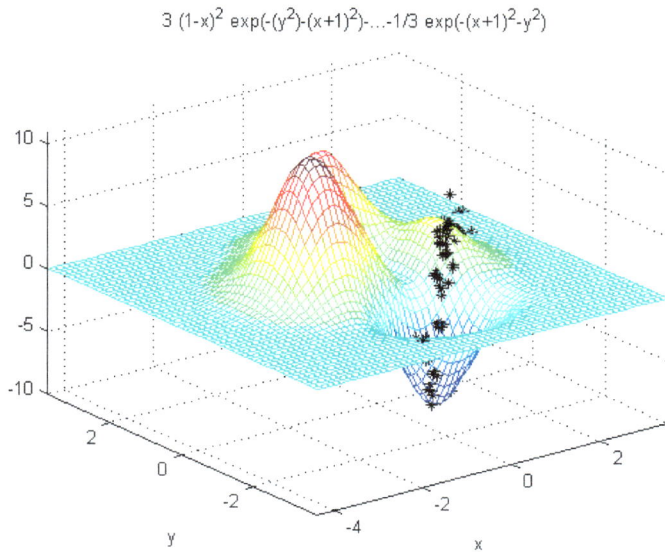

(e)

$$3 (1-x)^2 \exp(-(y^2)-(x+1)^2)-...-1/3 \exp(-(x+1)^2-y^2)$$

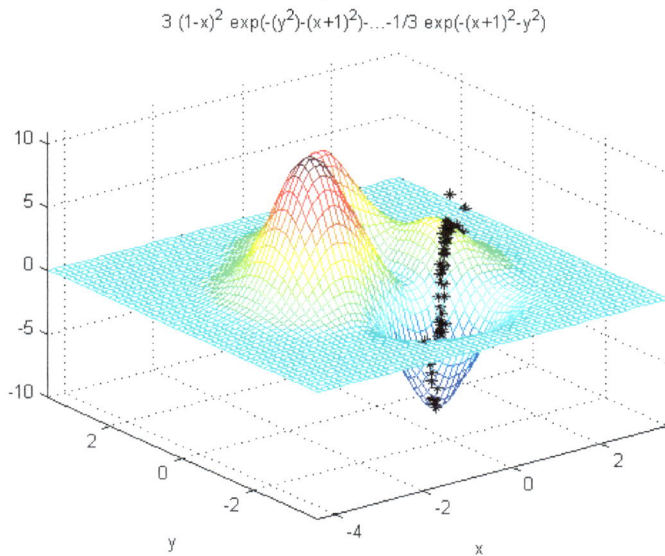

(f)

Fig. (20). Movement of chicks in proposed algorithm 2 on a fitness function and in different iterations.

In the first part, we present two suggested methods along with the chaotic optimization algorithms and based on the parameters of Table **10**.

Table 10. Parameters setting of algorithms.

Value	Parameter	Item No.
100	*pop*	*1*
100	*var*	*2*
-10	*Xmin*	*3*
+10	*Xmax*	*4*
2	*c*	*5*
100	*Iteration*	*6*
0.5	*Percent of crossover*	*7*
0.01	*Percent of mutation*	*8*
10	*Harmony memory size*	*9*
100	*New harmony memory size*	*10*
0.75	*Harmony memory*	*11*
0.05	*Pitch adjustment rate*	*12*
0.1	*Fret width*	*13*

The results are presented for 12 cost functions and based on Table **11**. In the first part, the results have been repeated with 5 known chaotic optimization algorithms and the results have been given in Table **12**. The results are based on the best cost in 100-th iteration, standard deviation of the cost of particles in iteration 100 and run times of 100 iterations. The results are taken from the average of 30 runs of algorithms in order to avoid random results.

Table 11. Fitness function that used in simulation.

F	Function	Dimension	Optima	Figure
F1	**Shifted Sphere**	N	0	
F2	**Shifted Schwefel's Problem 1.2**	N	0	
F3	**Shifted Rotated High Elliptic**	N	0	
F4	**Shifted Schwefel's Problem 1.2**	N	0	

(Table 11) cont.....

F	Function	Dimension	Optima	Figure
F5	**Schwefel's Problem 2.6**	N	0	
F6	**Shifted Rosenbrock's**	N	0	
F7	**Shifted Rotated Griewank's**	N	0	
F8	**Shifted Rotated Ackley's**	N	0	
F9	**Shifted Rastrigin's**	N	0	
F10	**Shifted Rotated Rastrigin's**	N	0	
F11	**Shifted Rotated Weierstrass**	N	0	
F12	**Schwefel's Problem 2.13**	N		

Table 12. Results based on best cost, standard deviation and run time of 5 chaotic algorithms and 2 proposed algorithm.

Function	Result	Chaotic PSO	Chaotic GA	Chaotic ABC	Chaotic BA	Chaotic HS	Chaotic SSPCO1	Chaotic SSPCO2
F1	Best Cost	0.6767	209.81	807.58 **W**	179.19	804.36	7.32E-06	7.12E-06 **B**
	STD	921.78	6.65E+03	799.79	279.59	313.65	277.54	1.18E+03
	Run Time	7.79	1.62	5.49	14.41	67.37	7.63	14.19
F2	Best Cost	0.4754	3.1984	9.5480 **W**	7.3486	9.9469	9.12E-05 **B**	2.25E-04
	STD	1.4009	6.5698	8.5565	0.0977	0.1061	1.8407	1.7087
	Run Time	7.61	2.06	6.11	15.37	70.30	6.96	13.88

(Table 11) cont.....

F3	Best Cost	9.32E+04	2.85E+06	2.41E+07 W	1.88E+06	9.07E+06	0.0873 B	0.3866
	STD	7.48E+07	8.20E+08	3.18E+08	6.85E+07	5.51E+07	1.94E+07	1.12E+08
	Run Time	9.66	2.71	7.50	25.22	74.71	8.72	17.69
F4	Best Cost	0.5947	3.9358	9.6390	7.7848	9.8694 W	7.64E-04	3.80E-05 B
	STD	1.4479	6.8912	9.2167	0.0997	0.0948	1.7107	1.5450
	Run Time	6.92	1.22	5.42	11.42	68.99	6.11	12.16
F5	Best Cost	2.53	1.63E+04	5.60E+05	3.56E+05	3.13E+06 W	0.0097 B	0.0447
	STD	1.88E+06	1.79E+09	5.31E+07	2.47E+06	2.56E+06	1.19E+06	6.800E+06
	Run Time	7.63	1.49	5.95	13.68	69.07	6.87	13.33
F6	Best Cost	462.54	5.91E+04	2.32E+05	2.38E+05	2.85E+06 W	98.99	98.15 B
	STD	5.39E+06	1.40E+09	8.19E+08	2.84E+06	2.52E+06	1.23E+06	1.08E+07
	Run Time	11.18	1.60	6.68	9.93	64.12	6.44	12.75
F7	Best Cost	0.0670	0.8599	1.3437 W	1.0164	1.2418	1.89E-08 B	3.04E-05
	STD	0.4779	2.2725	0.1029	0.0753	0.720	0.4929	0.6105
	Run Time	11.13	2.76	8.99	24.93	74.41	9.80	19.02
F8	Best Cost	1.8834	7.1044	11.3809 W	7.0984	10.7656	0.0013 B	0.018
	STD	2.0581	2.6044	0.6331	0.2995	0.3981	3.4023	3.3605
	Run Time	8.30	2.50	7.19	19.26	72.08	8.29	16.65
F9	Best Cost	185.15	649.88	1.95E+03	731.96 W	1.87E+03	0.0437 B	0.1483
	STD	968.75	8.29E+03	1.40E+03	298.79	340.11	647.81	958.37
	Run Time	7.21	1.38	5.67	11.29	67.91	6.92	13.61
F10	Best Cost	125.42	728.89	1.68E+03	785.50 W	1.84E+03	0.0084	0.0071 B
	STD	986.05	8.83E+03	1.40E+04	281.39	314.98	678.42	1.18E+03
	Run Time	8.19	2.50	7.04	18.35	68.21	7.79	15.78

(Table 11) cont.....

F11	Best Cost	2.37E-10	0.0097	0.0763 **W**	0.0097	0.0097	2.96E-05	0.00 **B**
	STD	0.3226	0.1223	0.2573	0.3069	0.3045	0.3538	0.3301
	Run Time	6.80	1.88	7.62	11.12	70.21	6.36	12.64
F12	Best Cost	1.1697	3.8628	9.6037 **W**	8.1495	9.9246	2.68E-04 **B**	0.0023
	STD	1.6551	7.9908	8.3561	0.1102	0.0875	1.7520	1.9852
	Run Time	8.05	1.35	5.61	11.83	72.04	6.73	13.19
		B=BEST ALGORITHM			**W**=WORST ALGORITHM			

The results are given based on the best cost at the end of estimations (Best Cost), the standard deviation of the cost of particles (STD) and run time. The results show that the proposed algorithms have had the best performance for each of 12 cost functions and have presented the best costs. For 7 functions, the first proposed method has the best cost among 7 algorithms, and for 5 functions, the second proposed method has the best cost. In function F1, algorithm Chaotic ABC has the worst cost with the cost of 807.58, while for the same function, the first proposed algorithm has the cost of 7.32E-06, and the second proposed algorithm has the cost of 7.12-E06, which has the best cost among other algorithms. The highest standard deviation for this cost function is associated to Chaotic SSPCO and the lowest standard deviation is associated to Chaotic SSPCO algorithm. For cost function F, the least and most run times are respectively associated to Chaotic GA method and Chaotic ABC algorithm. Due to the more complexity of the populating mechanism, the run time of this function for the second proposed method is higher than the first, and this run time procedure was equal for all 12 functions. Since the optimized answer of all functions, except for function F6, has been zero, for the rest of functions, two proposed methods have been able to reach to costs close to zero in the 100-th iteration, while for the most of these functions, other algorithms have reach the costs with much distances from zero. The graph of the best cost of chaotic algorithms is shown in Fig. (**21**). The graph of the best dispersion of these chaotic algorithms is also shown in Fig. (**21**). Fig. (**22**) also shows the runtime diagram for these algorithms. Fig. (**23**) shows the diagram of the time of execution of the two proposed methods and 5 other algorithms.

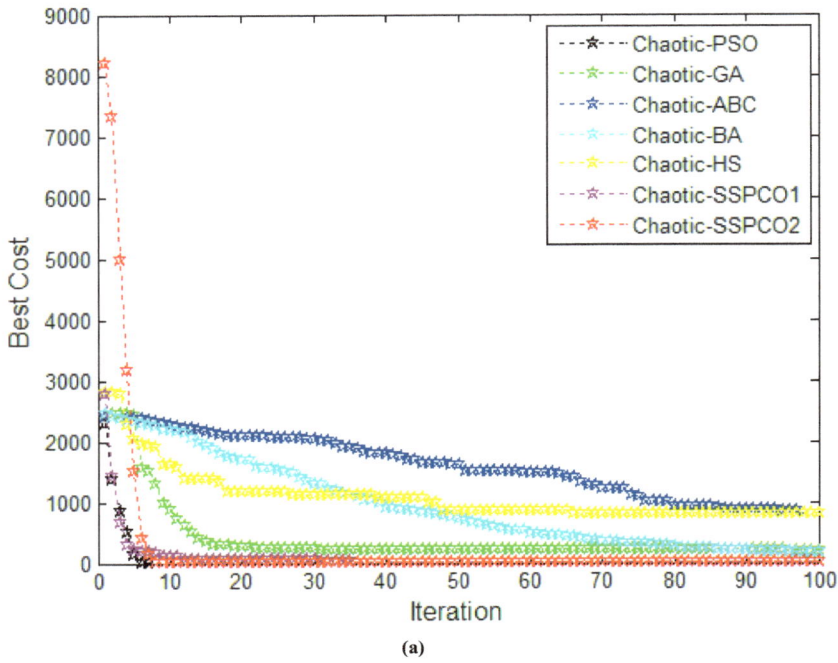

(a)

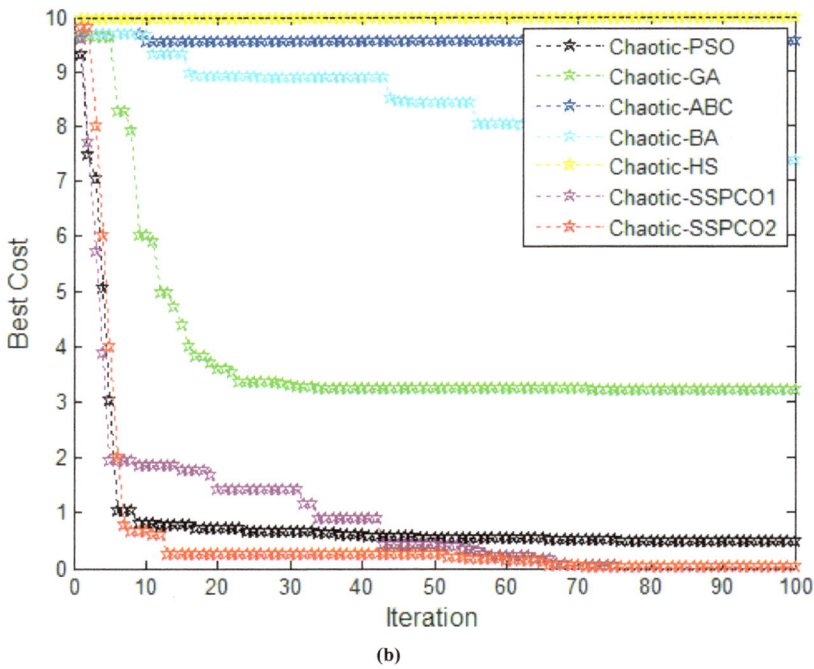

(b)

Fig. 21 cont.....

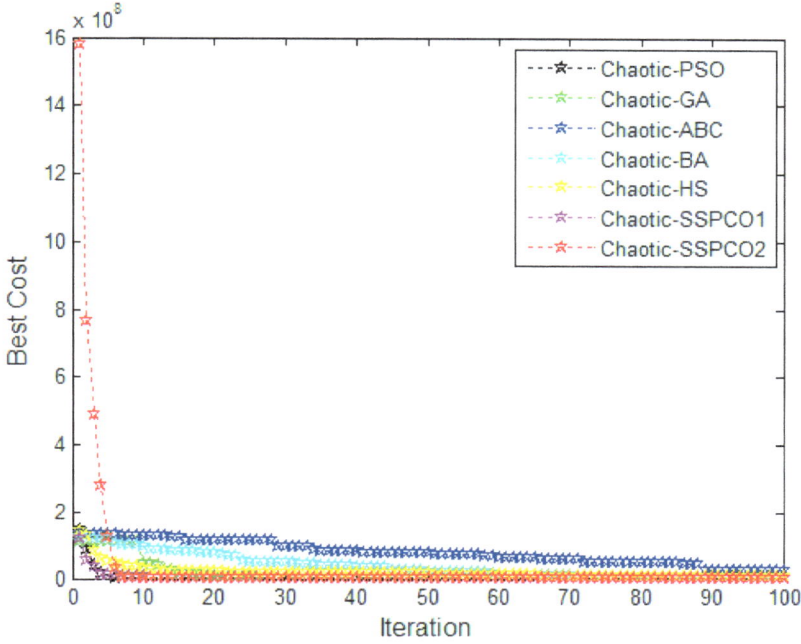

(c)

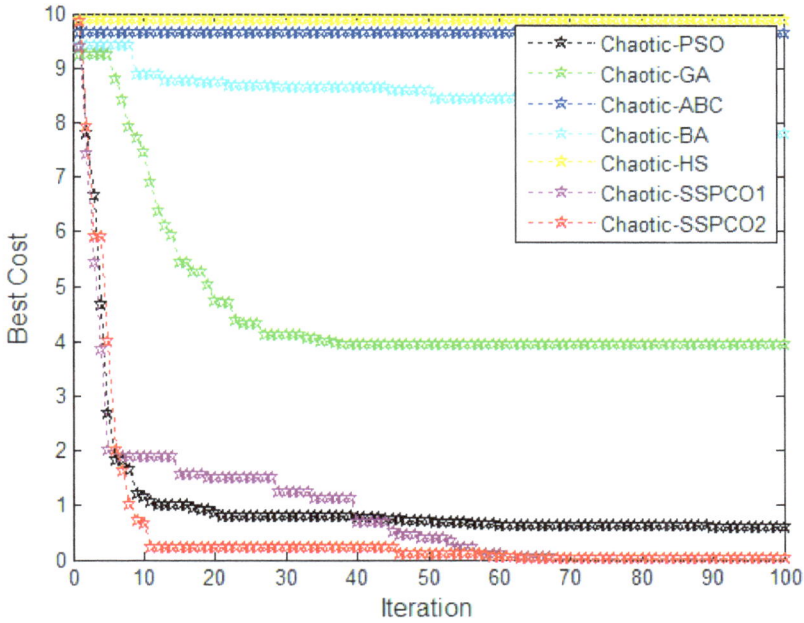

(d)

Fig. 21 cont.....

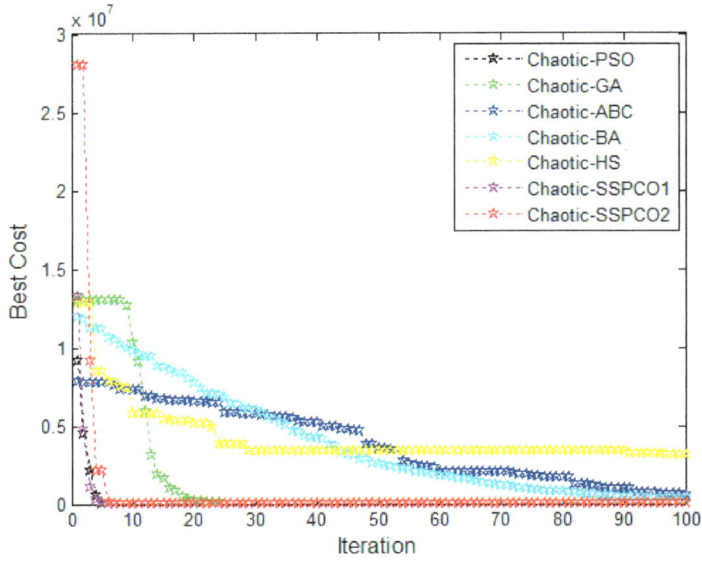

(e)

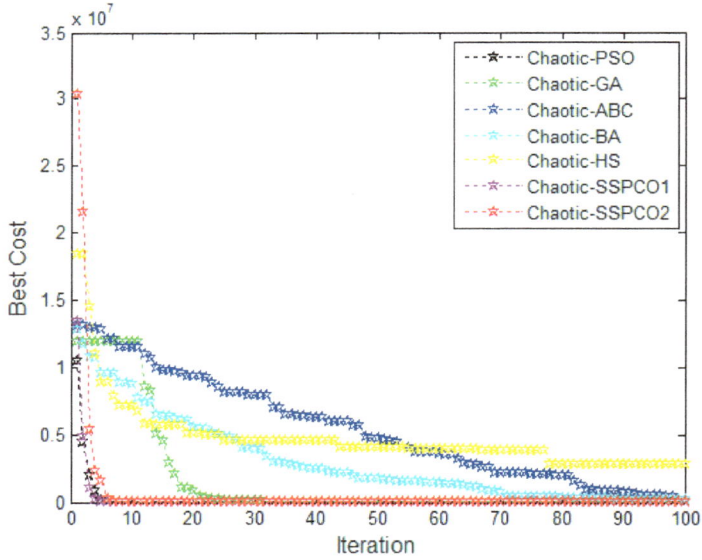

(f)

Fig. (21). Plot of best cost in 7 chaotic algorithms PSO, GA, BA, ABC, HS, SSPCO1 and SSPCO2 (**a**) F1. (**b**) F2.(**c**) F3. (**d**) F4. (**e**) F5. (**f**) F6. (**g**) F7. (**h**) F8. (**i**) F9. (**j**) F10. (**k**) F11. (**l**) F12.

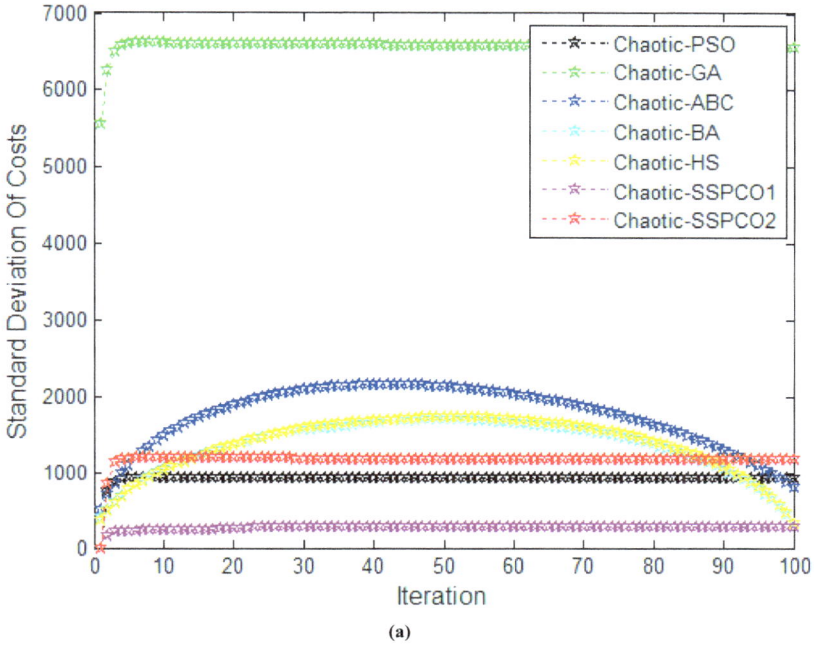

(a)

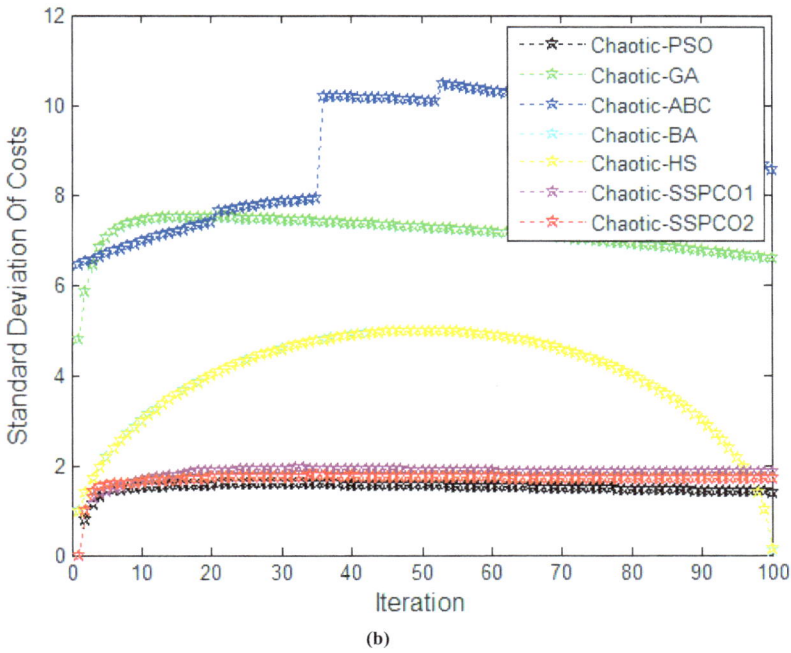

(b)

Fig. 22 cont.....

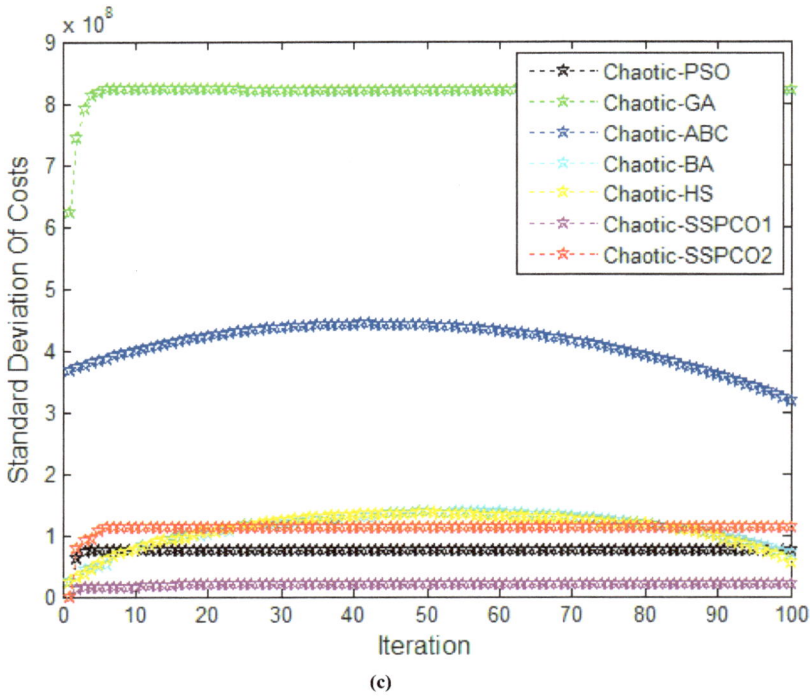

(c)

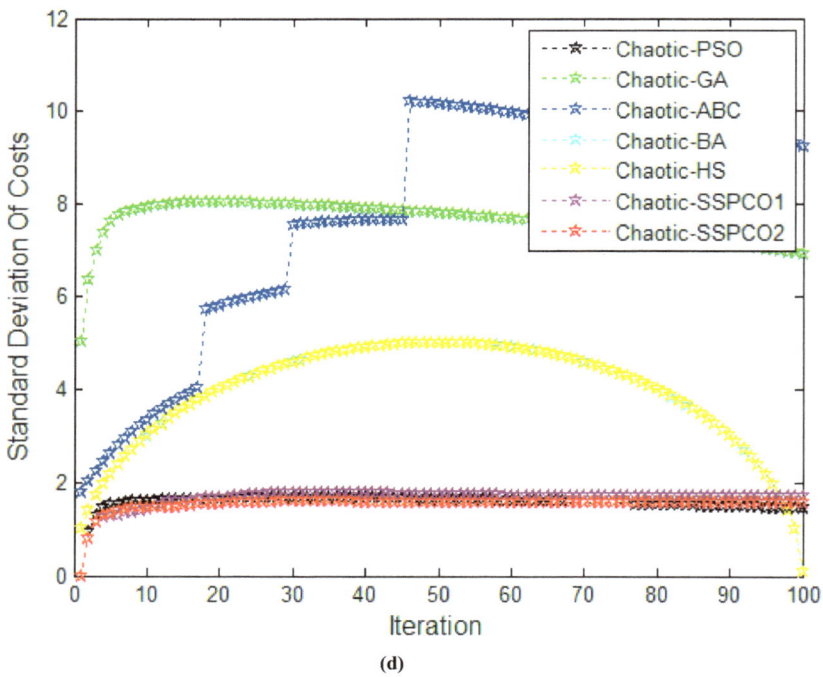

(d)

Fig. 22 cont.....

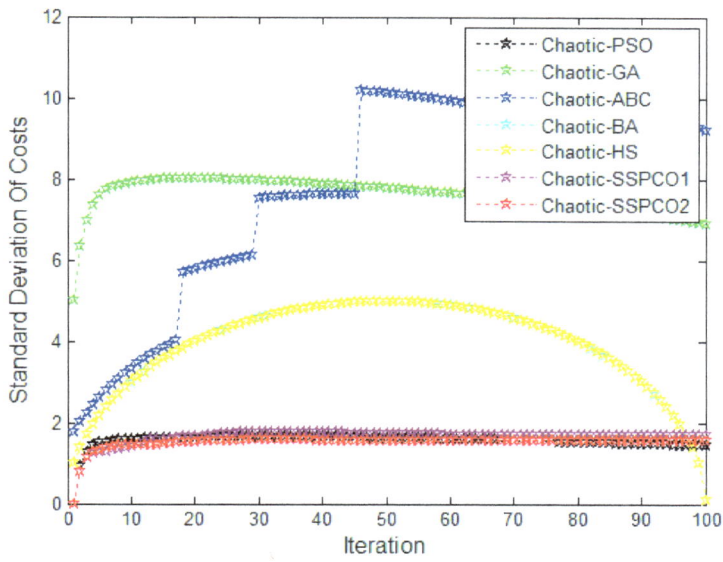

(e)

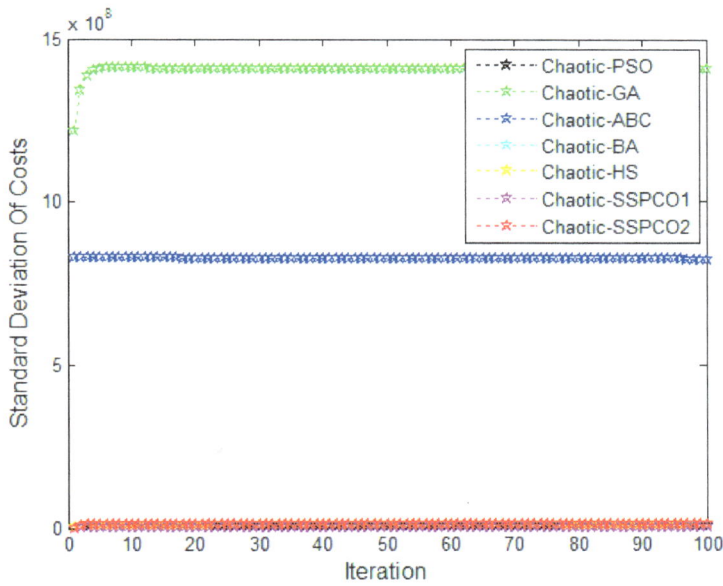

(f)

Fig. (22). Plot standard deviation in 7 chaotic algorithms PSO, GA, BA, ABC, HS, SSPCO1 and SSPCO2 (**a**) F1. (**b**) F2.(**c**) F3. (**d**) F4. (**e**) F5. (**f**) F6. (**g**) F7. (**h**) F8. (**i**) F9. (**j**) F10. (**k**) F11. (**l**) F12.

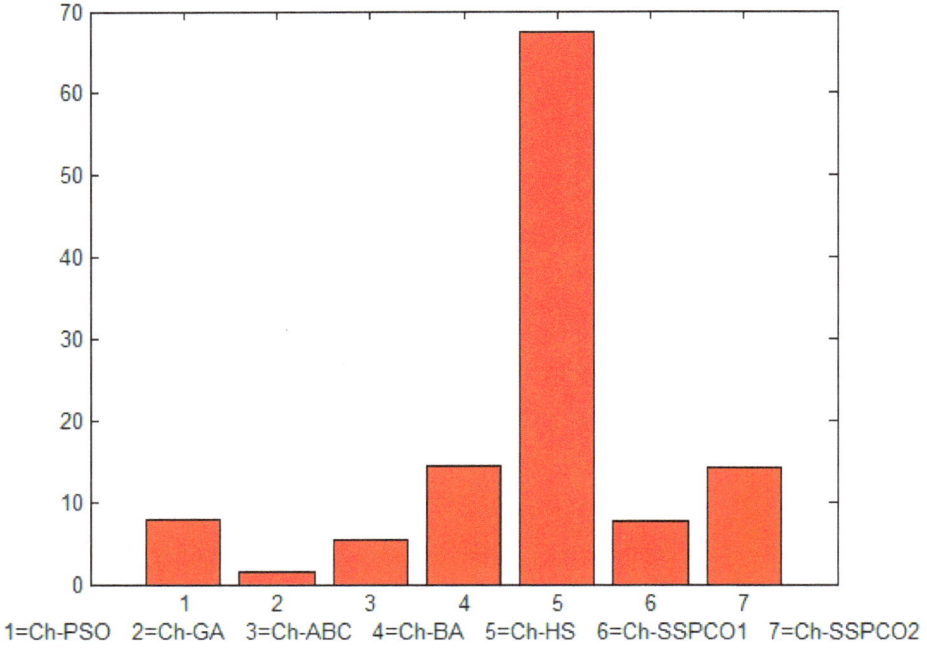

(a)

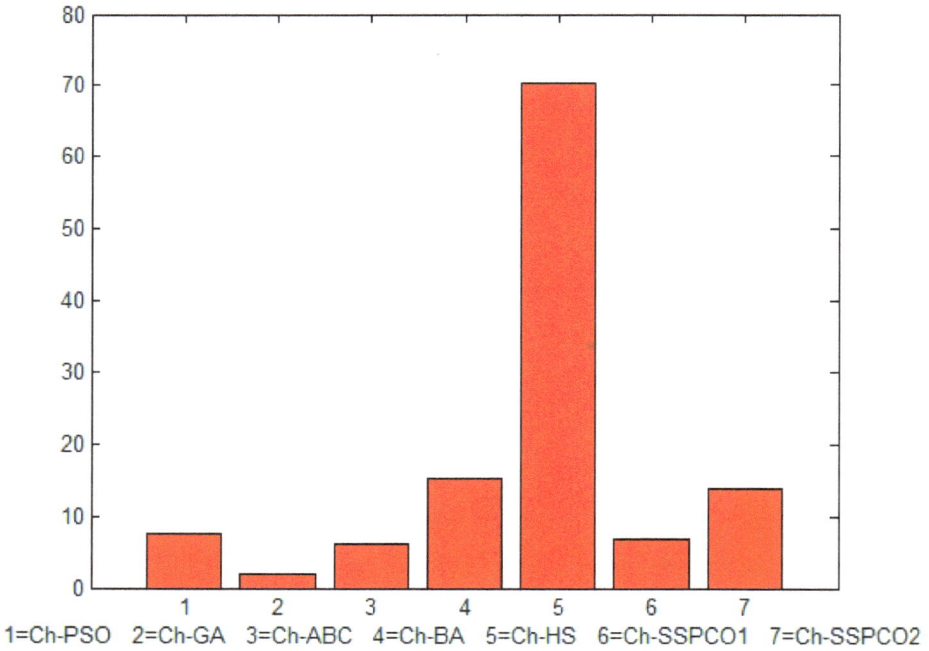

(b)

Fig. 23 cont.....

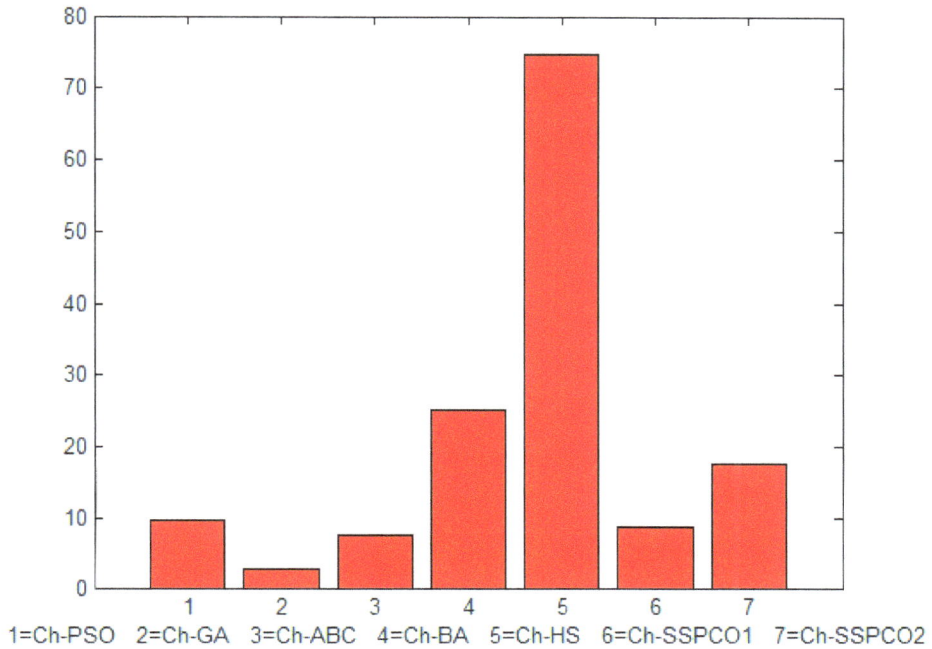

1=Ch-PSO   2=Ch-GA   3=Ch-ABC   4=Ch-BA   5=Ch-HS   6=Ch-SSPCO1   7=Ch-SSPCO2

(c)

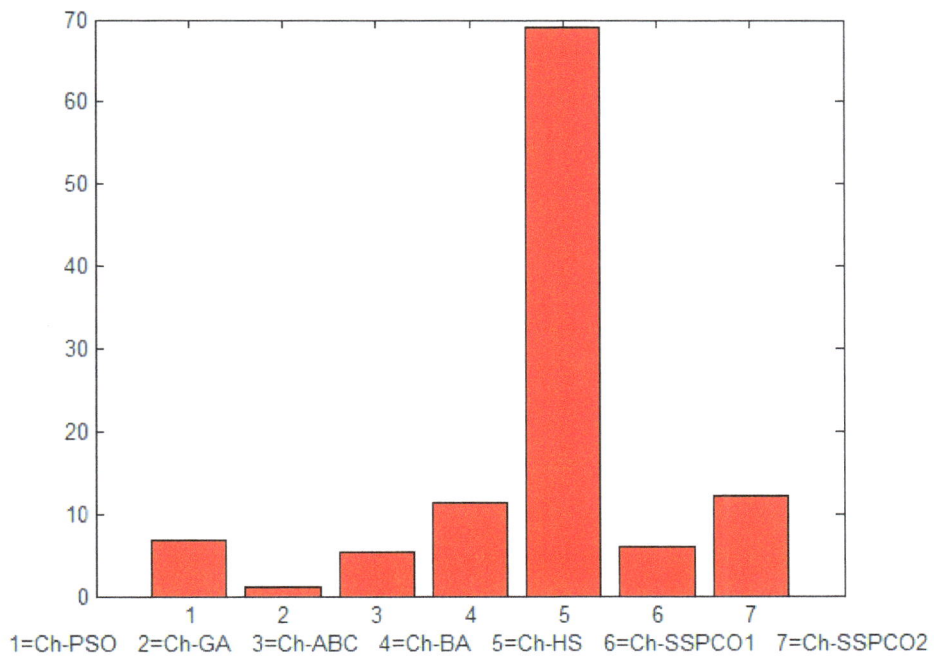

1=Ch-PSO   2=Ch-GA   3=Ch-ABC   4=Ch-BA   5=Ch-HS   6=Ch-SSPCO1   7=Ch-SSPCO2

(d)

Fig. 23 cont.....

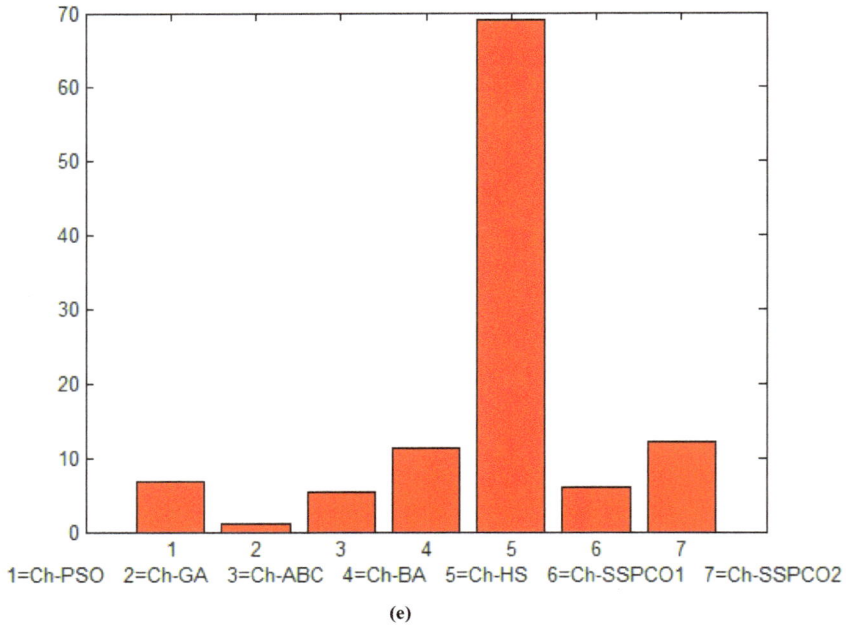

(e)

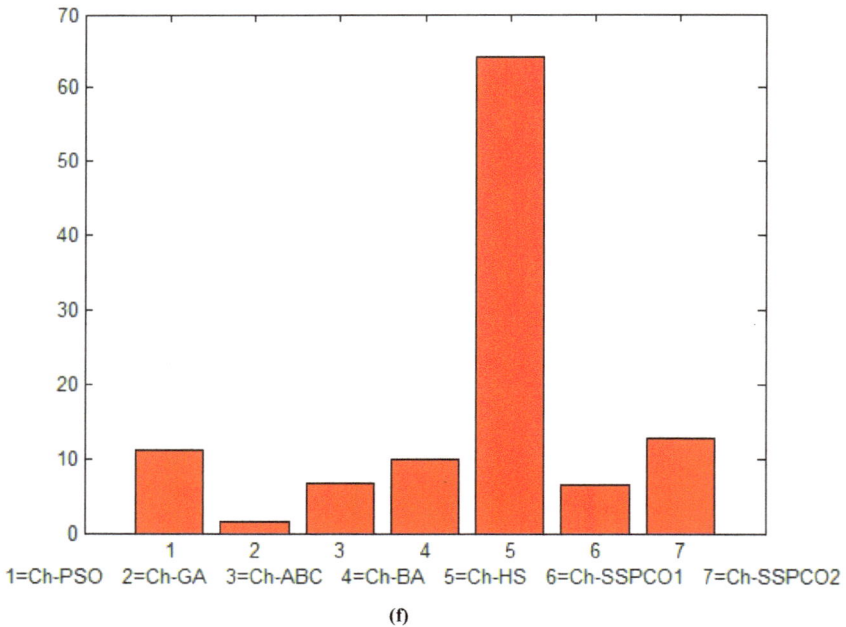

(f)

Fig. (23). Plot run time in 7 chaotic algorithms PSO, GA, BA, ABC, HS, SSPCO1 and SSPCO2 (**a**) F1. (**b**) F2.(**c**) F3. (**d**) F4. (**e**) F5. (**f**) F6. (**g**) F7. (**h**) F8. (**i**) F9. (**j**) F10. (**k**) F11. (**l**) F12.

In this section and in Table **13**, we compare the results of two chaotic methods, namely Chaotic SSPCO 1 and Chaotic SSPCO 2, with SSPCO algorithm with random populating to realize the difference between the performance of the algorithm with random populating and chaotic algorithm.

Table 13. Results based on best cost, standard deviation and run time of SSPCO algorithm with random population and two chaotic SSPCO algorithms.

Function	Result	Random SSPCO	Chaotic SSPCO1	Chaotic SSPCO2
F1	Best Cost	3.93e-05 **W**	7.32E-06	7.12E-06 **B**
	STD	288.27	277.54	1.18E+03
	Run Time	6.01	7.63	14.19
F2	Best Cost	1.19 e-05 **B**	9.12E-05	2.25E-04 **W**
	STD	5968.96	1.8407	1.7087
	Run Time	28.32	6.96	13.88
F3	Best Cost	1.20 **W**	0.0873 **B**	0.3866
	STD	17044818	1.94E+07	1.12E+08
	Run Time	12.89	8.72	17.69
F4	Best Cost	5.33 e-05	7.64E-04 **W**	3.80E-05 **B**
	STD	6698.88	1.7107	1.5450
	Run Time	26.16	6.11	12.16
F5	Best Cost	0.00017 **B**	0.0097	0.0447 **W**
	STD	1.95	1.19E+06	6.800E+06
	Run Time	6.74	6.87	13.33
F6	Best Cost	99.00 **W**	98.99	98.15 **B**
	STD	980107.8	1.23E+06	1.08E+07
	Run Time	5.74	6.44	12.75
F7	Best Cost	6.68e-08	1.89E-08 **B**	3.04E-05 **W**
	STD	0.48	0.4929	0.6105
	Run Time	6.52	9.80	19.02
F8	Best Cost	0.0017	0.0013 **B**	0.018**W**
	STD	3.37	3.4023	3.3605
	Run Time	6.23	8.29	16.65
F9	Best Cost	0.012	0.0437 **B**	0.1483 **W**
	STD	665.56	647.81	958.37
	Run Time	5.68	6.92	13.61

(Table 13) cont.....

F10	Best Cost	8.41e-05 **B**	0.0084 **W**	0.0071
	STD	626.74	678.42	1.18E+03
	Run Time	7.16	7.79	15.78
F11	Best Cost	6.44e-09	2.96E-05 **W**	0.00 **B**
	STD	0.49	0.3538	0.3301
	Run Time	10.36	6.36	12.64
F12	Best Cost	5.15e-05 **B**	2.68E-04	0.0023 **W**
	STD	27.23	1.7520	1.9852
	Run Time	42.64	6.73	13.19
B=BEST ALGORITHM			**W=WORST ALGORITHM**	

The results of this section show that SSPCO algorithm with random populating has the best performance for 4 functions and the worst performance for 3 functions. Unlike other optimization algorithms, the difference between results, in random populating and chaotic methods is low, which arises from the appropriate mechanism of this algorithm to reach the optimized solution. In the second part, the results of the proposed methods and optimization algorithms that have been proposed in recent years have been compared. We have compared the proposed methods with algorithms NPSO [53], FIPS [54], CPSO [55], CLPSO [56], PEECA [57], MRPSO [58] and E-ABC [59]. In this part, we have done the simulation with the number of population 500, the number of variables 30 and the number of times of estimation200000. We present the results based on two component, mean cost and standard deviation. The results based of mean cost () and standard deviation (*SD*) of particles have been presented at the end of estimations. In Table **14** the proposed method is compared with the other 7 algorithms in terms of average cost and dispersion rate.

Table 14. Results of proposed algorithms with FIPS, CPSO, CLPSO, EPSDE, NPSO, CCABC and MRPSO in 200000 iterations.

Function	Result	FIPS	CPSO	CLPSO	PEECA	NPSO	E-ABC	MRPSO	Chaotic SSPCO1	Chaotic SSPCO2
F1	F_{mean}	4.588E-02	5.14E-01W	0.00E+00B	2.02E-30	6.59E-21	1.11E-11	2.31E-27	0.00E+00B	0.00E+00B
	SD	1.95E-05	7.75E-02	0.00E+00	1.01E-29	1.63E-23	3.57E-18	3.41E-28	0.00E+00	0.00E+00
F2	F_{mean}	2.32E-01	1.25E-00	7.01E+02W	5.59E-26	2.50E-10	1.77E-15	4.99E-10	5.45E-027	4.13E-027B
	SD	1.14E-03	1.17E-01	1.18E+02	1.06E-25	4.33E-10	2.74E-15	7.72E-10	1.05E+06	1.01E+06
F3	F_{mean}	9.46E+00	1.88E-00	1.37E+07W	5.14E+06	5.45E-19	1.34E-12	4.82E+05	4.55E-21B	4.23E-020
	SD	2.59E+01	9.91E+00	4.37E+06	2.07E+07	9.24E-19	3.01E-14	2.01E+05	8.23E-18	6.54E-05
F4	F_{mean}	3.30E-00	1.07E-00	6.01E+03	2.48E+00	8.45E-00	3.13E+12W	1.25E+03	1.05E-00	5.54E-26B

(Table 14) cont.....

	SD	8.66E-00	2.76E-00	1.26E+03	7.60E+00	8.49E-00	3.98E+13	9.00E+02	1.08E+02	9.25E+06
F5	F_{mean}	2.67E+00	8.26E-00	3.97E+03	1.52E+03	3.06E-00	5.44E+08W	8.43E+03	3.33E-00	6.67E-19B
	SD	2.00E+00	2.34E+00	4.88E+02	1.03E+03	4.02E-00	8.47E+07	1.98E+03	4.54E+02	9.68E+08
F6	F_{mean}	0.00B	0.00B	3.34E+00	9.57E-01	0.00B	1.98E+05W	3.03E+01	0.00B	0.00B
	SD	0.00	0.00	5.01E+00	1.74E+00	0.00	5.89E+04	7.38E+01	0.00	0.00
F7	F_{mean}	5.85E+00	3.60E-01	4.40E-01	1.68E-02	0.00B	2.32E+08W	2.31E-02	0.00B	0.00B
	SD	1.91E+00	1.50E-02	6.99E-02	1.40E-02	0.00	1.33E+08	2.01E-02	0.00	0.00
F8	F_{mean}	6.18E+00	5.37E-01	2.09E+01	2.09E+01	4.04E-21	5.84E+07W	2.09E+01	2.10E-01	0.00B
	SD	1.40E+00	5.94E-02	6.14E-02	4.54E-02	1.55E-22	1.81E+05	5.19E-02	4.81E-02	0.00
F9	F_{mean}	1.38E-01	1.60E-00	0.00B	0.00B	-8.88E-01	3.77E+07W	1.17E+01	0.00 B	0.00 B
	SD	2.32E-02	7.86E-01	0.00E+00	0.00E+00	0.00	6.10E+06	4.28E+00	0.00	0.00
F10	F_{mean}	2.47E-00	2.12E-00	9.40E+01	4.65E+01	0.00B	4.94E+03W	1.13E+02	4.76E-19	0.00B
	SD	1.82E-00	6.31E-00	1.50E+01	9.44E+00	0.00	1.18E+02	3.04E+01	1.34E+01	0.00
F11	F_{mean}	-1.10E+00	-1.21E+00	2.55E+01	3.42E+01W	-1.25E+00	1.81E+00	1.64E+01	-1.87E+00B	-1.45+00
	SD	9.44E+00	3.37E+00	1.14E+00	3.48E+00	2.52E-00	1.33E-01	2.90E+00	5.68E+00	6.38E+00
F12	F_{mean}	2.60E+00	5.42E-01	1.42E+04	3.53E+04W	2.27E-19	4.02E+03	5.79E+03	2.87E-03	2.15E-21B
	SD	2.17E+00	8.28E-02	3.67E+03	6.95E+03	2.69E-18	2.87E+04	5.60E+03	3.26E+03	1.36E-15
		B=BEST ALGORITHM					W=WORST ALGORITHM			

The results show that among 9 algorithms, the first and second proposed algorithms have had the best performances efficiency respectively for 6 and 10 cost functions, where 4 functions were common in these two categories. The first proposed method was converged to the optimal solution for 4 functions and the second one could to obtain the global optimal point for 6 of cost functions at the end of evaluations. For cost function F1, CLPSO algorithm and the first proposed method commonly reached the optimal point and had the best efficiency performance. In this function, CPSO algorithm had the lowest efficiency and reached the mean cost of 5.14E-01. For cost function F2, the best mean cost was related to the first proposed algorithm with the mean cost of 4.13E-027. For this cost function, CLPSO algorithm had the worst mean cost. For cost function F3, the highest and lowest performances are respectively related to the first proposed and CLPSO algorithms. For cost function F4, the second proposed method has the best mean cost and CCABC algorithm that is an artificial bee colony based on chaos algorithm had the lowest performance. The same process is repeated for cost function F5. For cost function f6, FIPS, CPSO, NPSO and two proposed methods commonly had the best performance. For function F7, the first and second proposed and NPSO algorithms commonly had the best mean cost that was just the optimized point of the problem. Among algorithms, CCABC algorithm had the worst mean cost for functions F7, F8 and F9.

The left side of Fig. (**24**), represents the diagram of the best cost of random population-based SSPCO algorithm (SSPCO algorithm based on random population) and chaos-based SSOCO algorithms for various dimensions and the right side shows the diagram of the best cost respect to the total cost functions, over the various iterations of evaluations. In Fig. (**24**), the convergence characteristics of SSPCO, Chaotic SSPCO1 and Chaotic SSPCO2 algorithms are based on changes in the number of features of cost functions set. As we can see, chaotic algorithms are also not sensitive to changes in the size of features of set of cost functions.

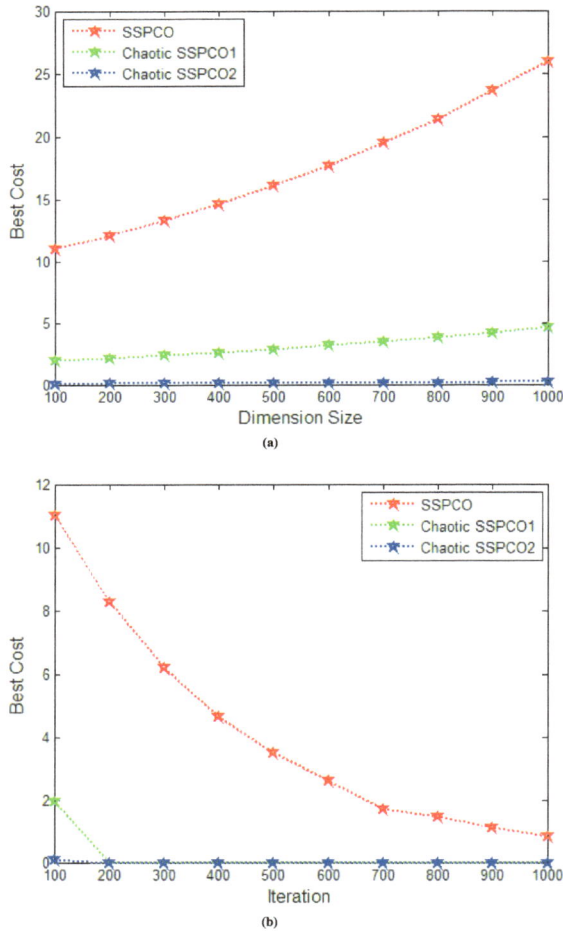

Fig. (24). Plot best cost on total of fitness function in SSPCO, SSPCO1 and SSPCO2 based on different dimension and iterations.

3.7. DATA CLUSTERING USING BY CHAOTIC SSPCO ALGORITHM

Given a database with C classes and N parameters, the classification problem can be seen as that of finding the optimal positions of C center in an N-dimensional space *i.e.* that of determining for any center its N coordinates, each of which can take on, in general, real values. With these premises, the i-th individual of the population is encoded as the equation No.17:

$$(p_i^{\rightarrow 1}, \dots, p_i^{\rightarrow C}, v_i^{\rightarrow 1}, \dots, v_i^{\rightarrow C}) \tag{17}$$

Where the position of the j-th center is constituted by N real numbers representing its N coordinates in the problem space:

$$p_i^{\rightarrow j} = \{p_{1,i}^j, \dots, p_{N,1}^j\} \tag{18}$$

And similarly the velocity of the j-th center is made up of N real numbers representing its N velocity components in the problem space:

$$v_i^{\rightarrow j} = \{v_{1,i}^j, \dots, v_{N,1}^j\} \tag{19}$$

Then, each individual in the population is composed of $2 \times C \times N$ components, each represented by a real value.

3.8. FITNESS FUNCTION

In symbols, i-th individual fitness is given by equation 14:

$$(i) = \frac{1}{D_{Train}} \sum_{j=1}^{D_{Train}} d(x_j^{\rightarrow}, p_i^{\rightarrow CL_{known}(x_j^{\rightarrow})}) \tag{20}$$

The fitness function is computed in one step as the sum on all training set instances of Euclidean distance in N-dimensional space between generic instance $x_j^{\rightarrow}$ and the centroid of the class, it belongs to database $(p_i^{\rightarrow CL_{known}(x_j^{\rightarrow})})$.

This sum is normalized with respect to D_{Train}.

When computing distance, any of its components in the N-dimensional space is normalized with respect to the maximal range in the dimension, and the sum of distance components is divided by N. With this choice, any distance can range within [0.0, 1.0].

3.9. EXPERIMENTAL STUDY

In this article, we compare the clustering algorithm with a two-clustering algorithm introduced earlier in this context. PSO clustering algorithm, in which the collective behavior of birds when flying was inspired by these parameters, has solved the problem of clustering: n = 50, T_{max} = 1000, v_{max} =. 05, v_{min} = -. 05, C_1 = 2, C_2 = 2, w_{max} = .09, w_{min} = .04. Artificial bee colony clustering algorithm has the following parameters [60]: the size of the colony is 20, the maximum ring is 1000, and a total of 20,000 is assessed. SSPCO algorithm has been exactly set according to PSO algorithm parameters. In this study, 13 datasets of known database UCI are tested for clustering problem [61]. Clustering of the 13 benchmark criteria is similar to and consistent with all algorithms, and the techniques are compared with SSPCO algorithm. 75% of the data for each data set is dedicated to education and 25% to testing. First, to briefly discuss data collections in this study, all the attributes are expressed and presented in Table **15** [60]:

Table 15. The properties of the problems.

Class	Input	Test	Train	Data	
3	4	156	469	625	Balance
2	30	142	427	569	Cancer
2	9	175	524	699	Cancer-Int
2	51	172	518	690	Credit
6	34	92	274	366	Dermatology
2	8	192	576	768	Diabetes
5	7	82	245	327	*E. coli*
6	9	53	161	214	Glass
2	35	76	227	303	Heart
3	58	91	273	364	Horse
3	4	38	112	150	Iris
3	5	53	162	215	Thyroid
3	13	45	133	178	Wine

3.10. RESULTS AND DISCUSSIONS

Benchmark comparison clustering techniques are based on the percentage error, and the percentage of models is sorted incorrectly. Each pattern should be part of the cluster closest to Euclidean distance with the cluster's center.-Margins of error classification criteria are compared in this paper based on Equation 21 and set to be [60]:

$$CEP(Classification\ Error\ Percentage) = 100 \times \frac{misclassification\ examples}{size\ of\ test\ data\ set} \qquad (21)$$

Results of PSO, ABC and SSPCO algorithms on the basis of the classification error on 13 issues of clustering are given in Table **15**. All of the results were obtained from an average of 20 runs. The clustering error rate of the proposed method is compared with PSO and ABC methods in Table **16**.

Table 16. Classification error percentages of the Meta-heuristic Algorithm.

PSO	ABC	SSPCO	
25.74	15.38	15.27	Balance
5.81	2.81	4.00	Cancer
2.87	0	4.17	Cancer-Int
22.96	13.37	15.12	Credit
5.76	5.43	7.02	Dermatology
22.50	22.39	15.23	Diabetes
14.63	13.41	13.55	*E. coli*
39.05	41.50	13.45	Glass
17.46	14.47	13.44	Heart
40.98	38.26	12.10	Horse
2.63	0	4..03	Iris
5.55	3.77	3.16	Thyroid
2.22	0	4.08	Wine

Fig. (**25**) shows an example of clustering using the proposed method. It can be seen that the clustering algorithm PSO in 6 data sets from ABC and PSO margins of error has fewer statistically significant errors in the data set compared to the other two algorithms, and the other data collection is ranked second on the error in the 4 clusters and only 3 of the data collection errors are higher than the other two algorithms. The average margin of error for all 13 data sets shows that the clustering algorithm is SSPCO that has the lowest percentage of error. The average margin of error on the full data set for clustering algorithm is with 10.04%, while the percentage errors of ABC and PSO are 13.13% and 15.99%, respectively. Table **17** compares the clustering error of the methods. In Table **18**, the overall ranking of the methods is compared.

Table 17. Classification error percentages of the techniques.

VFI	Ridor	NBTree	MultiBoost	Bagging	KStar	RBF	MlpAnn	BayesNet	PSO	ABC	SSPCO	
38.85	20.63	19.74	24.20	14.77	10.25	33.61	9.29	19.74	25.74	15.38	15.27	Balance
7.34	6.63	7.69	5.59	4.47	2.44	20.27	2.93	4.19	5.81	2.81	4.00	Cancer
5.71	5.48	5.71	5.14	3.93	4.57	8.17	5.25	3.42	2.87	0.00	4.17	Cancer- Int
16.47	12.65	16.18	12.71	10.68	19.18	43.29	13.81	12.13	22.96	13.37	15.12	Credit
7.60	7.92	1.08	53.26	3.47	4.66	34.66	3.26	1.08	5.76	5.43	7.02	Dermatology
34.37	29.31	25.52	27.08	26.87	34.05	39.16	29.16	25.52	22.50	22.39	15.23	Diabetes
17.07	17.07	20.73	31.70	15.36	18.29	24.38	13.53	17.07	14.63	13.41	13.55	*E. coli*
41.11	31.66	24.07	53.70	25.36	17.58	44.44	28.51	29.62	39.05	41.50	13.45	Glass
18.42	22.89	22.36	18.42	20.25	26.70	45.25	19.46	18.42	17.46	14.47	13.44	Heart
41.75	31.86	31.86	38.46	30.32	35.71	38.46	32.19	30.76	40.98	38.26	12.10	Horse
0.00	0.52	2.63	2.63	0.26	0.52	9.99	0.00	2.63	2.63	0	4..03	Iris
11.11	8.51	11.11	7.40	14.62	13.32	5.55	1.85	6.66	5.55	3.77	3.16	Thyroid
5.77	5.10	2.22	17.77	2.66	3.99	2.88	1.33	0.00	2.22	0	4.08	Wine

Table 18. The average classification error percentages and ranking of the techniques.

VFI	Ridor	NBTree	MultiBoost	Bagging	KStar	RBF	MlpAnn	BayesNet	PSO	ABC	SSPCO	
18.89	15.38	14.68	22.92	13.30	14.71	26.93	12.35	13.17	15.99	13.13	10.04	Average
10	8	7	11	5	6	12	2	4	9	3	1	Rank

Fig. (**26**) shows the clustering error graph. Also, Fig. (**27**) shows the average clustering error graph for all datasets. In Table **18**, 11% error clustering algorithm on 13 data sets [62] was found for SSPCO clustering algorithm. The proposed algorithm in 5 of the 12 data clustering techniques dwarfed, and 5 datasets with good performance and a good level of error have been clustered in three high sets of data error. The proposed algorithm in data collection Horse Glass and error clustering is very good compared to other techniques. In Table **3**, the average error clustering techniques on the entire data set are reviewed, and the best error clustering algorithm is SSPCO, the second is MlpAnn, and techniques of clustering algorithm clustering ABC is the third. Totally, SSPCO algorithm is better in good times compared to the mechanisms of the other clustering techniques. Table **19** shows the standard deviation clustering algorithm proposed in this paper on different benchmarks. Table **20** compares the mean distribution of the methods. Also, Table **21** shows the cluster execution time and Table **22** shows the general results of the methods.

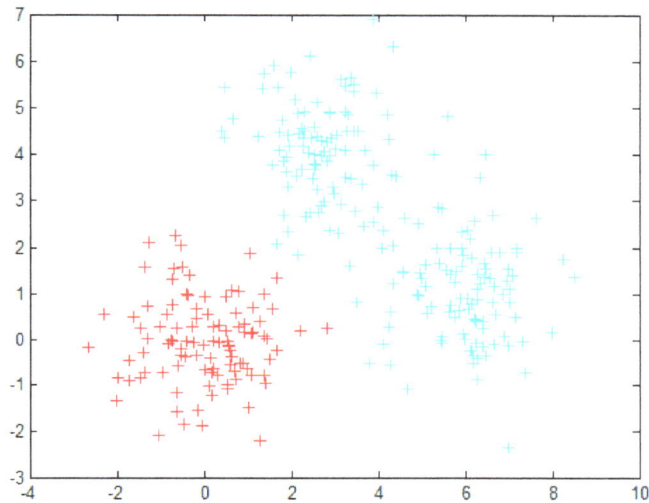

(a)

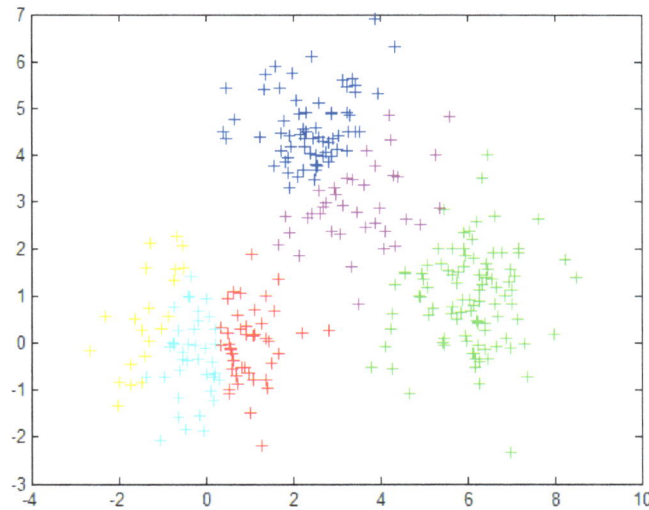

(b)

Fig. 25 cont.....

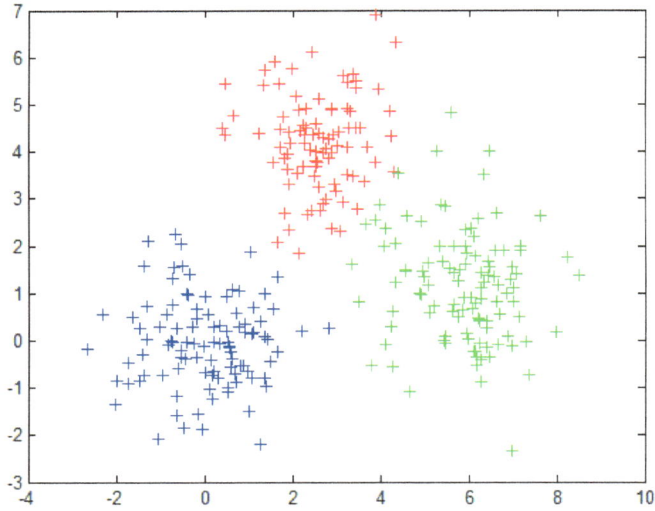

(c)

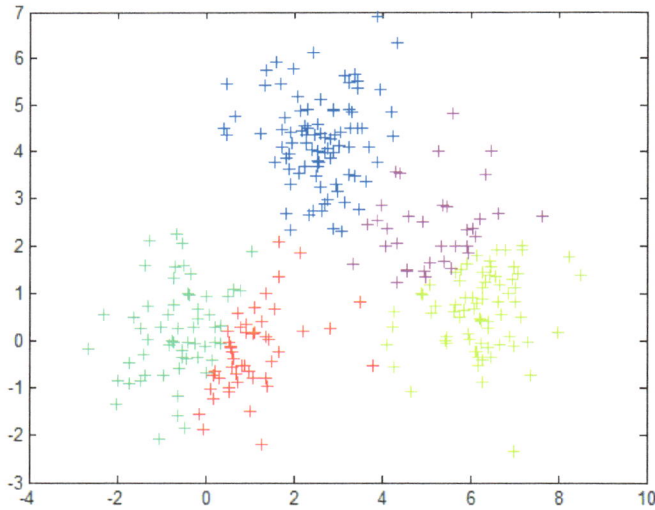

(d)

Fig. (25). Sample of Clustering Forms in SSPCO Algorithm.

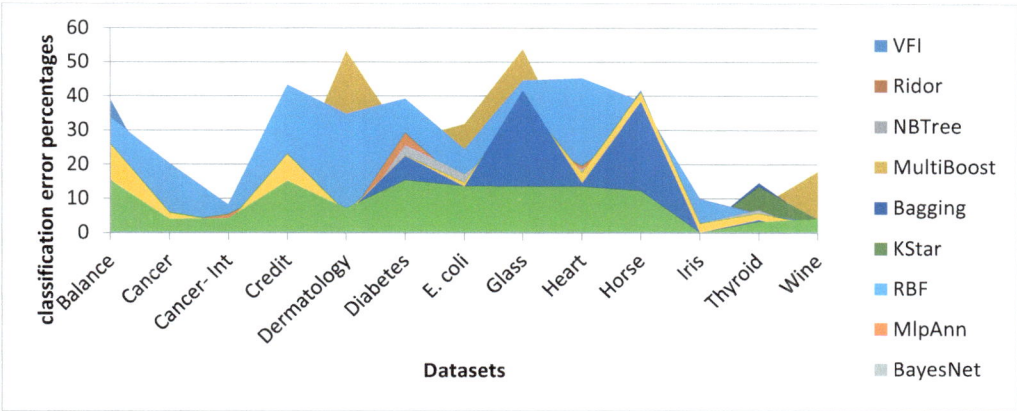

Fig. (26). Classification error percentages plot.

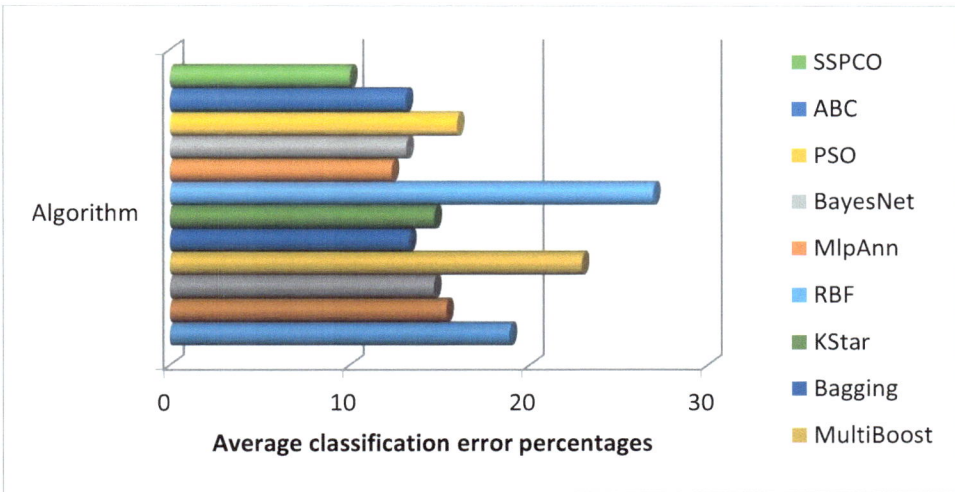

Fig. (27). The average classification error percentages and ranking of the techniques plot.

Table 19. Standard deviation classification in the techniques.

VFI	Ridor	NBTree	Multi-Boost	Bagging	KStar	RBF	MlpAnn	BayesNet	PSO	ABC	SSPCO	
3.36	9.33	7.03	5.55	6.30	3.35	5.85	4.25	8.86	9.23	7.23	6.30	Balance
0.11	1.03	0.88	0.22	0.33	0.77	0.71	0.96	0.13	1.22	0.21	0.22	Cancer
0.55	2.63	0.37	0.64	0.96	1.35	0.68	0.54	0.55	2.30	0.88	0.45	Cancer- Int
6.23	6.69	9.36	7.66	8.57	14.58	6.63	8.80	9.00	4.58	7.05	9.00	Credit
5.22	5.55	9.35	5.63	6.66	8.03	7.00	7.66	6.68	5.25	6.25	7.55	Dermatology
5.66	9.54	6.21	5.69	6.22	2.36	4.05	6.69	5.59	9.98	6.10	6.31	Diabetes

(Table 19) cont.....

VFI	Ridor	NBTree	Multi-Boost	Bagging	KStar	RBF	MlpAnn	BayesNet	PSO	ABC	SSPCO	
4.30	12.05	3.23	8.55	6.33	4.38	5.32	5.53	6.01	6.69	5.25	5.43	*E. coli*
6.28	9.23	6.35	7.35	4.69	3.36	7.05	7.22	7.00	9.35	6.68	6.38	Glass
4.41	8.32	4.33	6.65	4.66	2.20	4.45	5.02	6.52	7.78	4.47	7.14	Heart
6.60	8.00	6.61	4.63	9.98	2.68	7.50	6.69	7.04	10.03	6.68	6.35	Horse
0.88	3.02	1.08	0.69	0.99	1.58	0.78	1.01	0.98	0.22	0.98	0.77	Iris
0.22	1.50	1.00	0.36	0.65	0.20	0.44	0.65	0.44	0.55	0.55	0.26	Thyroid
3.03	1.01	1.32	2.03	1.10	0.69	2.00	0.65	1.56	1.11	2.30	1.02	Wine

Table 20. Mean of Standard deviation classification in the techniques.

VFI	Ridor	NBTree	MultiBoost	Bagging	KStar	RBF	MlpAnn	BayesNet	PSO	ABC	SSPCO	
9.99	13.65	9.14	10.65	13.10	13.30	9.38	8.64	14.29	11.65	14.65	12.33	Balance
1.00	4.29	1.26	0.88	6.31	1.03	3.33	4.02	1.25	3.35	3.32	4.33	Cancer
2.08	3.31	0.56	1.03	1.30	3.63	1.22	4.26	2.16	6.35	5.52	1.66	Cancer- Int
7.59	12.06	13.10	5.23	2.36	25.20	12.28	11.26	11.02	8.42	11.03	12.69	Credit
9.19	11.89	16.35	4.36	15.24	1.02	9.02	9.64	10.08	12.27	12.20	13.77	Dermatology
8.05	14.10	11.23	12.23	16.61	19.00	16.46	11.07	15.50	16.61	16.43	15.68	Diabetes
9.18	10.00	6.64	9.46	14.41	10.03	22.29	6.62	8.55	18.25	20.25	18.64	*E. coli*
14.88	12.21	11.90	13.64	16.55	16.66	14.59	9.18	14.20	16.44	17.20	12.38	Glass
7.78	9.91	6.55	9.80	8.89	8.92	9.94	6.64	9.68	8.29	10.00	9.35	Heart
12.75	15.15	10.71	20.06	11.06	4.42	12.03	9.75	15.28	22.29	25.31	13.77	Horse
1.73	6.44	6.45	1.06	6.68	8.84	6.30	6.89	6.64	6.54	2.56	8.37	Iris
0.88	2.69	4.22	0.85	4.26	2.22	2.05	4.21	2.24	2.23	6.25	3.65	Thyroid
7.17	6.64	6.44	1.06	6.64	8.48	7.89	1.88	3.65	4.02	4.58	5.66	Wine

Table 21. Run Time of classification in the techniques.

VFI	Ridor	NBTree	Multi-Boost	Bagging	KStar	RBF	MlpAnn	BayesNet	PSO	ABC	SSPCO	
3.36	9.33	7.03	5.55	6.30	33s	65s	105s	25s	27s	57s	14s	Balance
0.11	1.03	0.88	0.22	0.33	36s	54s	84s	28s	30s	33s	22s	Cancer
0.55	2.63	0.37	0.64	0.96	9s	16s	66s	89s	17s	53s	09s	Cancer- Int
6.23	6.69	9.36	7.66	8.57	33s	40s	94s	44s	21s	102s	18s	Credit
5.22	5.55	9.35	5.63	6.66	26s	28s	37s	25s	35s	85s	22s	Dermatology
5.66	9.54	6.21	5.69	6.22	58s	39s	115s	26s	39s	92s	19s	Diabetes
4.30	12.05	3.23	8.55	6.33	21s	28s	64s	18s	25s	51s	24s	*E. coli*
6.28	9.23	6.35	7.35	4.69	17s	25s	71s	14s	19s	41s	14s	Glass
4.41	8.32	4.33	6.65	4.66	09s	19s	95s	22s	15s	27s	08s	Heart
6.60	8.00	6.61	4.63	9.98	10s	52s	73s	66s	14s	18s	10s	Horse
0.88	3.02	1.08	0.69	0.99	19s	12s	112s	32s	13s	29s	09s	Iris
0.22	1.50	1.00	0.36	0.65	21s	16s	19s	17s	18s	17s	11s	Thyroid

(Table 21) cont.....

VFI	Ridor	NBTree	Multi-Boost	Bagging	KStar	RBF	MlpAnn	BayesNet	PSO	ABC	SSPCO	
3.03	1.01	1.32	2.03	1.10	22s	14s	71s	19s	9s	40s	08s	Wine

Table 22. The total results of the proposed algorithm.

Standard Deviation	Average Standard Deviation	Maximum Error	Average Error	Least Error	
6.30	12.33	15.99	15.22	15.27	Balance
0.22	4.33	4.90	4.58	4.00	Cancer
0.45	1.66	5.03	4.22	4.17	Cancer- Int
9.00	12.69	16.02	15.78	15.12	Credit
7.55	13.77	7.98	7.55	7.02	Dermatology
6.31	15.68	17.00	15.80	15.23	Diabetes
5.43	18.64	14.07	13.97	13.55	*E. coli*
6.38	12.38	13.93	13.64	13.45	Glass
7.14	9.35	14.06	13.77	13.44	Heart
6.35	13.77	13.15	12.80	12.10	Horse
0.77	8.37	4.97	4.66	4..03	Iris
0.26	3.65	6.58	3.64	3.16	Thyroid
1.02	5.66	4.99	4.71	4.08	Wine

3.11. T-TEST

The statistics t-test allows us to answer this question by using the t-test statistic to determine a p-value that indicates how likely we could have gotten these results by chance, if in fact the null hypothesis were true (*i.e.* no difference in the population) [63]. By convention, if there is less than 5% chance of getting the observed differences by chance, we reject the null hypothesis and say we found a statistically significant difference between the two groups. See Statistical Data Analysis for more information about hypothesis testing [64, 65]. In this study, H_1 is defined as follow: the obtained results are based on the random nature of the problem. If the value of the significant level for the example is zero, then it indicates that the probability of H_1 being incorrect will be zero. Therefore, in this particular example, it is safe to say that the obtained results are independent of the random circumstances of the problem. Tables **23** and **24** present the results of the T-test for the methods.

Table 23. T-Test results for classification error of SSPCO Algorithm.

H_0/H_1	p-value	Test Value	Confidence Interval 95%		Dataset
			Upper	Low	
H_1	0	17	24.95	9.29	Balance
H_1	0	3	5.203	0.747	Cancer
H_1	0	4.5	7.227	2.18	Cancer-Int
H_1	0	15.5	25.02	5.31	Credit
H_1	0	15.5	22.77	7.33	Dermatology
H_1	0	16	27.36	3.49	Diabetes
H_1	0	12.5	27.36	3.49	*E. coli*
H_1	0	13	22.22	5.10	Glass
H_1	0	13	23.92	1.61	Heart
H_1	0	22	27.00	14.00	Horse
H_1	0	4.5	6.146	2.404	Iris
H_1	0	3	3.627	2.11	Thyroid
H_1	0	3	5.909	1.518	Wine

Table 24. T-Test results For Standard deviation of SSPCO Algorithm.

H_0/H_1	p-value	Test Value	Confidence Interval 95%		Dataset
			Upper	Low	
H_1	0	17	6.43	0	Balance
H_1	0	3	0.898	0.275	Cancer
H_1	0	4.5	1.982	0.398	Cancer-Int
H_1	0	15.5	7.18	0.48	Credit
H_1	0	15.5	15.78	0.55	Dermatology
H_1	0	16	15.43	1.09	Diabetes
H_1	0	12.5	15.08	0	*E. coli*
H_1	0	13	19.19	4.66	Glass
H_1	0	13	7	1.07	Heart
H_1	0	22	15.84	3.03	Horse
H_1	0	4.5	0.97	0.026	Iris
H_1	0	3	1.773	0	Thyroid
H_1	0	3	1.313	0.317	Wine

3.12. FRIEDMAN TEST

We have to correct the results of the proposed clustering algorithm in order to ensure that a test is carried out on the results. Friedman test, a nonparametric test, is an analysis of variance with repeated measures and is equivalent to that of the comparison between the K variables used in the average rating. The test status variables are assessed in several related cases. More information about Friedman's test is available. We have to consider the validity of the results of the proposed algorithm. We have evaluated the results of the proposed algorithm in 4 different repetitions on each of the 13 benchmark Friedman tests. The main samples taken from Friedman test show this on 13 benchmarks. The final answer of this test is 0.502, because it is more indicative of the value of 0.50; this is the natural course that answers the same level and between different repetitions compliance on each of the 13 benchmarks, and the results are reliable. Table **25** presents the results of the Friedman test for the methods.

Table 25. Friedman test for Classification techniques of SSPCO algorithm in 4 times Descriptive Statistics.

Descriptive Statistics								
%	**N**	**Mean**	**Std. Deviation**	**Minimum**	**Maximum**	**Percentiles**		
						25th	**50th(Median)**	**75th**
Var00001	13	10.7154	5.41148	3.31	16.66	4.4850	13.5600	15.6400
Var00002	13	10.7646	5.67621	3.35	19.33	4.8200	12.0500	15.7800
Var00003	13	11.6962	7.56971	3.09	27.22	4.3750	9.5500	17.5800
Var00004	13	10.9092	5.36789	4.00	18.51	5.5200	13.2900	15.2100
Rank		**Test Statistics**			%			
Var00001	2.08	N		13	%			
Var00002	2.54	Chi-Square		2.354	%			
Var00003	2.54	df		3	%			
Var00004	2.85	Asymp. Sig.		.502	%			

3.13. A CLUSTERING APPROACH BY SSPCO OPTIMIZATION ALGORITHM BASED ON CHAOTIC INITIAL POPULATION

Given a database with C classes and N parameters, the classification problem can be seen as that of finding the optimal positions of C center in an N-dimensional space *i.e.* that of determining for any center its N coordinates, each of which can take on, in general, real values. With these premises, the i-th individual of the population is Encoded as it equation 22:

$$(p_i^{\to 1}, \dots, p_i^{\to C}, v_i^{\to 1}, \dots, v_i^{\to C}) \tag{22}$$

Where *pi* the position of the j-th center is constituted by N real numbers representing its N coordinates in the problem space:

$$p_i^{\to j} = \{p_{1,i}^j, \dots, p_{N,1}^j\} \tag{23}$$

And similarly the velocity of the j-th center is made up of N real numbers representing its N velocity components in the problem space:

$$v_i^{\to j} = \{v_{1,i}^j, \dots, v_{N,1}^j\} \tag{24}$$

Then, each individual in the population is composed of 2*C*N components, each represented by a real value.

In the flowchart of Fig. (**28**), input is a clustering form according chaotic theory, and output is the best clustering form that introduced by proposed algorithm.

3.14. FITNESS FUNCTION

The fitness function is computed in one step as the sum on all training set instances of Euclidean distance in N-dimensional space between generic instance

$\vec{x_j}$ and the centroid of the class it belongs to according to database $(p_i^{\to CL_{known}(\vec{x_j})})$. This sum is normalized with respect to D_{Train}. In symbols, i-th individual fitness is given by equation 25:

$$(i) = \frac{1}{D_{Train}} \sum_{j=1}^{D_{Train}} d(\vec{x_j}, p_i^{\to CL_{known}(\vec{x_j})}) \tag{25}$$

When computing distance, any of its components in the N-dimensional space is normalized with respect to the maximal range in the dimension, and the sum of distance components is divided by N. With this choice, any distance can range within [0.0,1.0].

1.//initialize all chicken by $k \times Cr_{(t)} \times (1 - Cr_{(t)})$ *(input is a clustering form according chaotic theory)*

2.Initialize by $k \times Cr_{(t)} \times (1 - Cr_{(t)})$

3.Repeat

4. For each chicken i

5.   //update the chicken's best position and priority

6. $(p_i^{\to 1}, \dots, p_i^{\to C}, v_i^{\to 1}, \dots, v_i^{\to C})$

$$p_i^{\to j} = \{p_{1,i}^j, \dots, p_{N,1}^j\}$$
$$v_i^{\to j} = \{v_{1,i}^j, \dots, v_{N,1}^j\}$$

7.   If $f(x_i) > f(pbest_i)$ then

8. $pbest_i = x_i$

9. $prioirity_i = prioirity_i + 1$

10.   End if

11.   //update the global best position and priority

12.   If $f(pbest_i) > f(gbest)$ then

13. $gbest = pbest_i$

14. $prioirity_i = prioirity_i + 1$

15.   End if

16. End for

17. //update chicken's velocity and position

18. For each chicken i

19.   For each dimension d

20. $X_i.velocity = w * X_i.velocity + c * rand() * [position(X_{i+1}.priority)] - X_i.position$

21. $x_{i,d} = x_{i,d} + v_{i,d}$

22.   End for

23. End for

24. //advance iteration

25. $itetation = itetation + 1$

26.Until $it > MaxIterations$

27. clustering form=gbest(index of cluster-heads and members)

Fig. (28). Pseudo-code of Proposed Method.

3.15. EXPERIMENTAL STUDY

In this chapter, we compare the clustering algorithm with a two-clustering algorithm introduced earlier in this context. PSO clustering algorithm, in which the collective behavior of birds when flying was inspired by these parameters, has solved the problem of clustering [19]: n = 50, T_{max} = 1000, v_{max} =. 05, v_{min} = -. 05, C_1 = 2, C_2 = 2, w_{max} = .09, w_{min} = .04. Artificial bee colony clustering algorithm has the following parameters: the size of the colony is 20, the maximum ring is 1000, and a total of 20,000 is assessed. SSPCO algorithm has been exactly set according to PSO algorithm parameters. In this study, 13 datasets of known database UCI are tested for clustering problem. Clustering of the 13 benchmark criteria is similar to and consistent with all algorithms, and the techniques are compared with SSPCO algorithm. 75% of the data for each data set is dedicated to education and 25% to testing. First, to briefly discuss data collections in this study, all the attributes are expressed and presented in Table **26**:

Table 26. Properties of the problems [17].

Class	Input	Test	Train	Data	%
3	4	156	469	625	Balance
2	30	142	427	569	Cancer
2	9	175	524	699	Cancer-Int
2	51	172	518	690	Credit
6	34	92	274	366	Dermatology
2	8	192	576	768	Diabetes
5	7	82	245	327	*E. coli*
6	9	53	161	214	Glass
2	35	76	227	303	Heart
3	58	91	273	364	Horse
3	4	38	112	150	Iris
3	5	53	162	215	Thyroid
3	13	45	133	178	Wine

3.16. RESULTS AND DISCUSSIONS

Benchmark comparison clustering techniques are based on the percentage error, and the percentage of models is sorted incorrectly. Each pattern should be part of the cluster closest to Euclidean distance with the cluster's center. The data is divided into two pieces, 75% of the training data and 25% of the final test data. Margins of error classification criteria are compared in this paper based on equation 26 and set to be:

$$CEP(Classification\ Error\ Percentage) = 100 \times \frac{misclassification\ examples}{size\ of\ test\ data\ set} \qquad (26)$$

It can be seen that the clustering algorithm PSO in 6 data sets from ABC and PSO margins of error has fewer statistically significant errors in the data set compared to the other two algorithms, and the other data collection is ranked second on the error in the 4 clusters and only 3 of the data collection errors are higher than the other two algorithms. The average margin of error for all 13 data sets shows that the clustering algorithm is SSPCO that has the lowest percentage of error. The average margin of error on the full data set for clustering algorithm is with 10.71%, while the percentage errors of ABC and PSO are 13.13% and 15.99%, respectively.

Table **27** shows the classification error percentages clustering algorithm proposed in this paper on different benchmarks. Also, Table **2** shows the average classification error percentages and ranking of the techniques.

Table 27. Classification error percentages of the techniques [17].

VFI	Ridor	NBTree	MultiBoost	Bagging	KStar	RBF	MlpAnn	BayesNet	PSO	ABC	SSPCO	
38.85	20.63	19.74	24.2	14.77	10.25	33.61	9.29	19.74	25.74	15.38	15.36	Balance
7.34	6.63	7.69	5.59	4.47	2.44	20.27	2.93	4.19	5.81	2.81	4.15	Cancer
5.71	5.48	5.71	5.14	3.93	4.57	8.17	5.25	3.42	2.87	0	4.49	Cancer- Int
16.47	12.65	16.18	12.71	10.68	19.18	43.29	13.81	12.13	22.96	13.37	15.92	Credit
7.6	7.92	1.08	53.26	3.47	4.66	34.66	3.26	1.08	5.76	5.43	16.11	Dermatology
34.37	29.31	25.52	27.08	26.87	34.05	39.16	29.16	25.52	22.5	22.39	16.66	Diabetes
17.07	17.07	20.73	31.7	15.36	18.29	24.38	13.53	17.07	14.63	13.41	13.89	*E. coli*
41.11	31.66	24.07	53.7	25.36	17.58	44.44	28.51	29.62	39.05	41.5	13.56	Glass
18.42	22.89	22.36	18.42	20.25	26.7	45.25	19.46	18.42	17.46	14.47	14.03	Heart
41.75	31.86	31.86	38.46	30.32	35.71	38.46	32.19	30.76	40.98	38.26	12.22	Horse
0	0.52	2.63	2.63	0.26	0.52	9.99	0	2.63	2.63	0	4.48	Iris
11.11	8.51	11.11	7.4	14.62	13.32	5.55	1.85	6.66	5.55	3.77	3.31	Thyroid
5.77	5.1	2.22	17.77	2.66	3.99	2.88	1.33	0	2.22	0	5.12	Wine

Table 28. Average classification error percentages and ranking of the techniques [17].

	SSPCO	ABC	PSO	BayesNet	MlpAnn	RBF	KStar	Bagging	MultiBoost	NBTree	Ridor	VFI
Average Rank	10.71	13.13	15.99	13.17	12.35	26.93	14.71	13.30	22.92	14.68	15.38	18.89
	1	3	9	4	2	12	6	5	11	7	8	10

3.17. T-TEST

The statistics t-test allows us to answer this question by using the t-test statistic to determine a p-value that indicates how likely we could have gotten these results by chance, if in fact the null hypothesis were true (*i.e.* no difference in the population). By convention, if there is less than 5% chance of getting the observed differences by chance, we reject the null hypothesis and say we found a statistically significant difference between the two groups. See Statistical Data Analysis for more information about hypothesis testing. In this study, H_1 is defined as follow: the obtained results are based on the random nature of the problem. If the value of the significant level for the example is zero, then it indicates that the probability of H_1 being incorrect will be zero. Therefore, in this particular example, it is safe to say that the obtained results are independent of the random circumstances of the problem. Table **28** presents the results of the T-test for the methods.

3.18. TRAVELING SALESMAN PROBLEM

Traveling salesman problem is the mechanism of finding the shortest route in traveling between the cities and returning to the first one. In the standard version of this problem which is in the form of symmetrical cost of travel and we have used this version to simulate, the cost of traveling from X to Y is equal with traveling Y to X.

In Fig. (**29**), each node is a city and the weight each graph edge is the cost of travelling from one city to another. According to this graph travelling salesman problem cost function will be calculated according to the equation 27:

$$T_C = \sum_{k=1}^{d} C_{ij} \qquad (27)$$

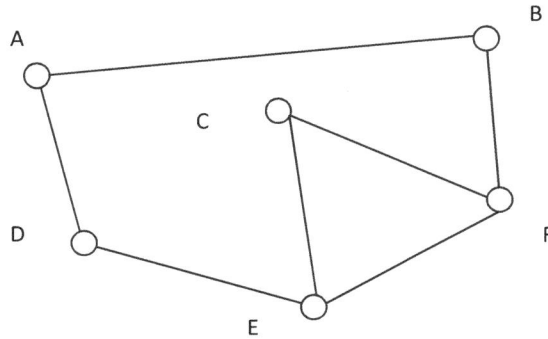

Fig. (29). Traveling salesman problem graph.

Where: C_{ij} is the cost of travel from city i to city j and k is the number of cities or sizes [66]. In this paper, the distance between cities i and j is set based on equation 28:

$$d(T[i], T[j]) = \sqrt{(x_i - x_j)^2 - (y_i - y_j)^2} \tag{28}$$

And a total tour is calculated based on the equation 29:

$$f = \sum_{i=1}^{n-1} d(T[i], T[j]) + d(T[n], T[1]) \tag{29}$$

Where n is the number of cities [67].

The basic idea of this optimization algorithm is taken from the behavior of the chicks of a type of bird called See-see partridge [68]. The chicks of this type of bird are located in a regular queue at the time of danger to reach a safe place and they start to move behind their mother to reach a safe point. To simulate the behavior of the chicks of this bird in the form of an optimization algorithm, each chick is considered as a particle of the suboptimal problem. The state of each particle should be according to the behavior of this type of chicks in a regular queue that we know this queue takes us to the best optimal point and this does not mean that minimizing the search space, but also, it is converging particles after some searches in a regular queue to the best point answers (bird mother). We consider a variable for each particle entitled as priority variable. For particle i, priority variable defined according equation 30:

$$chick_i \rightarrow X_i.priority \tag{30}$$

In every assessment, when a particle was better than the best personal experience or local optimum; a unit is added to the priority variable of that particle:

$$if \quad X_i.cost > P_{best} \quad \rightarrow \quad P_{best} = X_i.position \quad and \quad X_i.priority = X_i.priority + 1 \tag{31}$$

$X_i.cost$ The cost of each particle in the benchmark, P_{best} is the best personal experience of each particle, and $X_i.position$ is the location of each particle. In every time of assessment, if the local optimum is better than the global optimum and vice versa, the particle's priority variable goes higher and a unit is added to it:

$$if \quad P_{best} > G_{best} \quad \rightarrow G_{best} = P_{best} \quad and \quad X_i.priority = X_i.priority + 1 \tag{32}$$

G_{best} is the global optima. The motion equation of each particle is set almost similar to the particle swarm algorithm in the form of equation 33:

$$X_i.position = X_i.position + X_i.velocity \tag{33}$$

$X_i.velocity$ is the velocity of each particle or chick. Then, Chickens sorted in array based on priority variable. Now the particle velocity equation is calculated according to the equation 34:

$$X_i.velocity = w * X_i.velocity + c * rand() *$$
$$[position(X_{i+1}.priority)] - X_i.position \tag{34}$$

$X_i.velocity$ is the velocity of the particle, w is the coefficient impact of previous velocity in the current velocity equation of particle, c is the coefficient impact of position of particle with upper priority in the current velocity equation of particle, $rand()$ is a random number between 0 and one to create a random movement for particles, $[position(X_{i+1}.priority)]$ is the location of the particle with one level higher priority than the current particle that the current particle tries to adjust its velocity according to the particle, $X_i.position$ is the current location of the particle. To solve the traveling salesman problem using SSPCO optimization algorithm a priority variable is considered for each city. For example, a priority variable for city j is defined by equation 35:

$$priority_j \tag{35}$$

Then to travel between cities when we go to city *j*, we calculate the cost function of the tour's arriving to city *j* and whenever the function had lower cost one unit is added to priority variable of city *j*:

$$\text{if } T[j] > tourbest \quad \text{then} \quad priority_j = priority_j + 1 \tag{36}$$

In order to move between the cities, equation 37 is used:

$$d(T[i], T[j]) = (x_i - x_j)^2 - (y_i - y_j)^2 \rightarrow priority_j + 1 \tag{37}$$

In this equation $priority_j + 1$ is the location of the city the priority variable of which is one unit higher than the city *j*.

3.19. SIMULATION AND RESULTS

Problem simulation has been implemented in MATLAB software and by solving this problem by 4 the solution is compared with swarm, artificial bee colony, ants and genetic algorithms. The comparison index is the lowest tour cost and algorithms are compared based on the cost of a tour that logically the tour performed by the lowest cost is the most optimal one. The algorithms are set based on cable and tours cost in the 100th iteration is algorithm evaluation criteria for comparison. To avoid errors, the results were obtained by an average of 20 iterations. 25 cities are included in the problem space and the algorithms start traveling from a selected city and after a single pass from each city they will return to the starting point. All parameters are the same in every 5 intelligent optimization algorithms in Table **29** and comparisons are made in totally equal conditions. In the chart below, the cost of the best tours for each algorithm and optimal path of the proposed algorithm are presented.

Table 29. Parameters.

Parameter	Value
City number	25
iterations	100
Population	100
Variable	25

The arrangement of the cities in the problem is based on Fig. (**30**) and each city is defined by latitudinal and longitudinal coordinates.

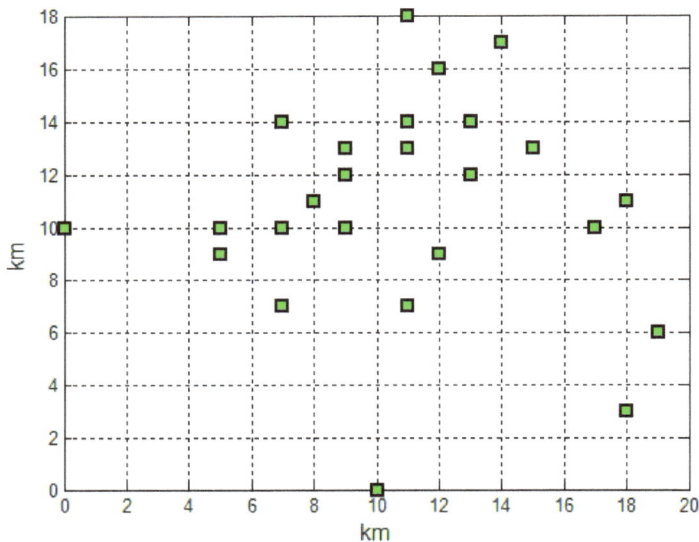

Fig. (30). Arrangement of the cities.

The type of movement from the initial point depends on the algorithm and is completely optional. Fig. (**31**) shows the optimal route obtained by the proposed algorithm which is a graph that presents the tour that had the lowest cost at the end of 100 times of algorithm evaluation. The tour that started moving from a city and returned to the starting point after passing through all the cities with the lowest cost at the end of 100 times of algorithm evaluation.

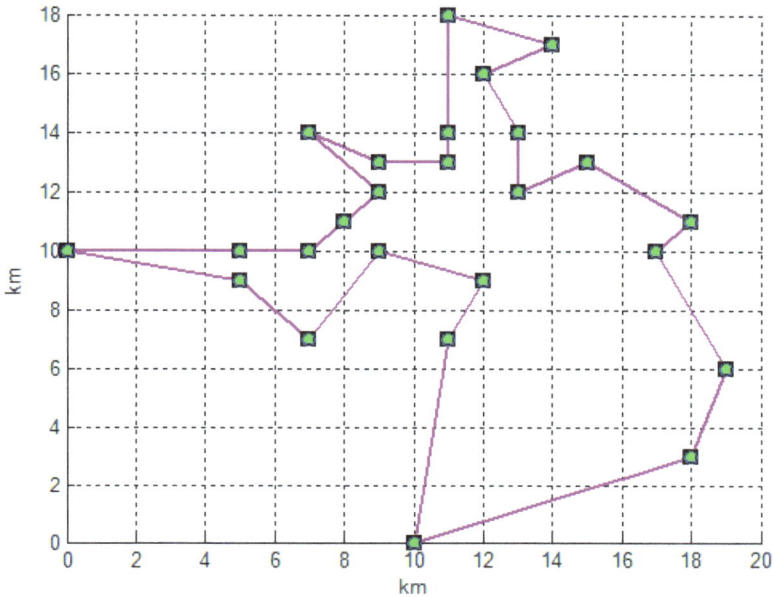

Fig. (31). Tour best in proposed algorithm in 100 iterations.

Fig. (**31**) shows a tour obtained by the proposed algorithm at the end of 100 evaluations and indicates the tour that has the lowest cost to move between 25 cities. Fig. (**32**) shows the graph of the distance matrix between cities. Fig. (**33**) indicates that the proposed method since the 15th iteration in all iteration has the tour in terms of the lowest cost. At the 50th iteration SSPCO algorithm achieved the lowest cost for a tour which is almost 55 while the swarm algorithm obtained the cost of 95, ant and genetic algorithms had the value of 105 and artificial bee colony obtained the cost of 110. After the 75th iteration until 100th all algorithms achieved a relative stability in the lowest tour cost between cities.

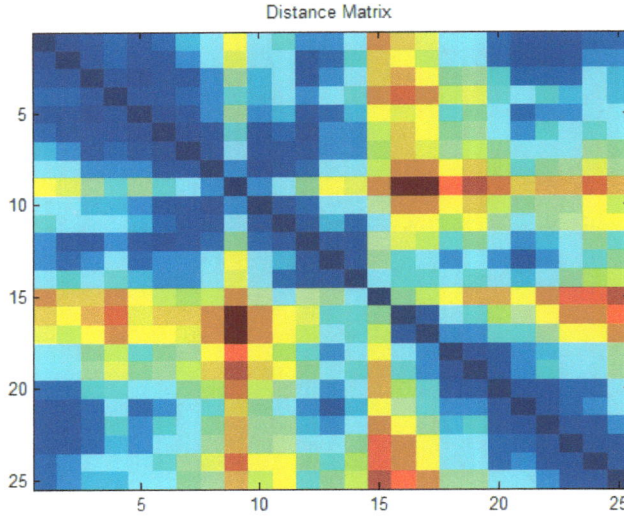

Fig. (32). Distance matrix of cities in proposed algorithm in 100 iterations.

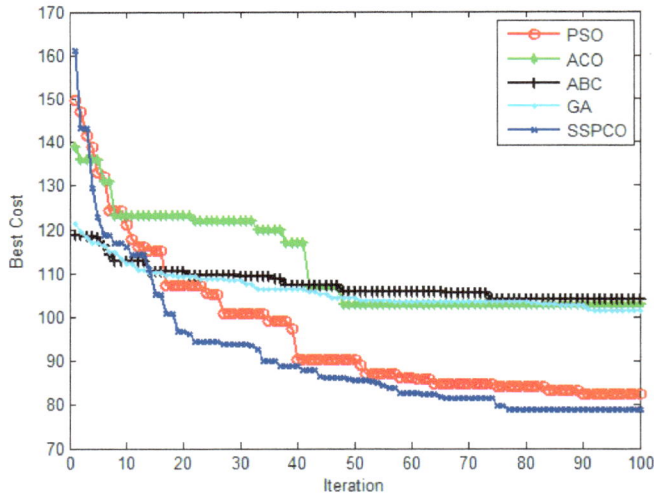

Fig. (33). Best cost of tours in PSO, ACO, ABC, GA and SSPCO in 100 iterations.

3.20. ESCAPE FROM HUNTER PARTICLE SWARM OPTIMIZATION

In intelligent algorithms, creating the initial population is effective for determining the optimal responses. Our proposed algorithm is defined as the following: the swarm passes a hunter, and the populated of the birds that are hunted by the hunter due to their inability would be removed from the swarm. The number of the dead birds is then replaced randomly by the others.

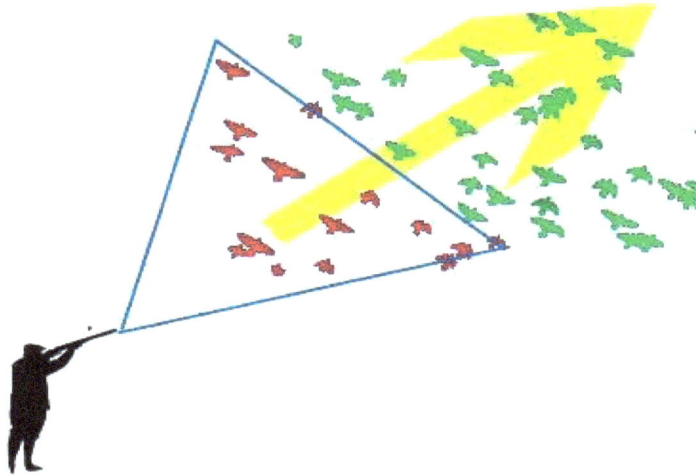

Fig. (34). How incompetent birds are hunted by a hunter in the proposed algorithm.

As shown in Fig. (**34**), the flock that is moving towards the optimized answer is exposed to a hunter. The birds marked with the red color are hunted due to their presence in an inappropriate area which is away from the optimal solution, and new birds replace them randomly. The birds marked with the green color pass the hunter due to their closeness to the optimal points and they will remain in the problem space. In fact, the populations that are not in a location appropriate to the optimal solution are removed from the problem space, and new populations accidentally replace them. The initial population defined in the problem is randomly given values. The location of the population in the cost function is assessed and the particle cost will be regulated according to the costs.

$$Cost\ Array = Sort(particle(i).cost) \tag{38}$$

The worst particle among the hunted birds or the first hunted bird is stored in a memory variable, called Hunt.

$$Hunt\ 1 = Cost\ Array(n) \tag{39}$$

In a minimizing problem, the costs are ordered in the second half and a number is randomly selected and then as many particles as this random number with inappropriate costs will be removed from the second half and from the end.

$$Delete(particle) \in Cost\ Array \tag{40}$$

Then, twice as much as the removed particles will be replaced by new particles randomly.

$$Replace(2 * particle(i).deleted) \rightarrow RandPop \tag{41}$$

In the next stage, all particles are again inserted in the cost function and the particle merit is measured. The particles are then ordered in a new array based on the merit of the cost function.

$$New\ Cost\ Array = Sort(particle(i).cost) \tag{42}$$

Now, as many as the number of early hunted birds are remove from the end of the array, and the size of our population reaches the normal size.

$$Pop = New\ Cost\ Array - Deleted(particle) \tag{43}$$

Then, the particle velocity equation will be set based on equation 40. The population-making mechanism seems to end here. After updating the local and general optimums, the particle speed is determine as follows: like in the birds algorithm, the particle is guided somewhere between the local and general optimums and an operator is added to the particle velocity equation so that the particle will be kept away from the place of the first hunted bird in the population-making stage.

$$V_{ij}(t+1) = w * (V_{ij}(t) + [c_1 r_{1,j}(t)[pbest_{ij} - X_{ij}(t)]]$$
$$+ [c_2 r_{2j}(t)[gbest_i(t) - X_{ij}(t)] * Hunt\ 1] \tag{44}$$

In this equation, w is the inertia weight that specifies the effectiveness of the current speed on the next one. c_1 and c_2 are the social constant coefficients, $r_{1,j}$ and $r_{2,j}$ are random numbers between zero and one, $pbest_{ij}$ is the best personal experience, $gbest_i(t)$ is the general optimum, $X_{ij}(t)$ the current location of the particle, and *Hunt 1* is the location of the first hunted bird in the population-making stage. Applying the first hunted bird with the worst location in the search phase to the particle speed equation will cause the particles not to be converging to the position of the first hunted bird, and in the case of converging to that position; they will get away from the position by applying this multiplication to the speed equation. When the speed equation is set based on equation 7, the particle position equation will be as equation 45 below:

$$X_{ij}(New) = V_{ij} + X_{ij} \tag{45}$$

In this equation, X_{ij} *(New)*, V_{ij} and X_{ij} are respectively the new particle position, the particle velocity and the particle current location. When the particles do their new positions in the search space according to equations 40 and 41, they will be put in the cost function again, their merit will be determined and the local and general optimums will be updated. The quasi-code of EHPSO algorithm is shown in Fig. (35). Fig. (36) shows the general steps of the proposed method(Flowchart).

1. Initialize random population
2. Fitness evaluations with cost function
3. Sort the particles based on fitness in a new array
4. Select a number of 1 to half main population randomly and delete particles to measure this number of particles array of end of particles array
5. Replace tow equal deleted particles of population with a randomly new particles
6. Sort the particles based on fitness in a new array
7. Delete particles to the number of birds hunted of end of new array
8. Update velocity equation
9. Update position equation
10. Evaluate new potion for particles in the target function and go to 3 step

Fig. (35). Code of EHPSO algorithm.

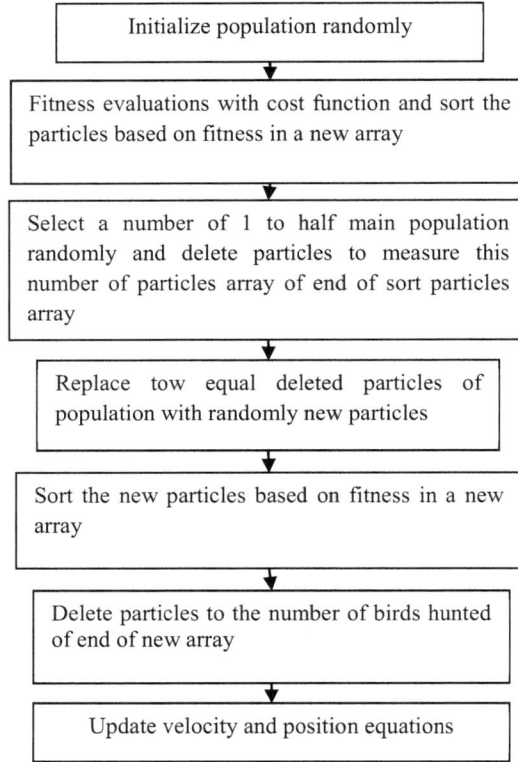

Fig. (36). EHPSO algorithm diagram.

3.21. EXPERIMENTAL RESULT

Simulation of the proposed method and other methods were carried out on 26 expanded benchmark functions [69]. These functions are presented in Table **30**.

Table 30. Introducing Benchmark functions.

Min	Range	D	Function
0	[-4.5,4.5]	2	F1(Beale)
-1	[-100,100]	2	F2(Easom)
0	[-10,10]	2	F3(Matyas)
0	[-10,10]	4	F4(Colville)
0	[-5,10]	10	F5(Zakharov)
0	[-10,10]	30	F6(Schwefel 2.22)
0	[-100,100]	30	F7(Schewefel 1.2)
0	[-10,10]	30	F8(Dixon-price)

(Table 30) cont.....

Min	Range	D	Function
0	[-5.12,5.12]	30	F9(Step)
0	[-100,100]	30	F10(Sphere)
0	[-10,10]	30	F11(SumSquares)
0	[-1.28,1.28]	30	F12(Quartic)
0	[-100,100]	2	F13(Schaffer)
-1.0316	[-5,5]	2	F14(6 H Camel)
0	[-100,100]	2	F15(Bohachevsky2)
0	[-100,100]	2	F16(Bohachevsky3)
-186.73	[-10,10]	2	F17(Shubert)
0	[-30,30]	30	F18(Rosenbrock)
0	[-600,600]	30	F19(Griewank)
0	[-32,32]	30	F20(Ackley)
0	[-100,100]	2	F21(Bohachevsky1)
0	[-10,10]	2	F22(Booth)
-1.8013	[0,π]	2	F23(Michalewicz2)
-4.6877	[0,π]	5	F24(Michalewicz5)
-9.6602	[0,π]	10	F25(Michalewicz10)
0	[-5.12,5.12]	30	F26(Rastrigin)

The proposed method was compared to genetic algorithm [70], differential evolution algorithm [71], particle swarm algorithm [72], bees algorithm [73], PBI algorithm [74], NPSO algorithm [75], MRPSO algorithm [76], EPSDE algorithm [77], CCABC algorithm [78]. The results were considered with the same parameters for all methods: population of 100, 30 variables, 500,000 evaluations. The results were also set on 26 functions introduced in Table **1** based on two criteria: the best particle cost (Mean) and the standard deviation of particles (StdDev). They are presented comprehensively in Table **31**. The Friedman test is also provided in this table to test the significance of the results for all methods.

Table 31. Results on 26 functions based on the best mean cost and standard deviation.

	Criteria	GA	DE	PSO	BA	PBA	FA	NPSO	MRPSO	CCABC	EPSDE	EHPSO
F1	Mean	0§	0§	0§	1.88E-05‡	0§	0§	0§	0§	0§	1.48E-05‡	0
	StdDev	0	0	0	1.94E-05	0	0	0	0	0	1.64E-05	0
F2	Mean	-1§	-1§	-1§	-0.99994‡	-1§	-1§	-1§	-1§	-1§	-0.8965‡	-1
	StdDev	0	0	0	4.50E-05	0	0	0	0	0	3.56E-05	0
F3	Mean	0§	0§	0§	0§	0§	0§	0§	0§	0§	0§	0
	StdDev	0	0	0	0	0	0	0	0	0	0	0

(Table 30) cont.....

	Criteria	GA	DE	PSO	BA	PBA	FA	NPSO	MRPSO	CCABC	EPSDE	EHPSO
F4	Mean	0.01494‡	0.04091‡	0§	1.11760‡	0§	0§	0§	1.13560‡	1.31760‡	0§	0
	StdDev	0.00736	0.08198	0	0.46623	0	0	0	0.45823	0.76643	0	0
F5	Mean	0.01336‡	0§	0§	0§	0§	0§	0§	0.01125‡	0§	0§	0
	StdDev	0.00453	0	0	0	0	0	0	0.00365	0	0	0
F6	Mean	11.0214‡	0§	0§	0§	7.59E-10‡	2.73028E-10‡	0§	7.268E-1‡	0§	0§	0
	StdDev	1.38686	0	0	0	7.10E-10	1.15E-11	0	7.30E-10	0	0	0
F7	Mean	7.40E+03‡	0§	0§	0§	0§	147.401395‡	8.51453‡	5.54478‡	6.56735‡	5.26235‡	0
	StdDev	1.14E+03	0	0	0	0	448.5712	8.768288	5.71233	6.1288	5.0354	0
F8	Mean	1.22E+03‡	0.66667‡	0.66667‡	0.66667‡	0.66667‡	0.66667‡	0.66667‡	0.4583‡	0.23467‡	0§	0
	StdDev	2.66E+02	E-9	E-8	1.16E-09	5.65E-10	0	0	E-8	2.66E-10	0	0
F9	Mean	1.17E+03‡	0§	0§	5.12370‡	0§	0§	0§	3.54970‡	0§	0§	0
	StdDev	76.56145	0	0	0.39209	0	0	0	0.312	0	0	0
F10	Mean	1.11E+03‡	0§	0§	0§	0§	0§	0§	1.12070‡	0§	0§	0
	StdDev	74.21447	0	0	0	0	0	0	0.44709	0	0	0
F11	Mean	1.48E+02‡	0§	0§	0§	0§	0§	0§	0§	0§	0§	0
	StdDev	12.40929	0	0	0	0	0	0	0	0	0	0
F12	Mean	0.18070‡	0.00136‡	0.00116‡	1.72E-06‡	0.00678‡	3.66E-03‡	9.70E-04‡	1.52E-05‡	0.00042‡	0.10233‡	0
	StdDev	0.02712	0.00042	0.00028	1.85E-06	0.00133	0.001401	0.00125	1.75E-05	0.00765	0.1555	0
F13	Mean	0.00424‡	0§	0§	0§	0§	0§	0§	0§	0§	0§	0
	StdDev	0.00476	0	0	0	0	0	0	0	0	0	0
F14	Mean	-1.03163§	-1.03163§	-1.03163§	-1.0316§	-1.0316§	-1.03163§	-1.0316§	-1.0316§	-1.0316§	-1.0316§	-1.03163
	StdDev	0	0	0	0	0	0	0	0	0	0	0
F15	Mean	0.06829‡	0§	0§	0§	0§	0§	0§	0§	0§	0§	0
	StdDev	0.07822	0	0	0	0	0	0	0	0	0	0
F16	Mean	0§	0§	0§	0§	0§	0§	0§	0§	0§	0§	0
	StdDev	0	0	0	0	0	0	0	0	0	0	0
F17	Mean	-186.73§	-186.73§	-186.73§	-186.73§	-186.73§	-186.73§	-186.73§	-186.73§	-186.73§	-186.73§	-186.73
	StdDev	0	0	0	0	0	0	0	0	0	0	0
F18	Mean	1.96E+05‡	18.20394‡	15.088617‡	28.834‡	4.2831‡	2.02E+01‡	1.04E-07‡	16.3261‡	14.4386‡	16.66861	0
	StdDev	3.85E+04	5.03619	24.1702	0.10597	5.7877	1.147947	2.95E-07	22.4319	29.57019	21.87019	0
F19	Mean	10.63346‡	0.00148‡	0.01739‡	0§	0.00468‡	0§	0§	0.45739‡	0.09739‡	0.08249‡	0
	StdDev	1.16146	0.00296	0.02081	0	0.00672	0	0	0.72081	0.09771	0.08691	0
F20	Mean	14.67178‡	0§	0.16462‡	0§	3.12E-08‡	6.56E-10‡	0§	0§	0.11432‡	0.21362‡	0
	StdDev	0.17814	0	0.49387	0	3.98E-08	1.24E-09	0	0	0.32587	0.549387	0
F21	Mean	0§	0§	0§	0§	0§	0§	0§	0§	0§	0§	0
	StdDev	0	0	0	0	0	0	0	0	0	0	0
F22	Mean	0§	0§	0§	0.00053‡	0§	0§	0§	0§	0§	0.00132‡	0
	StdDev	0	0	0	0.00074	0	0	0	0	0	0.00149	0
F23	Mean	-1.8013§	-1.8013§	-1.57287‡	-1.8013§	-1.8013§	-1.8013§	-1.8013§	-1.8013§	-1.8013§	-1.8013§	-1.8013
	StdDev	0	0	0.11986	0	0	0	0	0	0	0	0
F24	Mean	-4.64483‡	-4.68348‡	-2.4908‡	-4.6877§	-4.6877§	-4.60E+00‡	-4.6877§	-1.3577‡	-3.64483‡	-2.4468‡	-4.6877
	StdDev	0.09785	0.01253	0.25695	0	0	0.092696	0	0.78615	0.00785	0.03597	0
F25	Mean	-9.49683‡	-9.59115‡	-4.0071‡	-9.6602§	-9.6602§	-9.2952172‡	-9.65352‡	-9.77525‡	-9.11525‡	-9.65352‡	-9.6602
	StdDev	0.14112	0.06421	0.50263	0	0	0.282019	0.014947	0.019947	0.028947	0.014947	0
F26	Mean	52.92259‡	11.71673‡	43.97714‡	0§	0§	47.884069‡	0§	33.5561‡	44.9664‡	38.7871‡	0
	StdDev	4.56486	2.53817	11.72868	0	0	16.132	0	21.78868	11.8868	11.09868	0

(Table 30) cont.....

	Criteria	GA	DE	PSO	BA	PBA	FA	NPSO	MRPSO	CCABC	EPSDE	EHPSO
	"‡" sign denotes EHPSO efficiency is better than the given algorithm, "†" sign denotes EHPSO efficiency is worse than the given algorithm, and "§" sign denotes EHPSO efficiency is equal to the given algorithm.											
	Friedman Test											
		5.65	3.65	4.08	3.85	3.56	4.06	3.15	3.11	4.12	3.77	4.02
	p-value	3.45E-07										
	Statistic	40.609										

According to the results obtained, the proposed method in all 26 benchmark functions has been able to converge to the optimal point of the function. The results showed that since the average cost of the particles was counted rather than the best cost, it can be said that the EHPSO algorithm could fully converge to the optimum in all 26 functions. Hence, it seems logical that at the end of the determined assessment (here 1000), the standard deviation of the particles would be zero. In some functions, the proposed method along with several other methods has had the best performance in terms of the quality of results. Fig. (**37**) shows the best cost in different dimensions.

In functions F11, F13 and F15, all methods except the genetic algorithm converged to the optimal point. In functions F3, F14, F17 and F21, all methods could converge to the optimal point. The proposed method in functions F8, F12 and F18 could alone achieve the optimal solution. The Friedman test conducted on the results of all methods indicated the normal process of the results as well as the independence on the random process.

The results of the compared methods were measured based on different sizes and presented in Fig. (**37**). The sizes were changed on the values 20, 30, 40, 50, 80 and 100, and they were tested on 26 benchmark functions for all methods. The results showed that the convergence to optimum was almost identical in all aspects for the proposed algorithm. They also indicated that the EHPSO algorithm had the best quality of results in all tests. Naturally, with the increase of the number of variables or the size of the problem, the results have changed from the better quality to the worse one due to the complicatedness of the mechanism of the discussed problem.

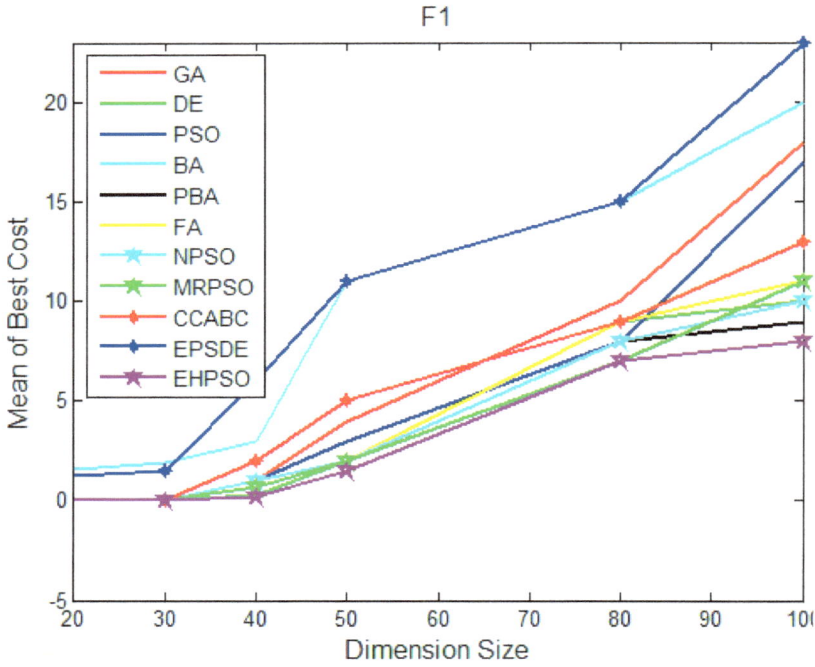

(a)

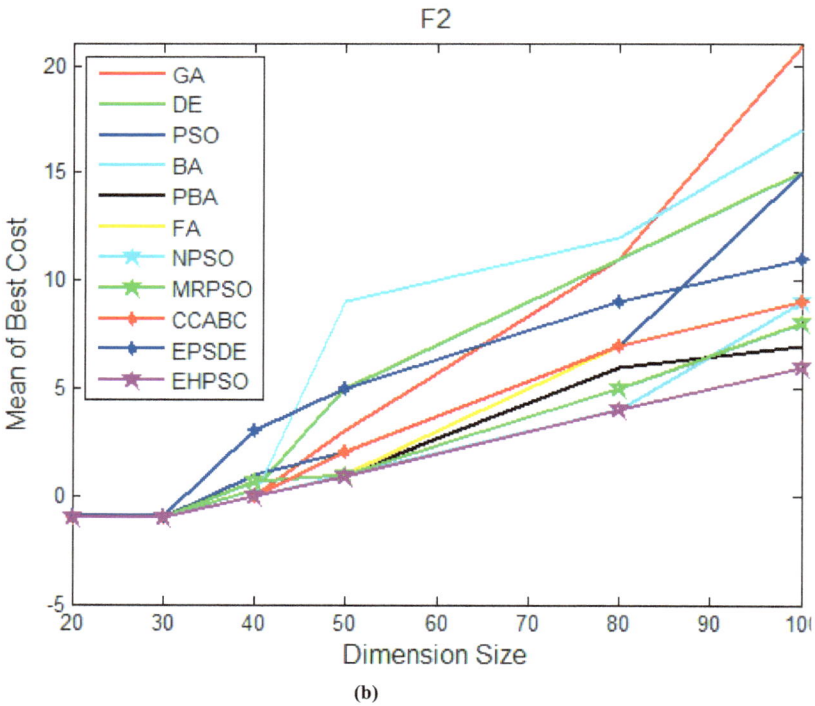

(b)

Fig. 37 cont.....

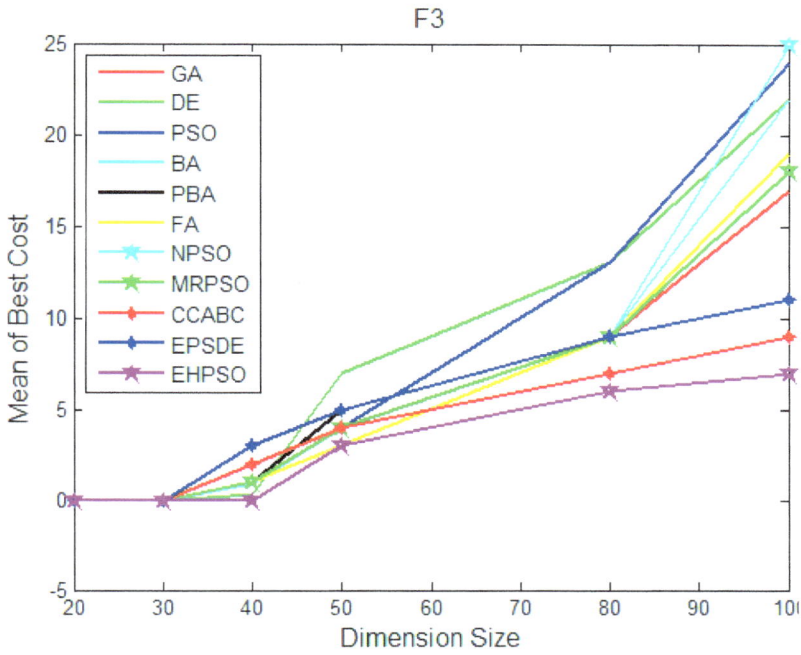

(c)

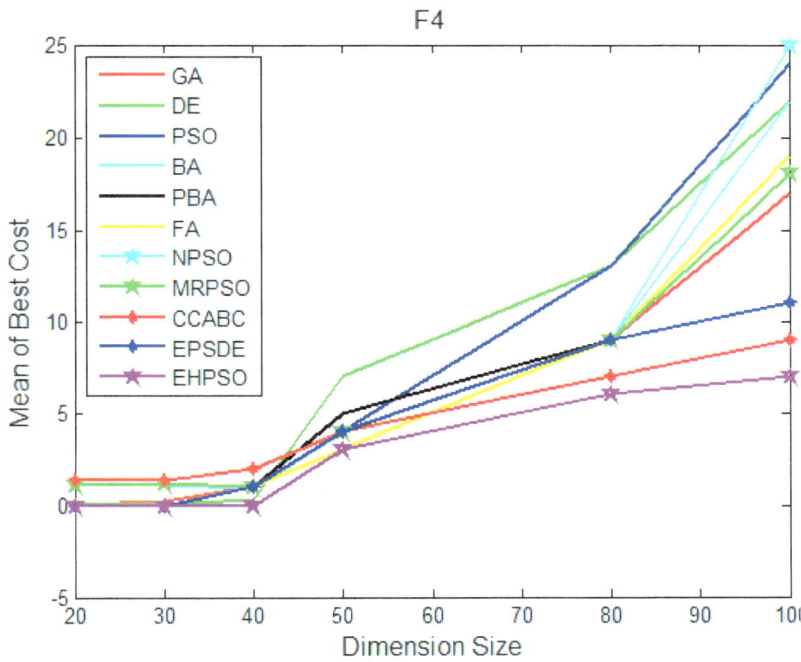

(d)

Fig. 37 cont.....

(e)

(f)

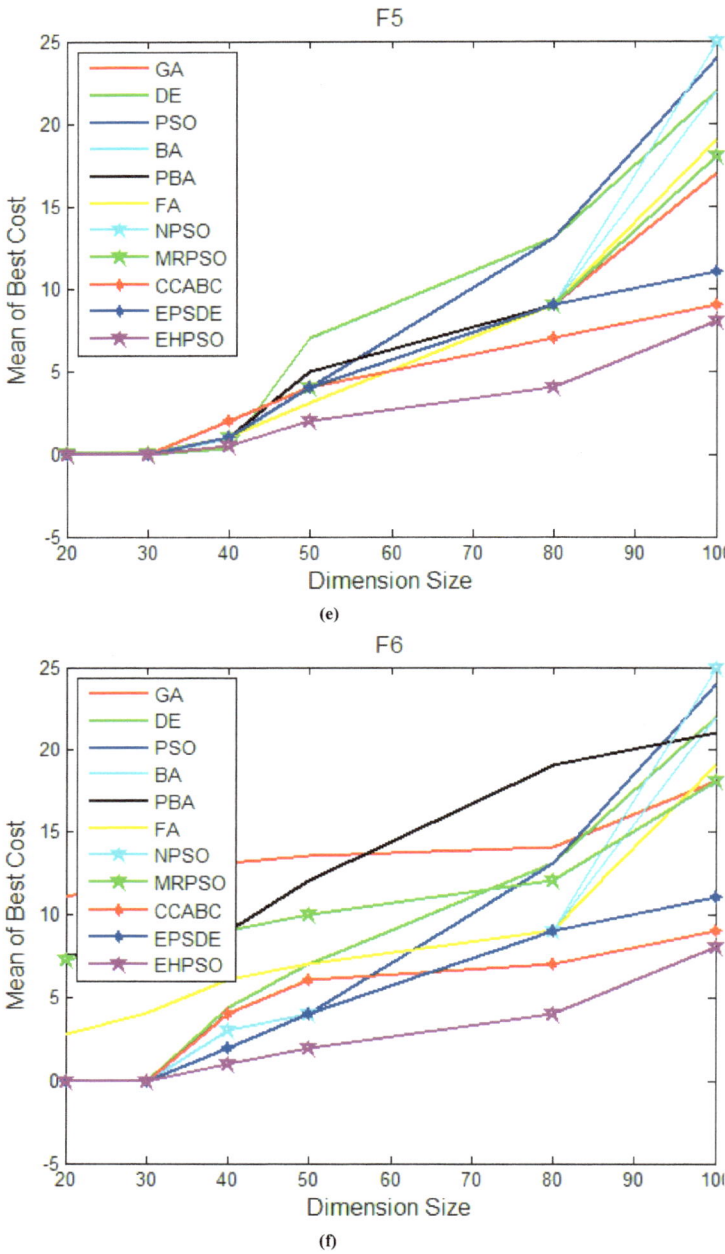

Fig. (37). The results of compared methods in sizes 20, 30, 40, 50, 80 and 100 on 26 benchmark functions.

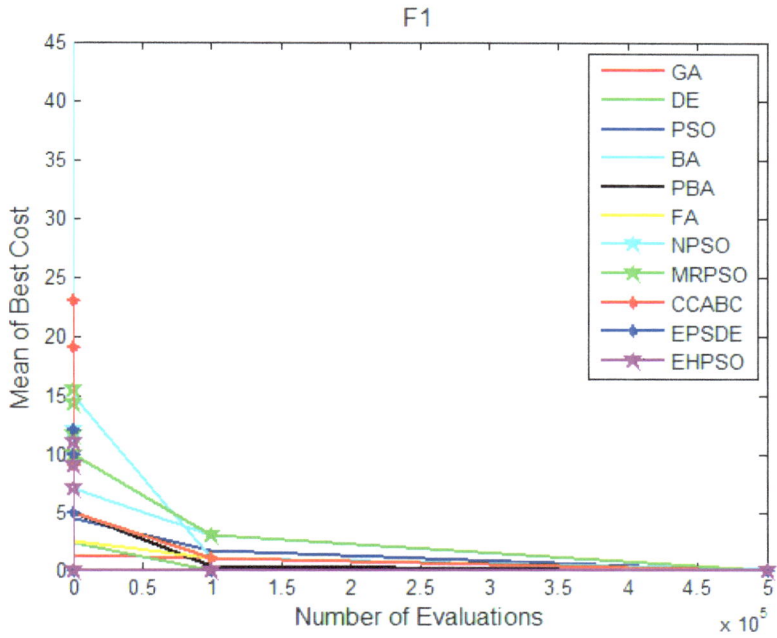

(a)

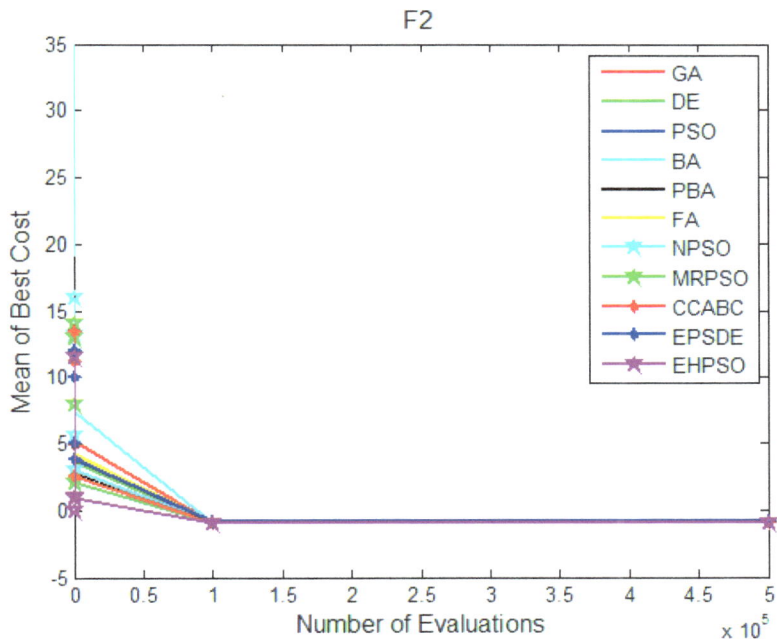

(b)

Fig. 38 cont.....

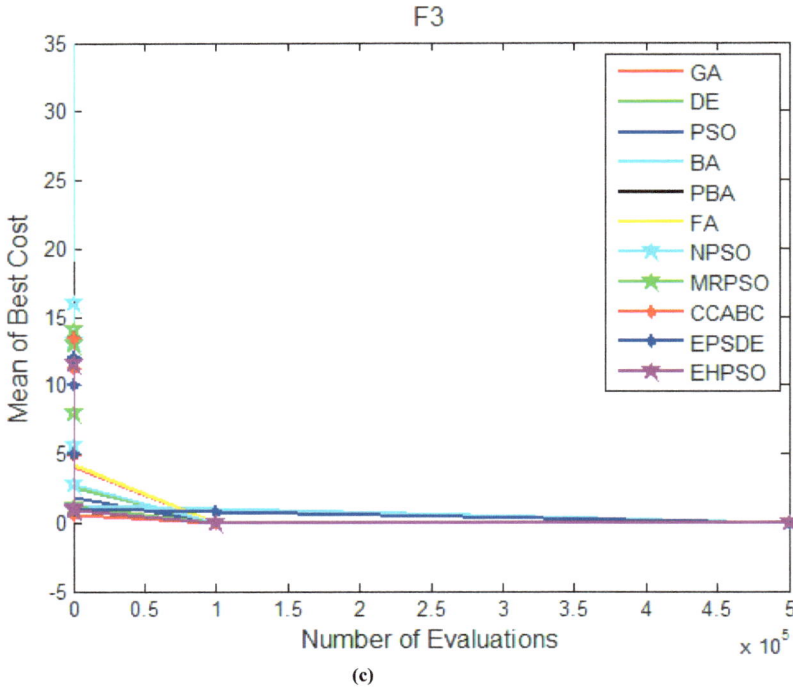

(c)

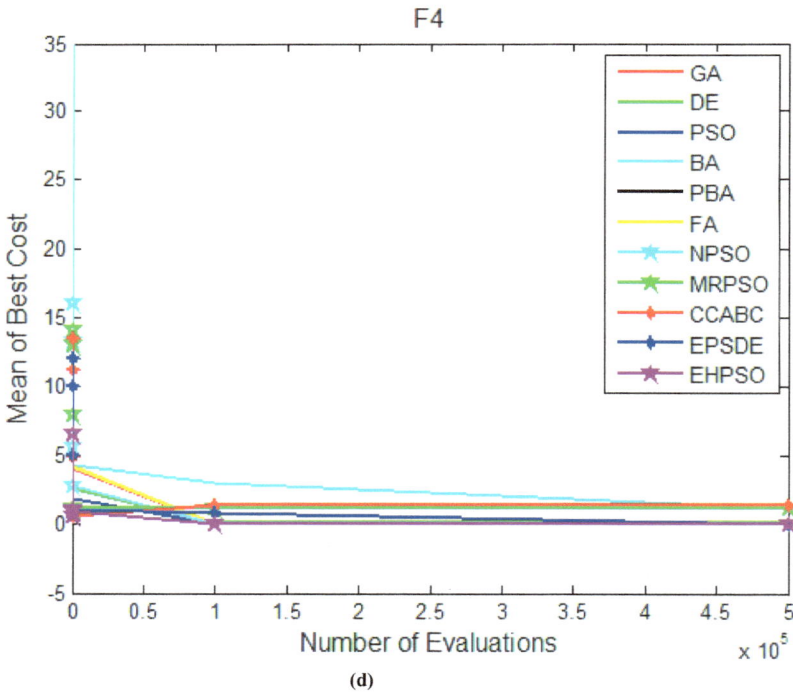

(d)

Fig. 38 cont.....

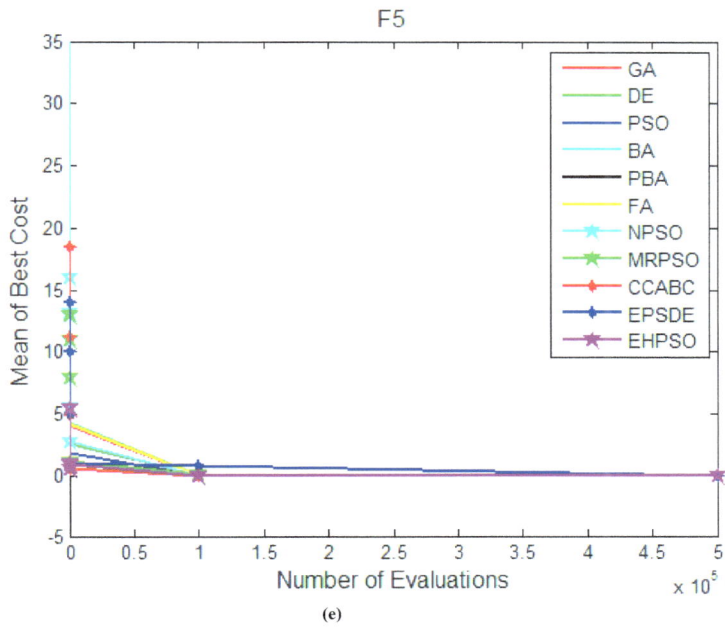

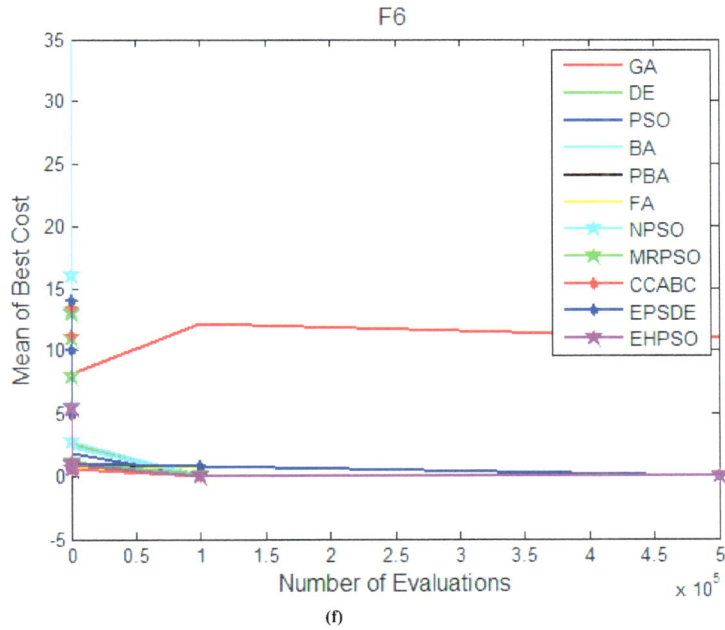

Fig. (38). Results of the compared methods in assessments 100, 200, 500, 1000, 100000 and 500000 on 26 benchmark functions.

Fig. (**38**) shows the results of testing all methods on different assessment values. Different assessments indicate that in this diagram, the convergence of the proposed algorithm in various assessment values has gradually converged towards the optimal response as the assessment has increased. The assessment values for all methods were tested on 100, 200, 500, 1000, 100000 and 500000. The results of 26 functions showed that the EHPSO algorithm has had the best performance on all different assessment values and has been able to find the best cost in all assessments. The results trend has move towards getting better as the assessment value has increased. To be able to measure the algorithm efficiency compared to similar new algorithms, the algorithm was also compared with GSO [79], CS [80], IMPSO-FNN [81], DSA [82] and BMO [83] algorithms. This comparison was done 25 times based on the average best cost (Mean) and the standard deviation (StdDev) from an average. The results were tested on 25 benchmark functions [84] algorithms. This comparison was done 25 times based on the average best cost (Mean) and the standard deviation (StdDev) from an average. The results were tested on 25 benchmark functions [85] and 300000 evaluations with 30 variables. Table **32** shows the results of all methods.

Table 32. Results of the comparison with newer algorithms on 26 functions based on the mean best cost and the StdDev.

	Criteria	GSO		CS	IMPSO-FNN	DSA			BMO		EHPSO
F1	Mean	2.63E-05 ‡		0§	3.64E-27 ‡	1.23E-28 ‡			1.23E-28 ‡		0
	StdDev	5.15E-05		0	5.82E-27	0			0		0
F2	Mean	8.46E+02‡		1.40E-03‡	1.79E-09‡	1.56E+03‡			1.36E+00‡		1.88E-09
	StdDev	1.83E+02		2.49E-03	4.50E-09	5.64E+02			1.45E+00		4.69E-09
F3	Mean	1.90E+06‡		2.06E+06‡	1.05E+06‡	1.19E+07‡			5.48E+06‡		1.01E+06
	StdDev	6.20E+05		6.83E+05	6.64E+05	5.55E+06			2.42E+06		6.72E+05
F4	Mean	1.39E+04‡		1.51E+03‡	2.73E+02‡	8.46E+03‡			3.87E+03‡		1.67E+02
	StdDev	2.93E+03		1.19E+03	8.31E+02	2.01E+03			4.32E+03		7.78E+03
F5	Mean	9.51E+03‡		2.96E+03‡	3.24E+03‡	3.24E+03‡			4.22E+03‡		1.49E+03
	StdDev	1.89E+03		7.17E+02	7.64E+02	4.99E+02			1.30E+03		6.87E+02
F6	Mean	1.16E+02‡		1.52E+01‡	3.13E+01‡	5.18E+01‡			4.42E+01‡		1.33E+01
	StdDev	3.10E+01		2.10E+01	4.51E+01	3.37E+01			4.91E+01		2.56E+01
F7	Mean	6.70E-01‡		3.24E-03‡	2.77E-02‡	2.28E-02‡			2.15E-02‡		3.17E-03
	StdDev	1.76E-01		5.52E-03	4.12E-02	8.43E-03			1.66E-02		5.22E-03
F8	Mean	2.03E+01‡		2.09E+01‡	2.09E+01‡	2.09E+01‡			2.05E+01‡		2.01E+01
	StdDev	9.33E-02		5.83E-02	5.01E-02	5.15E-02			5.58E-02		8.44E-02
F9	Mean	8.03E+00‡		2.21E+01‡	9.78E+01‡	0§			3.27E+00‡		0
	StdDev	2.28E+00		4.72E+00	2.38E+01	0			2.57E+00		0

(Table 32) cont.....

	Criteria	GSO		CS	IMPSO-FNN	DSA		BMO	EHPSO
F10	Mean	3.37E+02‡		1.64E+02‡	1.18E+02‡	8.93E+01‡		6.79E+01‡	4.38E+01
	StdDev	6.85E+01		3.85E+01	3.33E+01	2.03E+01		1.88E+01	2.23E+01
F11	Mean	3.32E+01‡		2.94E+01‡	3.02E+01‡	2.71E+01‡		2.52E+01‡	2.33E+01
	StdDev	3.02E+00		1.32E+00	5.30E+00	2.10E+00		3.76E+00	4.39E+00
F12	Mean	1.06E+04‡		2.59E+04‡	9.49E+03‡	2.09E+04‡		1.13E+04‡	9.82E+03
	StdDev	9.22E+03		7.13E+03	1.13E+04	5.03E+03		5.85E+03	3.53E+04
F13	Mean	1.96E+00‡		5.96E+00‡	4.62E+00‡	1.83E+00‡		2.14E+00‡	1.03E+00
	StdDev	4.26E-01		1.32E+00	1.42E+00	1.25E-01		5.29E-01	5.45E-01
F14	Mean	1.29E+01‡		1.30E+01‡	1.28E+01‡	1.29E+01‡		1.22E+01‡	1.19E+01
	StdDev	3.92E-01		2.10E-01	3.99E-01	2.43E-01		6.65E-01	7.43E-01
F15	Mean	4.12E+02‡		2.85E+02‡	4.62E+02‡	3.96E+01‡		3.04E+02‡	2.55E+01
	StdDev	1.98E+02		7.52E+01	5.62E+01	2.38E+01		1.14E+02	2.38E+01
F16	Mean	4.15E+02‡		2.05E+02‡	2.55E+02‡	1.63E+02‡		1.19E+02‡	1.07E+02
	StdDev	1.59E+02		5.72E+01	1.35E+02	3.77E+01		3.98E+01	6.98E+01
F17	Mean	4.76E+02‡		2.36E+02‡	2.61E+02‡	2.26E+02‡		1.45E+02‡	1.22E+02
	StdDev	8.39E+01		5.84E+01	1.59E+02	3.48E+01		7.51E+01	6.53E+01
F18	Mean	1.04E+03‡		9.09E+02‡	9.34E+02‡	9.09E+02‡		9.06E+02‡	8.79E+02
	StdDev	8.90E+01		1.96E+00	3.78E+01	1.48E+00		1.23E+00	1.73E+00
F19	Mean	1.05E+03‡		9.09E+02‡	9.51E+02‡	9.10E+02‡		9.06E+02‡	7.29E+02
	StdDev	5.16E+01		1.63E+00	2.98E+01	1.28E+00		1.75E+00	1.88E+00
F20	Mean	1.06E+03‡		9.09E+02‡	9.47E+02‡	9.09E+02‡		9.06E+02‡	9.04E+02
	StdDev	8.00E+01		1.96E+00	2.30E+01	1.58E+00		1.79E+00	1.11E+00
F21	Mean	1.13E+03‡		5.12E+02‡	1.01E+03‡	5.00E+02‡		1.09E+03‡	4.79E+02
	StdDev	2.80E+02		6.00E+01	3.14E+02	9.21E-14		4.49E+00	5.33E-14
F22	Mean	1.22E+03‡		9.20E+02‡	9.38E+02‡	9.38E+02‡		8.64E+02‡	8.51E+02
	StdDev	6.95E+01		2.80E+01	3.88E+01	1.53E+01		3.08E+01	4.76E+01
F23	Mean	1.16E+03‡		5.66E+02‡	1.12E+03‡	5.34E+02‡		1.10E+03‡	5.17E+02
	StdDev	2.33E+02		1.08E+02	1.97E+02	3.70E-04		3.59E+00	3.66E-04
F24	Mean	1.15E+03‡		6.20E+02‡	2.66E+02‡	2.00E+02‡		9.42E+02‡	1.44E+02
	StdDev	4.24E+02		3.60E+02	2.29E+02	6.27E-13		4.04E+00	6.83E-13
F25	Mean	1.18E+03‡		2.13E+02‡	4.49E+02‡	2.21E+02‡		2.17E+02‡	2.00E+02
	StdDev	4.06E+02		1.67E+00	4.31E+02	2.32E+00		1.70E+00	3.69E+00

"‡" sign denote EHPSO efficiency is best, "†" sign denote EHPSO efficiency is worse, "§" sign denote EHPSO efficiency is equal.

Friedman Test

		GSO		CS	IMPSO-FNN	DSA		BMO	EHPSO
		4.21	4.29			3.85	4.53	3.11	4.12
	p-value	3.38E-06							
	Statistic	40.32							

Results of comparing the proposed algorithm with new methods showed that in all 25 functions the quality algorithm has had better results. In both F1 and F9 functions the proposed method jointly with another algorithm could have the best performance. In the F1 function, the CS algorithm and the proposed method have had the best performance by reaching the optimal point of zero. The same process was seen for the proposed algorithm and the DSA algorithm in the F9 function. Totally, the EHPSO proposed algorithm was tested in 51 benchmark functions and compared with 15 optimization algorithms and could have the best performance in all cases. The standard deviation values of the proposed method were high in most comparisons and this indicates the ability of a diverse search by the algorithm in the problem space. The statistical test conducted on the results in Table **34** shows that the values of the results obtained from the methods had no significant relationship with the random process.

3.22. PROVIDING A BIRD ALGORITHM BASED ON CLASSICAL CONDITIONING LEARNING BEHAVIOR

Due to using a number of bird swarms in our proposed method, the determined population was divided into the intended categories (Fig. **39**). In general, we divided the birds into categories, and implemented the proposed method's mechanism in each category and in the entire categories. We finally determined the solutions produced in the entire swarms as the optimal solution. Table **33** defines the parameters of each population.

Fig. (39). Bird swarm movement.

Table 33. Definition of parameters.

Parameter	Definition
n Var section	Area number of problem space
Var Min	The upper limit of the problem space
Var Max	The lower limit of the problem space
Var Size	Number of variables any population
n Population section	Number of categories

In the first phase, we will define the range of variables in each population. The reason is to divide the variables of each population in certain ranges and allow them to move in that range.

$$n\, Var\ section \tag{46}$$

In this equation, we will define the determined number in the variable. In this simulation, the number of *n Var section* equale 10; that is to say we will assume the range of variables to be 10. Now the length of each range is calculated by the equation 47.

$$L = \frac{(Var\ Max - Var\ Min)}{n\, Var\ section} \tag{47}$$

In this equation, *Var Max* and *Var Min* are the upper and lower limits, and *n Var section* is the number of variable ranges. In the next step, the population is divided into several parts or categories.

$$n\, Population\ section = x \tag{48}$$

In this simulation we divided the population into 4 categories. Therefore, equations 47-48 can be written as:

$$n\, Population\ section = 4 \tag{49}$$

To define the parameters, a threshold parameter is defined to determine the standard deviation of bird swarms. At the stage of generating the population randomly and as large as the population determined based on the upper limit, we create the lower limit and the number of variables to generate the initial population.

$$Particle(i).Position = Random(Var\ Max, Var\ Min, Var\ Size) \qquad \textbf{(50)}$$

In this equation, *Var Size* is the number of the population, and *unifrnd* is also used because we want to create unique random numbers and the particles' locations in the search space should not be duplicated. The produced population is inserted in the cost function and the cost of particles will be obtained.

$$Particle(i).Cost = Fitness(Particle(i).Position) \qquad \textbf{(51)}$$

We also determined where in the space the variables of each population were located. We divided the dimensions of the problem space into sections so that the space could be classified based on the value of the area. Thus, it was necessary to determine in which areas, there was any variable of the population.

$$for\ k = 1:nPopulation$$

$$for\ i = 1:nVar$$

$$for\ j = 1:nVar\ Section \qquad \textbf{(52)}$$

$$if\ VarMin + (j-1)*L \le Particle(i).Position(j)\ and\ Particle(i).Position(j) <$$
$$(VarMin + j*L) \to Space(k,i) = j$$

Birds that have good energy and good nutrition will have a better performance in flight. We modeled this behavior of birds and removed the particles with inappropriate conditions from the problem space when deciding on the initial population and replaced them with the same number of random population. To do so, we first arranged the initially generated population in an array according to their costs.

$$Cost\ Array = Sort(Particle(i).Cost) \qquad \textbf{(53)}$$

And from the end of the array, the specified number of replacements was done. In this study, we replaced one third of the arranged costs of the particles from the end of the array.

$$for\ i = 1: index\left(\frac{2}{3} \times nPopulation\right): end$$

$$Particle(i).Position = unifrnd(Var\ Max, Var\ Min, Var\ Size)$$

(54)

The cost of new population is estimated, and the particle location is the local optimum for each particle in the first evaluation.

$$PBest = (Particle(i).Position)$$

(55)

The general optimum is the best value in the entire particles. For the static functions in this study, the minimum value was the best cost.

$$GBest = min(Particle(i).Cost)$$

(56)

After determining the general optimum of the entire particles, the general optimum of each category will be determined separately. To do this, for each category we will initially put the costs of the particles in an array.

$$for\ i = 1: nPopulation\ Section$$

$$C = (Particle.Cost)$$

$$T = \frac{(i-1)\times Population\ Number}{nPopulation\ Section} + 1: \frac{i\times Population\ Number}{nPopulation\ Section}$$

(57)

We specify the population of each category in parameter T and put them in parameter C in order to separately compare the population in each category.

$$C = C(T)$$

(58)

Now the minimum cost per category will be determined as the general optimum of that category.

$$GBest(i) = min(C) \tag{59}$$

We used the idea of birds; sensitivity to the environment, and after dividing the land dimensions into several sections for variables, rated each space on the grounds that every time a particle was placed in a space and it was also the optimum. We added the velocity of particles in the space by 1 unit.

$$for\ i = 1:nVar\ Section$$
$$if\ GBest\ in\ i\ \rightarrow Space\ Rate(i) = Space\ Rate(i) + 1 \tag{60}$$

In the next stage, the standard deviation of each category was measured in order to be able to implement our idea of classical conditioning learning behavior.

$$if\ STD(i) \geq Threshold$$
$$C1 = 0.9 \times C1 \quad C2 = 1.1 \times C2 \tag{61}$$

$$Else$$
$$C1 = 1.1 \times C1 \quad C2 = 0.9 \times C2 \tag{62}$$

In this equation, the coefficients before and after the local optimum are used in the velocity equation. According to the above equations if the standard deviation of the category is high, we can lead the particle towards the general optimum and make it far from the local optimum by placing a number higher than 1 for the coefficient before the general optimum and a number lower than 1. Conversely, if the diversity or standard deviation of the category is low, we can put a less-than-1 coefficient before the local optimum and a more-than-1 coefficient before the general optimum to send the particle away from the general optimum and lead it towards the local optimum. This is done because if the diversity of the bird swarm is greater than the defined threshold, as the particles have searched in a larger space, going towards its general optimum might be more beneficial.

In Fig. (**40**), it is shown that categories 1 and 3 have the least and the most diversity, respectively. In categories 1 and 2, the particles mainly move towards a local optimum while in Fig. (**59**), the particles in categories 3 and 4, according to the defined mechanism in this study, will mainly move towards the general optimum. We will define this idea in the form of classical conditioning learning behavior of birds for particles. According to the learned behavior, birds learn to move more eagerly towards the general optimum whenever they feel that the diversity of their categories is high. The particle velocity equation will be set as follows:

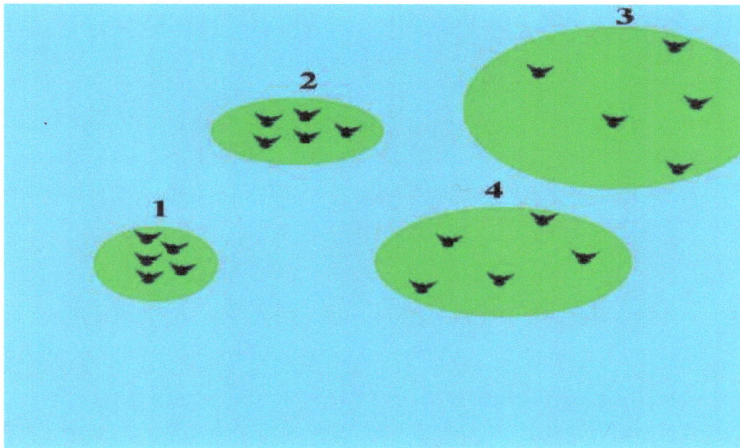

Fig. (40). Variation of the categories.

$$for\ i = 1: nPopulation$$

$$for\ j = 1: nVar$$

$$Velocity(i) = \left(1 - \frac{Space\ Rate\ (1,j,Space\ Rate(i,j))}{sum(Space\ Rate(1,j,x))}\right) \times w \times Particle(i).Velocity + c1 \times \quad \text{(63)}$$
$$rand(Var\ Size) \times (Particle(i).PBest - Particle(i).Position) + c2 \times rand(Var\ Size) \times$$
$$(Particle(i).GBest - Particle(i).Position)$$

In this equation, $\left(1 - \frac{Space\ Rate\ (1,j,Space\ Rate(i,j))}{sum(Space\ Rate(1,j,x))}\right)$ is used to control the speed of the particles in high-value and low-value spaces. This part of the velocity equation produces lower numbers for the particles in the spaces with higher values. Multiplying this lower number by inertia weight will reduce the velocity. Through this mechanism, the particles will move at a slower rate and do more search in the more valuable space. *w* is the inertia weight used to determine the impact of the previous speed on the current one, *Particle(i).Velocity* is the current speed of the particle, *c1* is the coefficient that specifies the ratio of particles' tendency towards the local optimum, *rand(Var Size)* is a random number for non-linear motion of the particle, *Particle(i).PBest* is the local optimum or the best personal experience and the best place a particle has had so far. *Particle(i).Position* is the current location of the particle, *c2* is the coefficient that specifies the ratio of particles' tendency towards the general optimum, and *Particle(i).GBest* is the general optimum or the best particle in the entire population of the birds. With this equation, if the particles that are going to move in the next step find their standard deviation and category diversity to be high, they will move towards the general optimum, and if the category diversity is low and the particles involved in a category are searching in a smaller space, they will try to incline towards the local optimum or their best personal experience. Determining the particle velocity equation, we can specify the motion equation in accordance with equation 64.

$$Particle(i).NewPosition = Particle(i).Position + Particle(i).Velocity \quad (64)$$

In this equation, *Particle(i).NewPosition* is the next location of the particle while *Particle(i).Position* and *Particle(i).Velocity* are the particle's current location and velocity, respectively.

According to Fig. (**41**), assuming that particle *e* is the general optimum of category 3, particle *b* in category 3 wants to move in the next step and due to the high diversity of the categories tries to set its velocity equation so that it will move toward the general optimum of the category. This is done by setting the number of coefficients *c1* and *c2*. Fig. (**42**) shows how to value the problem space. The parts marked in bold have greater value and probably more general optimums have been found in the evaluations in these areas. In the proposed method we try to move the particles in these spaces at a slower speed so that the particles could do more search in these areas. The first part of the equation will apply the speed of the proposed method of this mechanism.

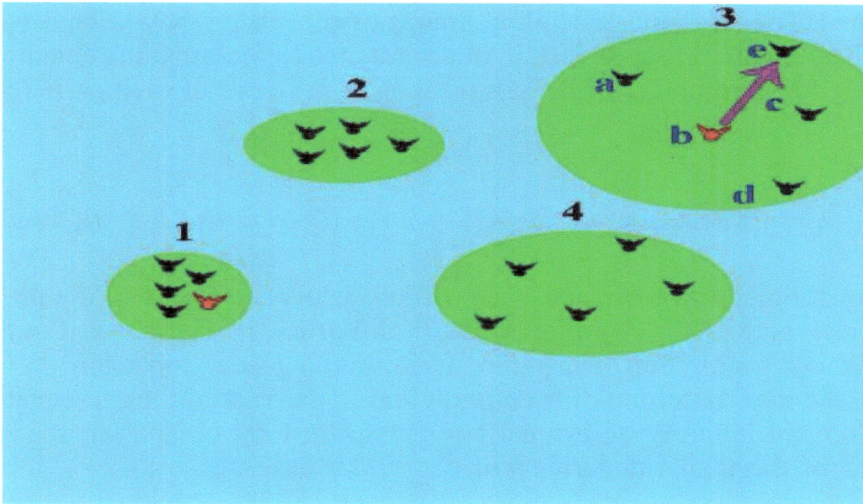

Fig. (41). Particle motion mechanism within each category.

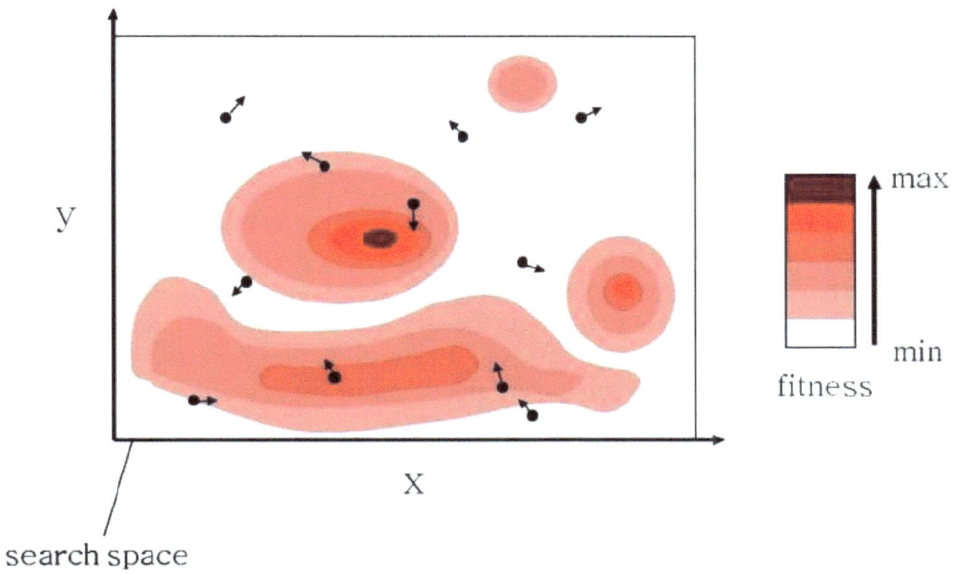

Fig. (42). How to value the problem space.

After the particle motion according to equation 46 and getting located in a new place, they will be put in the cost function again and the cost of the particles will be obtained. The local and general optimums of each category will be determined again. The general optimum will be in accordance to the previous equations and finding the local optimum or the best personal experience of each particle can be achieved through equation 65.

$$if\ Cost(Particle(i).NewPosition) < Pbest(i) \rightarrow Pbest(i) = Particle(i).NewPosition \quad \textbf{(65)}$$

In this equation, *Cost(Particle(i).NewPosition)* is the cost of the bird's new place and *Pbest (i)* is the local optimum of the bird. Earlier, it was said that in the first stage, the local optimum of any bird is its initial place, and from the second iteration, the local optimum of each particle is updated according to equation 66. In the end, the number of evaluations determined by comparing the general optimums of the total categories will obtain the best cost.

$$for\ i = 1: nPopulation\ Section$$

$$Best\ Cost = min(Gbest(Population\ Section(i)))$$

$\textbf{(66)}$

Fig. (**43**) shows the general diagram of the proposed method. In this Figure, first the initial random population is generated and then a third of the bad population will be removed. In the next step, a random population as large as the removed one will replace it. The population is then divided into a number of particle categories. In this Figure, the particles in the red category will mainly move towards their personal experience due to the low diversity. This motion that will be combined with a random and free motion may change the same category into a category with higher diversity in the next assessments. Due to the higher diversity, the particles in the green category will converge to the general optimum of their category. In this Figure, the particles in high-value spaces identified in bold will move slower in order to do more search in those points. Here, the conditioned stimulus of bird swarm diversity and the natural work that the birds do as they see the condition is to go to the local or general optimums of the categories.

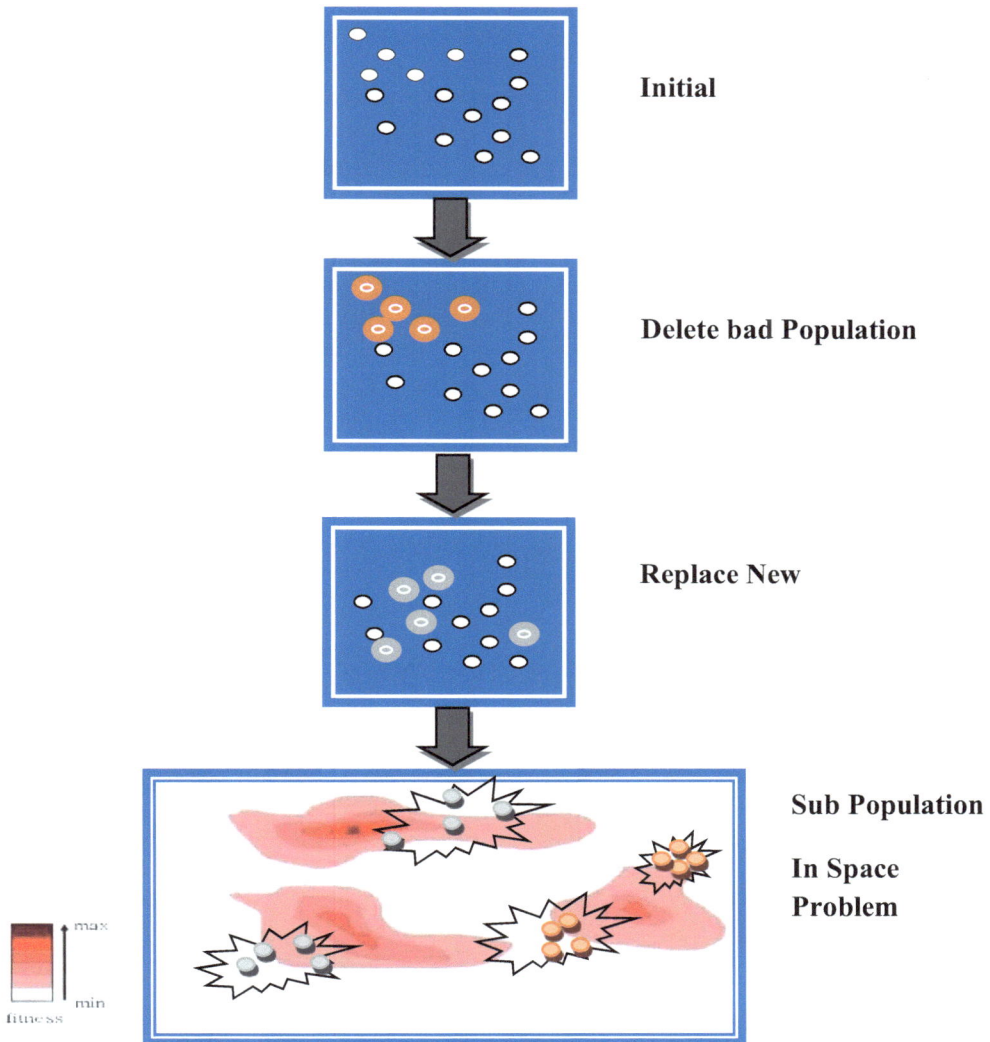

Fig. (43). General diagram of the proposed method.

Fig. (**44**) shows the pseudo-code of the proposed method. In line 1 create population based on randomly, line 2 Determine the suitability of the initial population, line 3 Sort the population according to their merits, in line 4 Removing 1/3 from the worst population and replacing it randomly, line 5 Recalculate the size of the merit of the population, in line 6 Split the population into several categories, line 7 will determine the region of the variable of each population, line 8 determine pbest any categories, line 9 determine gbest any categories, line 10 determine the appropriate number for coefficients C1and C2 based on the dispersion rate of each category, line 11 determine the velocity of population, line 12 determine the new position of population, line 13 move any population to new position and in line 14 determine the merit of new position for any population.

---

1. Generate the initial population randomly.

2. Insert the initial population in the cost function and calculate the cost of the particles.

3. Arrange the particles in an array based on their costs.

4. Remove stage 3 and 1/3 of the particles respectively from the arranged array and the end of it and replace them with random particles.

5. Put the new population in the cost function and calculate the cost of the particles.

6. Divide the particles into several categories.

7. Specify the variable areas of each population.

8. For each category, put the initial place of the particles as their local optimum.
9. Specify the general optimum of each category as its best local optimum and add one unit to the value of the particle's space.
10. Set the values of parameters C1 and C2 based on standard deviation and diversity of the categories.

11. For each particle, update the velocity equation based on the speed of the space at which they are.

12. Calculate the equation of particles' motion.

13. Move the population to a new location.

14. Calculate the cost of the particles for new locations of the particles.

15. If the new location of the particles is better than their local optimum, put the new location as a local optimum.

16. Find the general optimum for each category.

17. Select the best general optimum of the categories as the best cost.

18. If the current iteration is less than the determined iteration, go to Step 5; otherwise, go to Step 19.

19. The end

Fig. (44). Pseudo-code of the proposed method.

3.23. SIMULATION AND RESULTS

We implemented the proposed method in MATLAB software and assessed the results in different sections and various similar methods using different sets of tests. The results were classified into three sections and various comparison methods were used in each section. In the first section, the results were obtained through CEC 2009 tests. In the second section, the series of CEC 2005 [84] tests were used and in the third section we tested the compared methods on CEC 2013 tests.

In the first section, we applied the methods on CEC 2009 series of tests [85] presented in Table **34**.

Table 34. Introducing CEC 2009 test series.

Min	Range	D	Function
0	[-4.5,4.5]	2	F1(Beale)
-1	[-100,100]	2	F2(Easom)
0	[-10,10]	2	F3(Matyas)
0	[-10,10]	4	F4(Colville)
0	[-5,10]	10	F5(Zakharov)
0	[-10,10]	30	F6(Schwefel 2.22)
0	[-100,100]	30	F7(Schewefel 1.2)
0	[-10,10]	30	F8(Dixon-price)
0	[-5.12,5.12]	30	F9(Step)
0	[-100,100]	30	F10(Sphere)
0	[-10,10]	30	F11(SumSquares)
0	[-1.28,1.28]	30	F12(Quartic)
0	[-100,100]	2	F13(Schaffer)
-1.0316	[-5,5]	2	F14(6 H Camel)
0	[-100,100]	2	F15(Bohachevsky2)
0	[-100,100]	2	F16(Bohachevsky3)
-186.73	[-10,10]	2	F17(Shubert)
0	[-30,30]	30	F18(Rosenbrock)
0	[-600,600]	30	F19(Griewank)
0	[-32,32]	30	F20(Ackley)
0	[-100,100]	2	F21(Bohachevsky1)
0	[-10,10]	2	F22(Booth)
-1.8013	$[0,\pi]$	2	F23(Michalewicz2)
-4.6877	$[0,\pi]$	5	F24(Michalewicz5)
-9.6602	$[0,\pi]$	10	F25(Michalewicz10)
0	[-5.12,5.12]	30	F26(Rastrigin)

In this section, we compared the proposed approach with genetic methods [86], random evolution [87], SSA Algorithm [88], bees algorithm [89], Co-e PSO algorithm [90], JA-ABC5 algorithm [91] and firefly algorithm [92]. We implemented the results with equal parameters for all methods, including the population of 100, 30 variables, and 500000 evaluations. Table **35** also shows the parameters of the algorithms. The results were set based on two criteria: the best cost of the particles (Mean) and the standard deviation of the particles (StdDev) on 26 functions introduced in Table **36**. Table **37** shows the results comprehensively. In this table, the Friedman test is presented to test the significance of the results for all methods.

Table 35. Parameter setting.

Item No.	Parameter	Value
1	pop	100
2	var	30
3	Xmin	-10
4	Xmax	10
5	c	2
6	Iteration	500000
7	Percent of crossover	0.5
8	Percent of mutation	0.01
9	Harmony memory size	10
10	New harmony memory size	100
11	Harmony memory	0.75
12	Pitch adjustment rate	0.05
13	Fret width	0.1
14	Number imperialist	10

Table 36. Comparison of the methods in CEC 2009 test series.

	Criteria	GA	DE	PSO	BA	PBA	FA	NPSO	MRPSO	JA-ABC5	Co-e PSO	Proposed
F1	Mean	0§	0§	0§	1.88E-05‡	0§	0§	0§	0§	0§	1.48E-05‡	0
	StdDev	0	0	0	1.94E-05	0	0	0	0	0	1.64E-05	0
F2	Mean	-1§	-1§	-1§	-0.99994‡	-1§	-1§	-1§	-1§	-1§	-0.8965‡	-1
	StdDev	0	0	0	4.50E-05	0	0	0	0	0	3.56E-05	0
F3	Mean	0§	0§	0§	0§	0§	0§	0§	0§	0§	0§	0
	StdDev	0	0	0	0	0	0	0	0	0	0	0
F4	Mean	0.01494‡	0.04091‡	0§	1.11760‡	0§	0§	0§	1.13560‡	1.31760‡	0§	0
	StdDev	0.00736	0.08198	0	0.46623	0	0	0	0.45823	0.76643	0	0
F5	Mean	0.01336‡	0§	0§	0§	0§	0§	0§	0.01125‡	0§	0§	0

(Table 36) cont.....

	Criteria	GA	DE	PSO	BA	PBA	FA	NPSO	MRPSO	JA-ABC5	Co-e PSO	Proposed
	StdDev	0.00453	0	0	0	0	0	0	0.00365	0	0	0
F6	Mean	11.0214‡	0§	0§	0§	7.59E-10‡	2.73028E-10‡	0§	7.268E-1‡	0§	0§	0
	StdDev	1.38686	0	0	0	7.10E-10	1.15E-11	0	7.30E-10	0	0	0
F7	Mean	7.40E+03‡	0§	0§	0§	0§	147.401395‡	8.51453‡	5.54478‡	6.56735‡	5.26235‡	0
	StdDev	1.14E+03	0	0	0	0	448.5712	8.768288	5.71233	6.1288	5.0354	0
F8	Mean	1.22E+03‡	0.66667‡	0.66667‡	0.66667‡	0.66667‡	0.66667‡	0.66667‡	0.4583‡	0.23467‡	0§	0
	StdDev	2.66E+02	E-9	E-8	1.16E-09	5.65E-10	0	0	E-8	2.66E-10	0	0
F9	Mean	1.17E+03‡	0§	0§	5.12370‡	0§	0§	0§	3.54970‡	0§	0§	0
	StdDev	76.56145	0	0	0.39209	0	0	0	0.312	0	0	0
F10	Mean	1.11E+03‡	0§	0§	0§	0§	0§	0§	1.12070‡	0§	0§	0
	StdDev	74.21447	0	0	0	0	0	0	0.44709	0	0	0
F11	Mean	1.48E+02‡	0§	0§	0§	0§	0§	0§	0§	0§	0§	0
	StdDev	12.40929	0	0	0	0	0	0	0	0	0	0
F12	Mean	0.18070‡	0.00136‡	0.00116‡	1.72E-06‡	0.00678‡	3.66E-03‡	9.70E-04‡	1.52E-05‡	0.00042‡	0.10233‡	0
	StdDev	0.02712	0.00042	0.00028	1.85E-06	0.00133	0.001401	0.00125	1.75E-05	0.00765	0.1555	0
F13	Mean	0.00424‡	0§	0§	0§	0§	0§	0§	0§	0§	0§	0
	StdDev	0.00476	0	0	0	0	0	0	0	0	0	0
F14	Mean	-1.03163§	-1.03163§	-1.03163§	-1.0316§	-1.0316§	-1.03163§	-1.0316§	-1.0316§	-1.0316§	-1.0316§	-1.03163
	StdDev	0	0	0	0	0	0	0	0	0	0	0
F15	Mean	0.06829‡	0§	0§	0§	0§	0§	0§	0§	0§	0§	0
	StdDev	0.07822	0	0	0	0	0	0	0	0	0	0
F16	Mean	0§	0§	0§	0§	0§	0§	0§	0§	0§	0§	0
	StdDev	0	0	0	0	0	0	0	0	0	0	0
F17	Mean	-186.73§	-186.73§	-186.73§	-186.73§	-186.73§	-186.73§	-186.73§	-186.73§	-186.73§	-186.73§	-186.73
	StdDev	0	0	0	0	0	0	0	0	0	0	0
F18	Mean	1.96E+05‡	18.20394‡	15.088617‡	28.834‡	4.2831‡	2.02E+01‡	1.04E-07‡	16.3261‡	14.4386‡	16.66861	0
	StdDev	3.85E+04	5.03619	24.1702	0.10597	5.7877	1.147947	2.95E-07	22.4319	29.57019	21.87019	0
F19	Mean	10.63346‡	0.00148‡	0.01739‡	0§	0.00468‡	0§	0§	0.45739‡	0.09739‡	0.08249‡	0
	StdDev	1.16146	0.00296	0.02081	0	0.00672	0	0	0.72081	0.09771	0.08691	0
F20	Mean	14.67178‡	0§	0.16462‡	0§	3.12E-08‡	6.56E-10‡	0§	0§	0.11432‡	0.21362‡	0
	StdDev	0.17814	0	0.49387	0	3.98E-08	1.24E-09	0	0	0.32587	0.549387	0
F21	Mean	0§	0§	0§	0§	0§	0§	0§	0§	0§	0§	0
	StdDev	0	0	0	0	0	0	0	0	0	0	0
F22	Mean	0§	0§	0§	0.00053‡	0§	0§	0§	0§	0§	0.00132‡	0
	StdDev	0	0	0	0.00074	0	0	0	0	0	0.00149	0
F23	Mean	-1.8013§	-1.8013§	-1.57287‡	-1.8013§	-1.8013§	-1.8013§	-1.8013§	-1.8013§	-1.8013§	-1.8013§	-1.8013
	StdDev	0	0	0.11986	0	0	0	0	0	0	0	0
F24	Mean	-4.64483‡	-4.68348‡	-2.4908‡	-4.6877§	-4.6877§	-4.60E+00‡	-4.6877§	-1.3577‡	-3.64483‡	-2.4468‡	-4.6877
	StdDev	0.09785	0.01253	0.25695	0	0	0.092696	0	0.78615	0.00785	0.03597	0
F25	Mean	-9.49683‡	-9.59115‡	-4.0071‡	-9.6602§	-9.6602§	-9.2952172‡	-9.65352‡	-9.77525‡	-9.11525‡	-9.65352‡	-9.6602
	StdDev	0.14112	0.06421	0.50263	0	0	0.282019	0.014947	0.019947	0.028947	0.014947	0
F26	Mean	52.92259‡	11.71673‡	43.97714‡	0§	0§	47.884069‡	0§	33.5561‡	44.9664‡	38.7871‡	0
	StdDev	4.56486	2.53817	11.72868	0	0	16.132	0	21.78868	11.8868	11.09868	0

The sign "‡" indicates the proposed algorithm outperforms the given algorithm, the sign "†" indicates the given algorithm outperforms the proposed algorithm and finally "§" indicates the difference in performance of the given algorithm and that of the proposed algorithm are meaningless

(Table 36) cont.....

Friedman Test												
		5.65	3.65	4.08	3.85	3.56	4.06	3.15	3.11	4.12	3.77	4.02
	p-value	3.45E-07										
	Statistic	40.609										

According to the obtained results, the proposed method in all 26 benchmark functions has been able to converge to the optimal point. The results show that, since the average cost of the particles was to be counted, it can be said that the proposed algorithm in all 26 functions could fully converge to the optimum. Hence, it seems logical that the standard deviation of the particles becomes zero at the end of the assessment which was set 1000 in here. The proposed method jointly with several other methods has had the best performance in the quality of the results. In functions F11, F13 and F15 all methods except for genetic algorithm converged to the optimal point. In functions F3, F14, F17 and F21, all methods could converge to the optimal point. The proposed method alone in functions F8, F12 and F18 could achieve the optimal solution. The Friedman test conducted on the results of all methods indicated the normal process of the results and the lack of dependence on the random process. Results of the methods compared on the basis of different dimensions were measured and shown in Fig. (**45**). The dimensions were changed on the values of 20, 30, 40, 50, 80 and 100, and the results of all methods were tested on 26 benchmark functions. Here, "dimension" refers to the number of algorithm variables. The results showed that the convergence to the optimum was almost identical in all aspects for the proposed algorithm. The results showed that the proposed algorithm had the best quality results in all tests carried out. Naturally, as the variables or the problem dimensions increased, the results changed from better quality to worse quality because the problem mechanism got more complicated.

Fig. (**45**) shows the results of testing all methods on different evaluation levels. Different evaluations show that in this diagram, the convergence of the proposed algorithm in varying amounts of evaluations converged to the optimal solution as the number of evaluations had increased. In Fig. (**46**) we tested the assessment values for all methods on 100, 200, 500, 1000, 100000 and 500000. Results of 26 functions showed that the proposed algorithm had the best performance on all different assessment values and could find the best cost in all assessments. As the assessment values increased, the results were towards getting better.

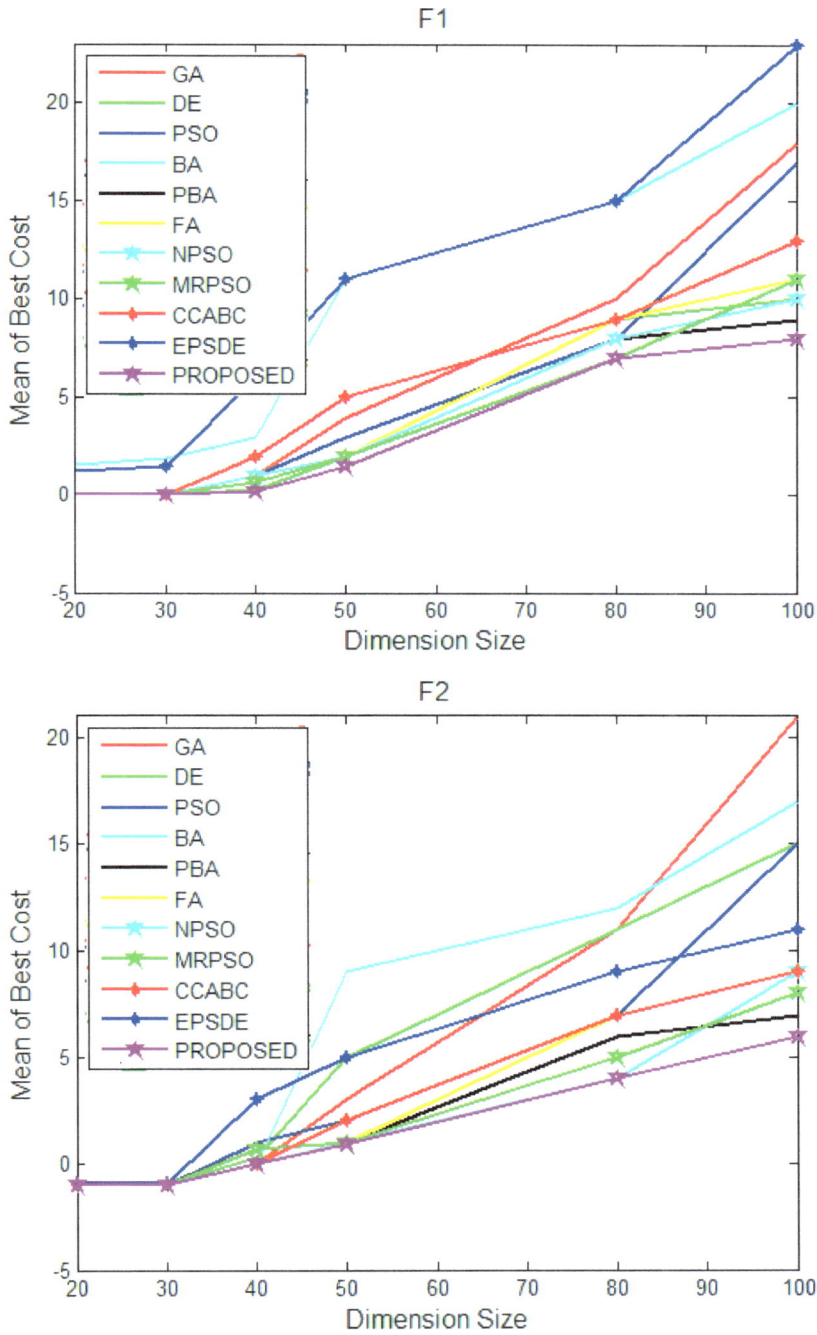

Fig. 45 cont.....

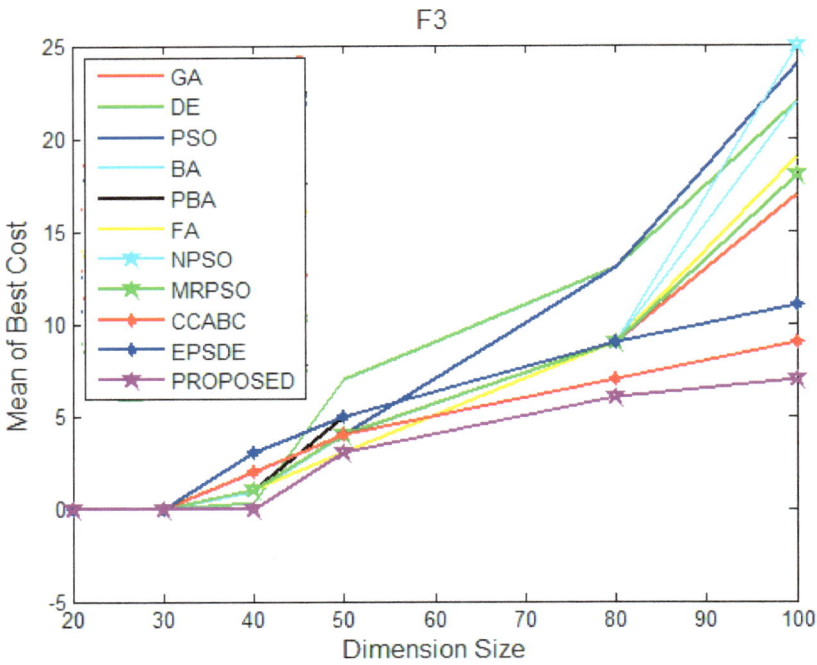

F3

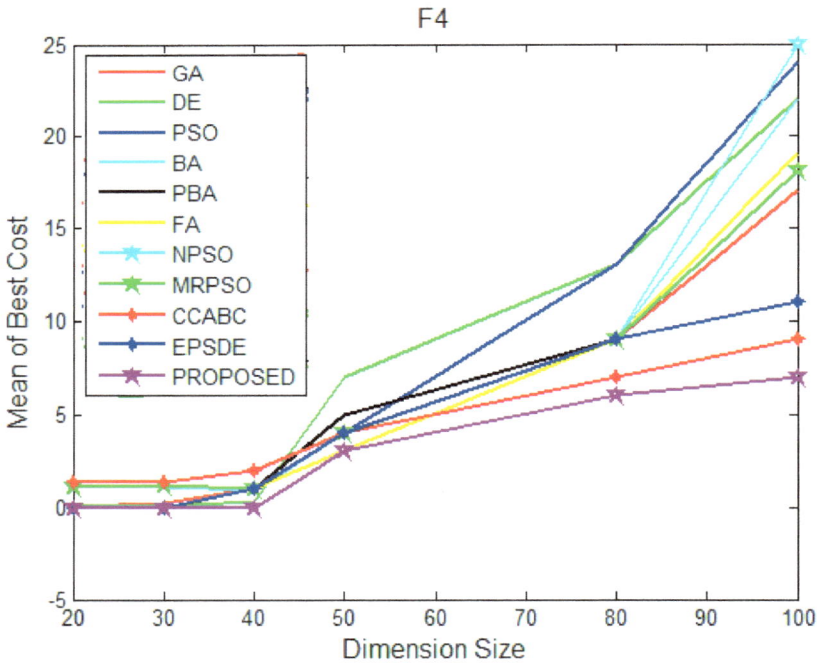

F4

Fig. 45 cont.....

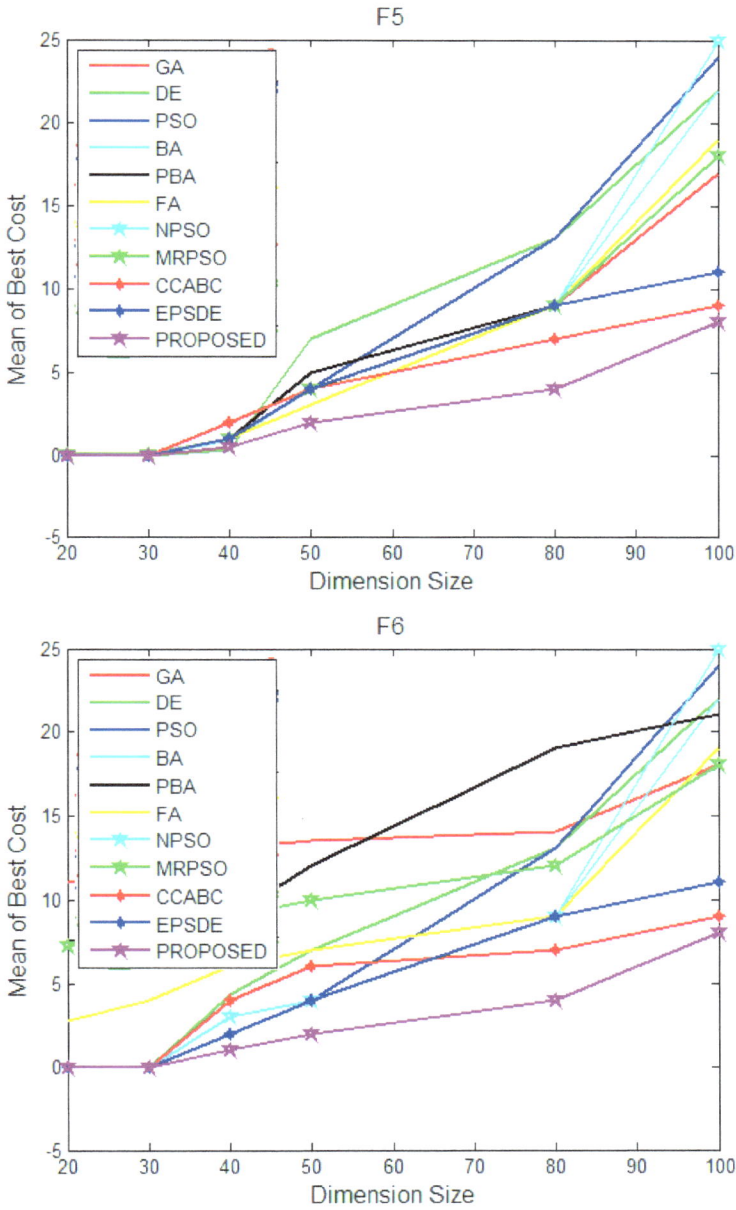

Fig. (45). Results of the compared methods in dimensions 20, 30, 40, 50, 80 and 100 on 26 benchmark functions.

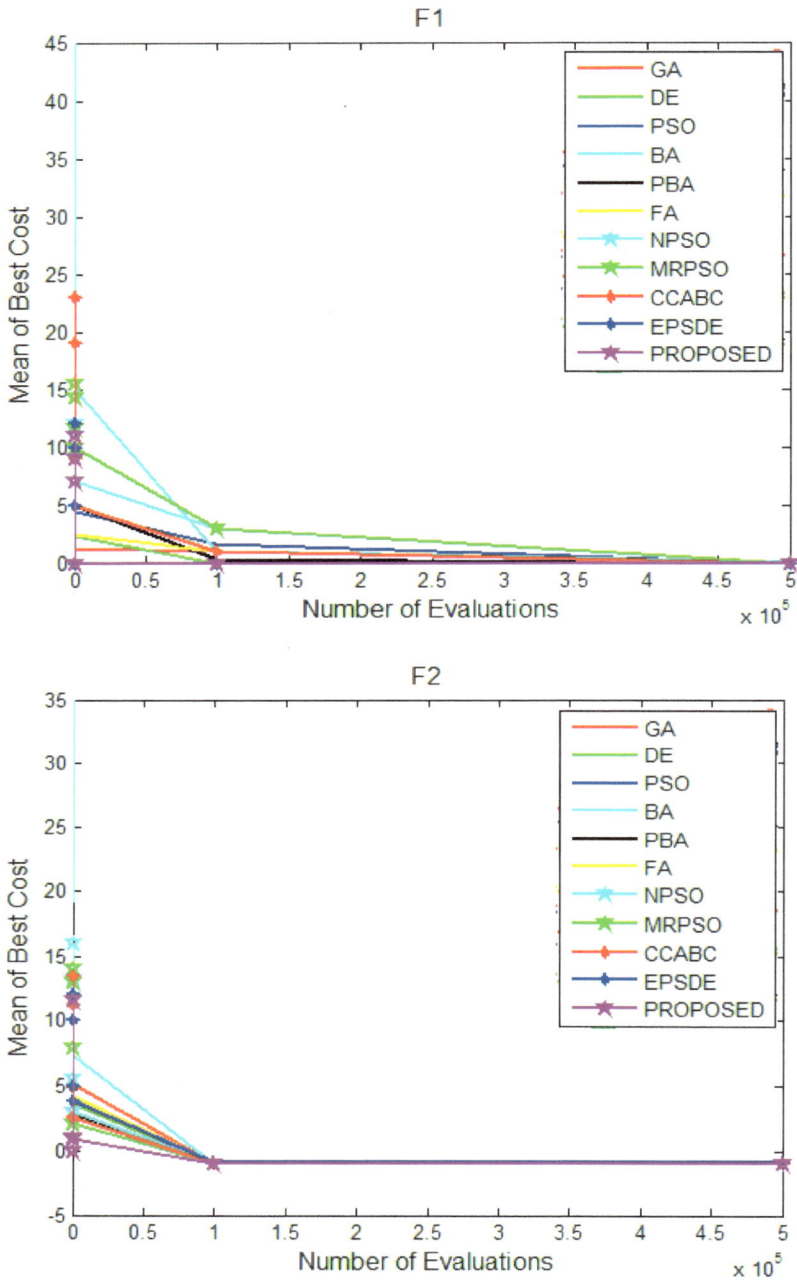

Fig. 46 cont.....

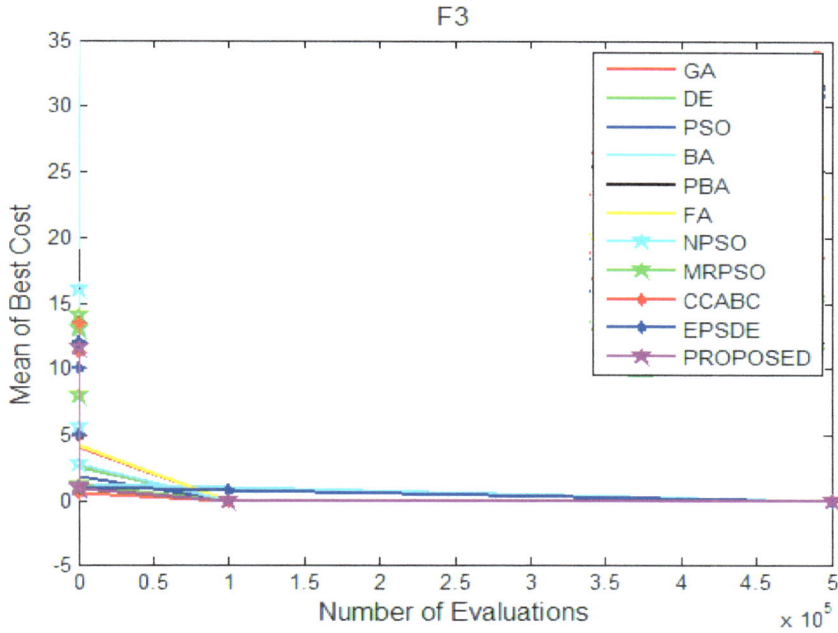

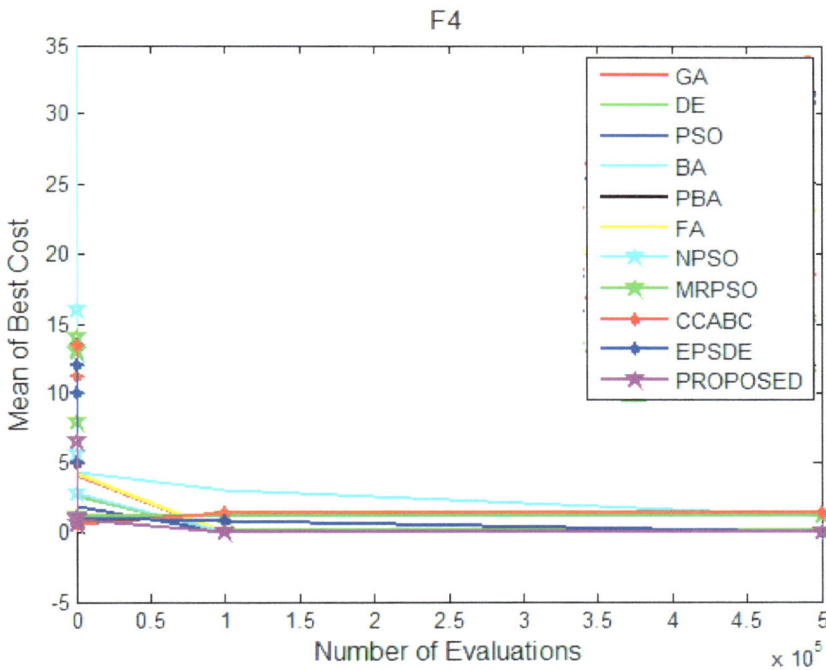

Fig. 46 cont.....

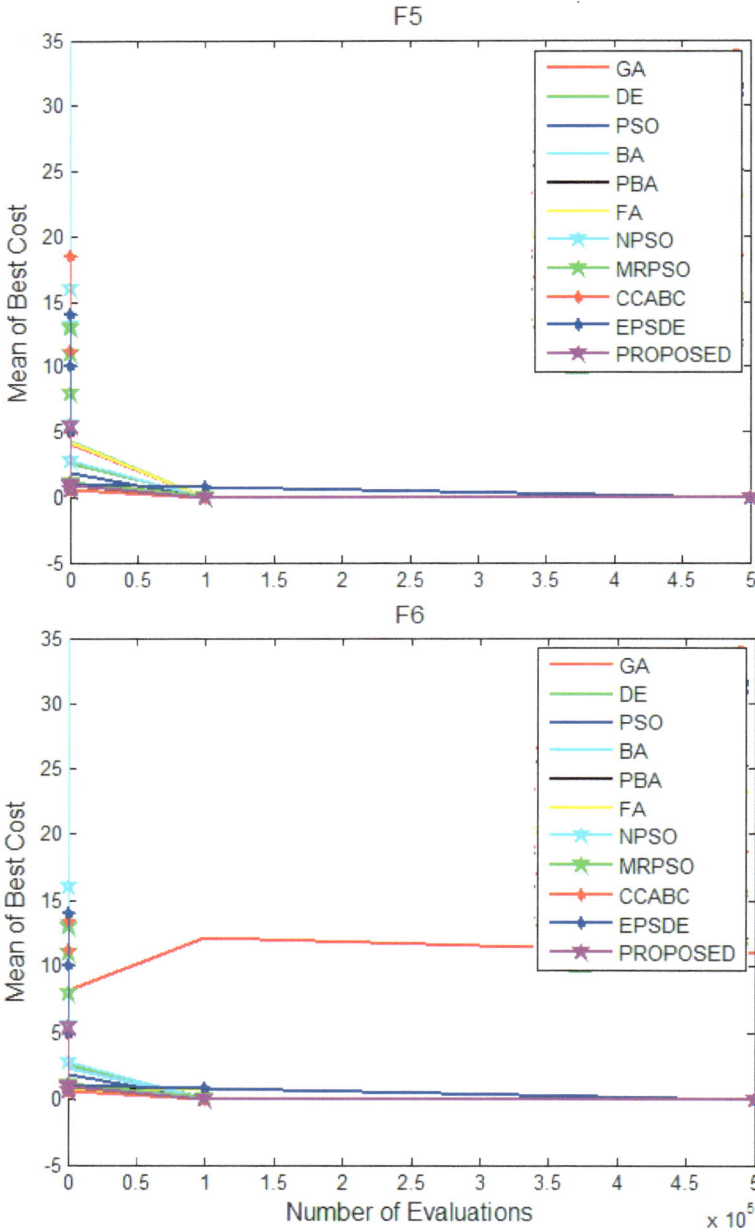

Fig. (46). Results of the compared methods in evaluations 100, 200, 500, 1000, 100000 and 500000 on 26 benchmark functions.

Fig. (**47**) shows the population distribution diagram of the proposed method for 9 functions. To measure the particle convergence in the proposed method, we select 9 functions and show the standard deviation of particles on them. The particle convergence curve in the 9 functions showed that particles in the middle of the evaluation are very diverse and converge at the end of the evaluation to the optimal answer point. This plot shows the rationale of the proposed method in the particle search in the problem space.

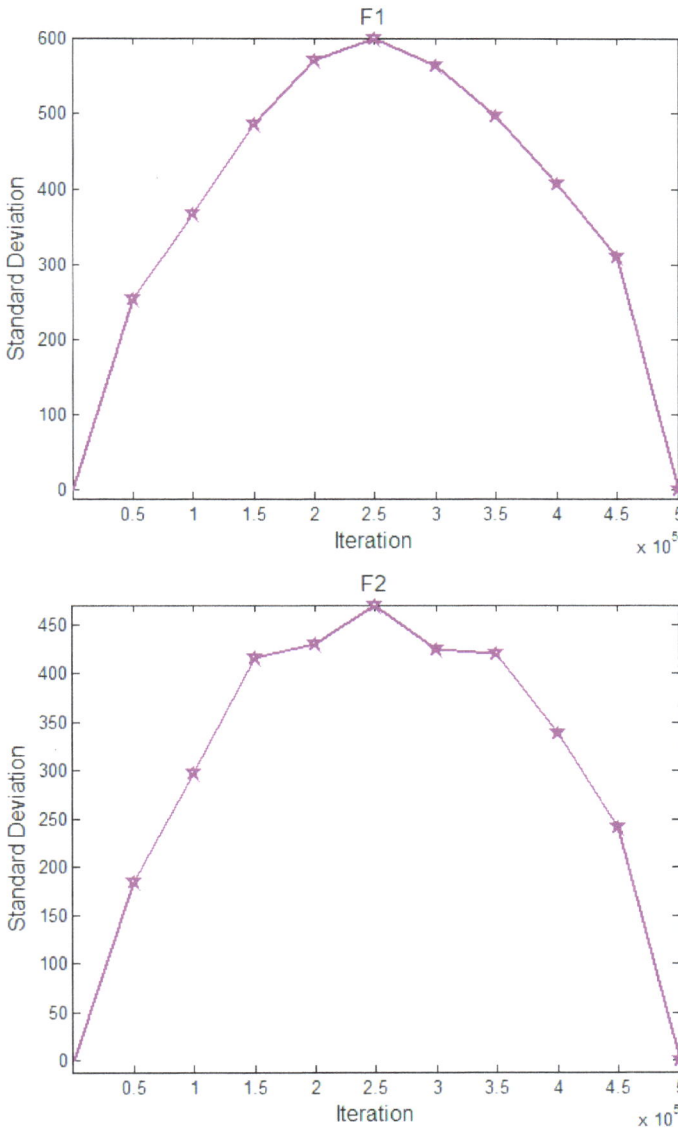

Fig. 47 cont.....

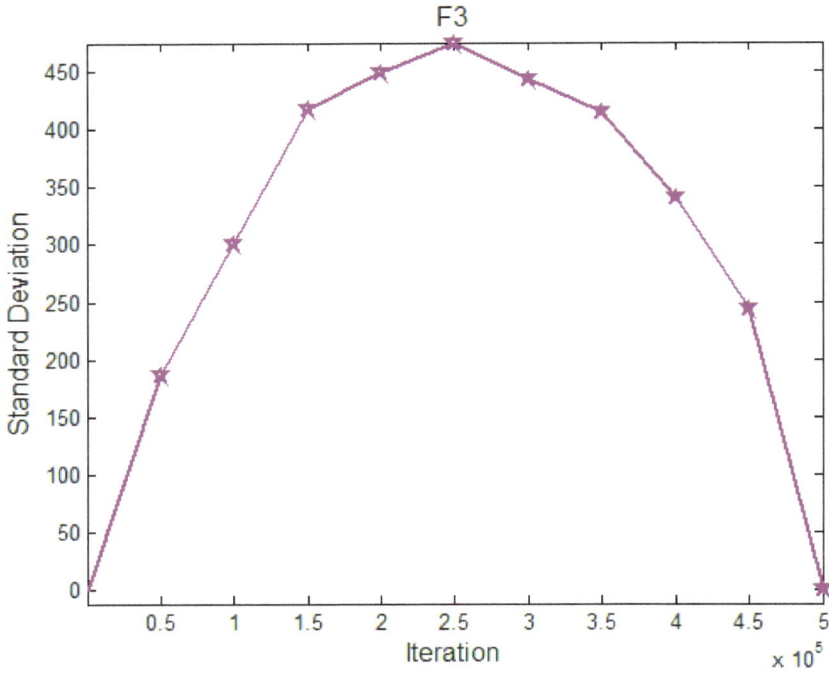

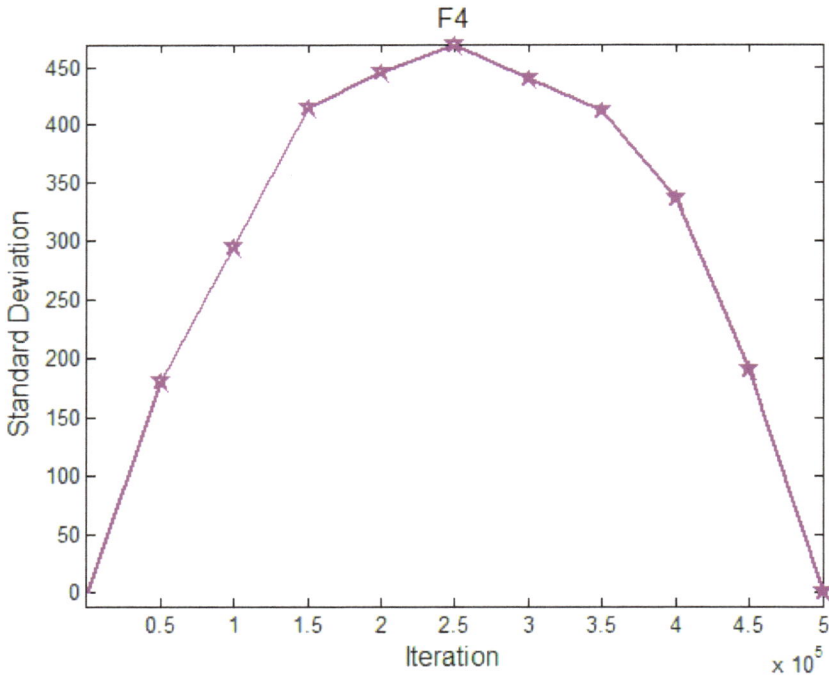

Fig. 47 cont.....

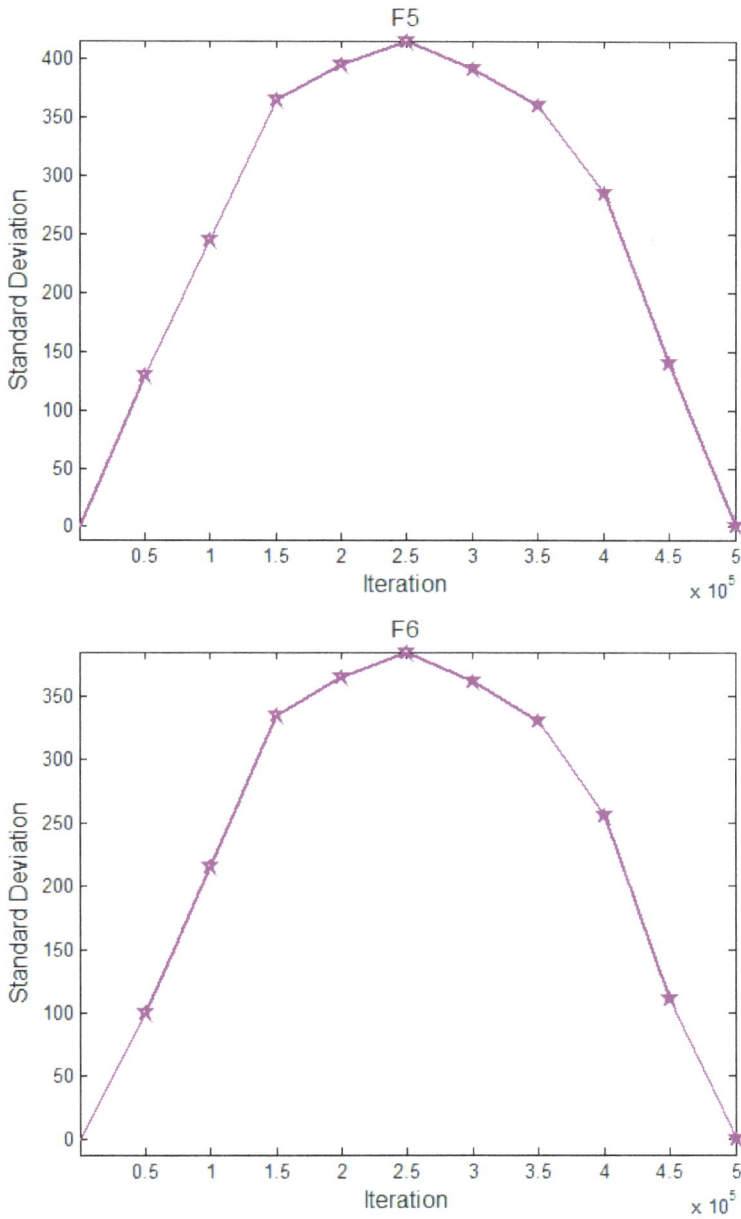

Fig. (47). Standard Deviation of proposed algorithm on 9 functions from benchmark functions.

In this section, the proposed method was compared to the following methods in Table **37**: CS [93], TLBO [94], SC-BR-APSO algorithm [95] and BMO [96]. We tested these methods on the test series CEC 2005 [84]. This comparison was done based on the average best cost (Mean) and the standard deviation (StdDev) of averagely 25 times and on the basis of 300000 evaluations with 30 variables and a population of 40.

Table 37. Results of comparison with newer algorithms on 26 functions based on the mean best cost and standard deviation.

	Criteria	Rain Drop		CS	TLBO	DSA		BMO		Proposed
F1	Mean	2.63E-05 ‡		0§	3.64E-27 ‡	1.23E-28 ‡		1.23E-28 ‡		0
	StdDev	5.15E-05		0	5.82E-27	0		0		0
F2	Mean	8.46E+02‡		1.40E-03‡	1.79E-09‡	1.56E+03‡		1.36E+00‡		1.88E-09
	StdDev	1.83E+02		2.49E-03	4.50E-09	5.64E+02		1.45E+00		4.69E-09
F3	Mean	1.90E+06‡		2.06E+06‡	1.05E+06‡	1.19E+07‡		5.48E+06‡		1.01E+06
	StdDev	6.20E+05		6.83E+05	6.64E+05	5.55E+06		2.42E+06		6.72E+05
F4	Mean	1.39E+04‡		1.51E+03‡	2.73E+02‡	8.46E+03‡		3.87E+03‡		1.67E+02
	StdDev	2.93E+03		1.19E+03	8.31E+02	2.01E+03		4.32E+03		7.78E+03
F5	Mean	9.51E+03‡		2.96E+03‡	3.24E+03‡	3.24E+03‡		4.22E+03‡		1.49E+03
	StdDev	1.89E+03		7.17E+02	7.64E+02	4.99E+02		1.30E+03		6.87E+02
F6	Mean	1.16E+02‡		1.52E+01‡	3.13E+01‡	5.18E+01‡		4.42E+01‡		1.33E+01
	StdDev	3.10E+01		2.10E+01	4.51E+01	3.37E+01		4.91E+01		2.56E+01
F7	Mean	6.70E-01‡		3.24E-03‡	2.77E-02‡	2.28E-02‡		2.15E-02‡		3.17E-03
	StdDev	1.76E-01		5.52E-03	4.12E-02	8.43E-03		1.66E-02		5.22E-03
F8	Mean	2.03E+01‡		2.09E+01‡	2.09E+01‡	2.09E+01‡		2.05E+01‡		2.01E+01
	StdDev	9.33E-02		5.83E-02	5.01E-02	5.15E-02		5.58E-02		8.44E-02
F9	Mean	8.03E+00‡		2.21E+01‡	9.78E+01‡	0§		3.27E+00‡		0
	StdDev	2.28E+00		4.72E+00	2.38E+01	0		2.57E+00		0
F10	Mean	3.37E+02‡		1.64E+02‡	1.18E+02‡	8.93E+01‡		6.79E+01‡		4.38E+01
	StdDev	6.85E+01		3.85E+01	3.33E+01	2.03E+01		1.88E+01		2.23E+01
F11	Mean	3.32E+01‡		2.94E+01‡	3.02E+01‡	2.71E+01‡		2.52E+01‡		2.33E+01
	StdDev	3.02E+00		1.32E+00	5.30E+00	2.10E+00		3.76E+00		4.39E+00
F12	Mean	1.06E+04‡		2.59E+04‡	9.49E+03‡	2.09E+04‡		1.13E+04‡		9.82E+03
	StdDev	9.22E+03		7.13E+03	1.13E+04	5.03E+03		5.85E+03		3.53E+04
F13	Mean	1.96E+00‡		5.96E+00‡	4.62E+00‡	1.83E+00‡		2.14E+00‡		1.03E+00
	StdDev	4.26E-01		1.32E+00	1.42E+00	1.25E-01		5.29E-01		5.45E-01
F14	Mean	1.29E+01‡		1.30E+01‡	1.28E+01‡	1.29E+01‡		1.22E+01‡		1.19E+01

(Table 37) cont.....

	Criteria	Rain Drop		CS	TLBO		DSA			BMO		Proposed
	StdDev	3.92E-01		2.10E-01	3.99E-01		2.43E-01			6.65E-01		7.43E-01
F15	Mean	4.12E+02‡		2.85E+02‡	4.62E+02‡		3.96E+01‡			3.04E+02‡		2.55E+01
	StdDev	1.98E+02		7.52E+01	5.62E+01		2.38E+01			1.14E+02		2.38E+01
F16	Mean	4.15E+02‡		2.05E+02‡	2.55E+02‡		1.63E+02‡			1.19E+02‡		1.07E+02
	StdDev	1.59E+02		5.72E+01	1.35E+02		3.77E+01			3.98E+01		6.98E+01
F17	Mean	4.76E+02‡		2.36E+02‡	2.61E+02‡		2.26E+02‡			1.45E+02‡		1.22E+02
	StdDev	8.39E+01		5.84E+01	1.59E+02		3.48E+01			7.51E+01		6.53E+01
F18	Mean	1.04E+03‡		9.09E+02‡	9.34E+02‡		9.09E+02‡			9.06E+02‡		8.79E+02
	StdDev	8.90E+01		1.96E+00	3.78E+01		1.48E+00			1.23E+00		1.73E+00
F19	Mean	1.05E+03‡		9.09E+02‡	9.51E+02‡		9.10E+02‡			9.06E+02‡		7.29E+02
	StdDev	5.16E+01		1.63E+00	2.98E+01		1.28E+00			1.75E+00		1.88E+00
F20	Mean	1.06E+03‡		9.09E+02‡	9.47E+02‡		9.09E+02‡			9.06E+02‡		9.04E+02
	StdDev	8.00E+01		1.96E+00	2.30E+01		1.58E+00			1.79E+00		1.11E+00
F21	Mean	1.13E+03‡		5.12E+02‡	1.01E+03‡		5.00E+02‡			1.09E+03‡		4.79E+02
	StdDev	2.80E+02		6.00E+01	3.14E+02		9.21E-14			4.49E+00		5.33E-14
F22	Mean	1.22E+03‡		9.20E+02‡	9.38E+02‡		9.38E+02‡			8.64E+02‡		8.51E+02
	StdDev	6.95E+01		2.80E+01	3.88E+01		1.53E+01			3.08E+01		4.76E+01
F23	Mean	1.16E+03‡		5.66E+02‡	1.12E+03‡		5.34E+02‡			1.10E+03‡		5.17E+02
	StdDev	2.33E+02		1.08E+02	1.97E+02		3.70E-04			3.59E+00		3.66E-04
F24	Mean	1.15E+03‡		6.20E+02‡	2.66E+02‡		2.00E+02‡			9.42E+02‡		1.44E+02
	StdDev	4.24E+02		3.60E+02	2.29E+02		6.27E-13			4.04E+00		6.83E-13
F25	Mean	1.18E+03‡		2.13E+02‡	4.49E+02‡		2.21E+02‡			2.17E+02‡		2.00E+02
	StdDev	4.06E+02		1.67E+00	4.31E+02		2.32E+00			1.70E+00		3.69E+00

The sign "‡" indicates the proposed algorithm outperforms the given algorithm, the sign "†" indicates the given algorithm outperforms the proposed algorithm and finally "§" indicates the difference in performance of the given algorithm and that of the proposed algorithm are meaningless

Friedman Test												
		4.21	4.29			3.85		4.53	3.11		4.12	
	p-value	3.38E-06										
	Statistic	40.32										

Results of the comparison between the proposed algorithm and new methods showed that in all 25 functions the proposed algorithm had better quality. In functions F1 and F9 the proposed method jointly with another algorithm could have the best performance. In function F1, the CS algorithm and the proposed approach had the best performance due to reaching the optimal point zero. The same process was found in the proposed algorithm and DSA algorithm in function

F9. The standard deviation values of the proposed method were often high in most comparisons and this indicates the ability of algorithms search diversity in the problem space. The statistical test applied on the results of Table **37** shows that the values of the results obtained by the methods had no significant relationship with the random process. Fig. (**48**) shows the proposed method diagram for 14 tested functions on different values of dimensions or number of variables. The results showed that as the number of dimensions increased and the problem became more complicated to resolve, the value of the best cost will be ascending. The diagrams were applied for 20 populations, 10000 times assessments and 10, 20, 30, 40 and 50 variables.

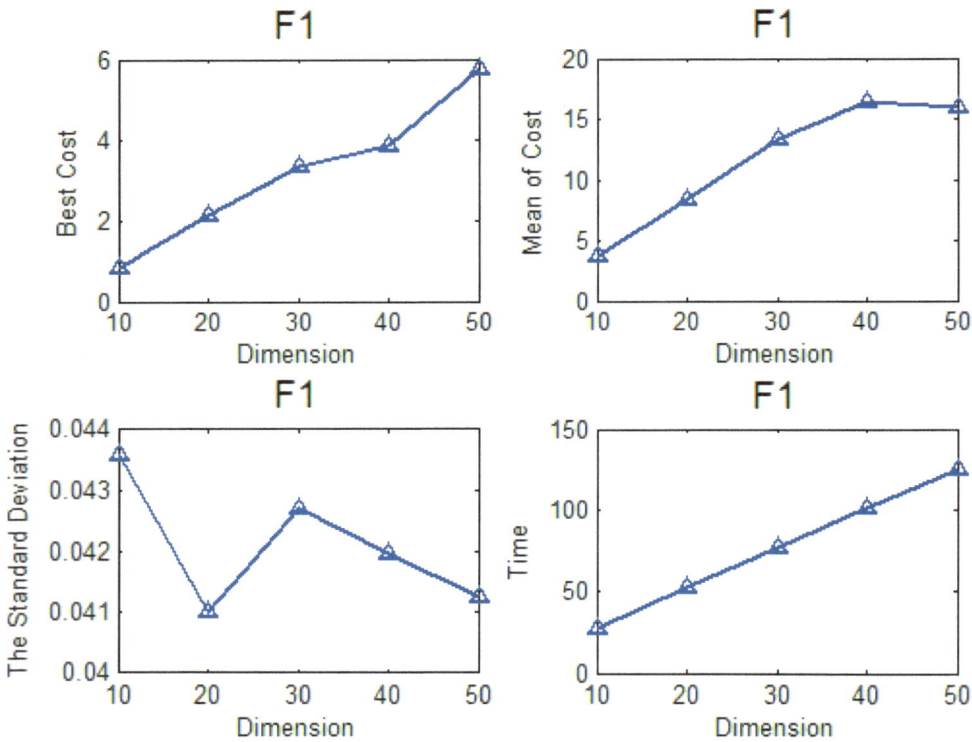

Fig. 48 cont.....

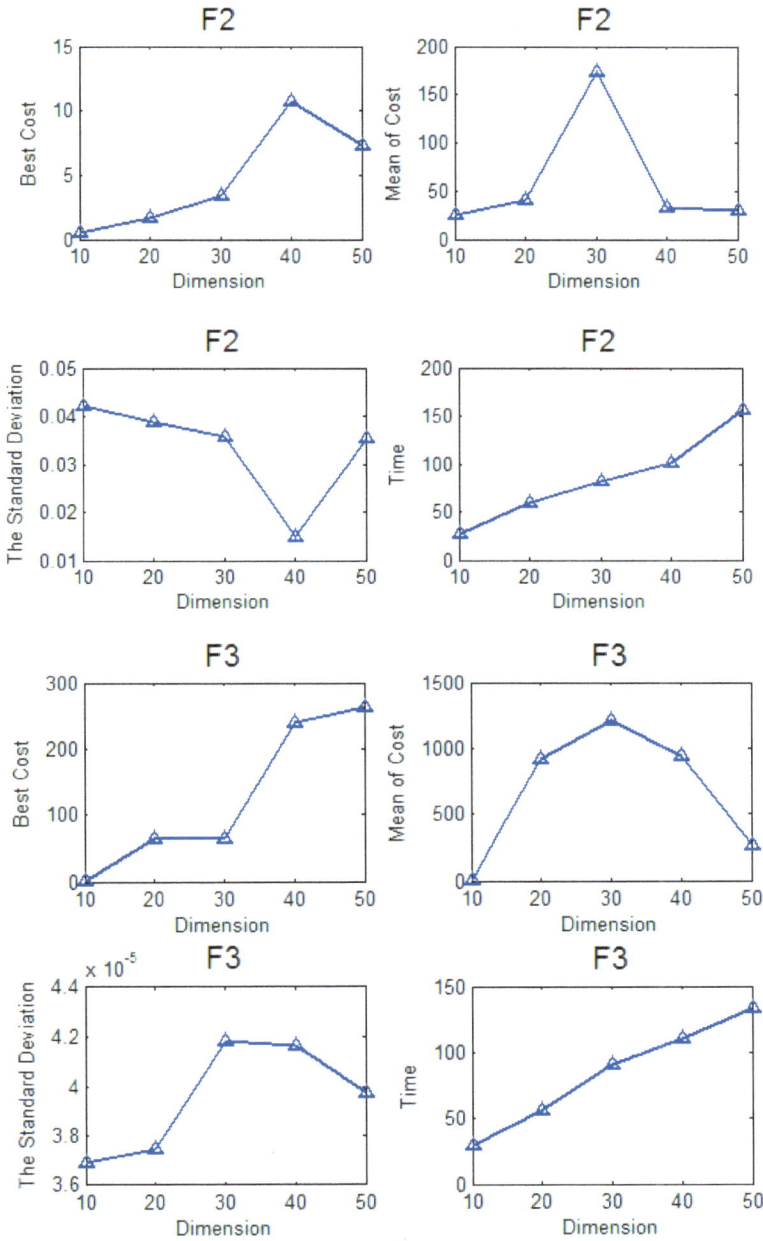

Fig. 48 cont.....

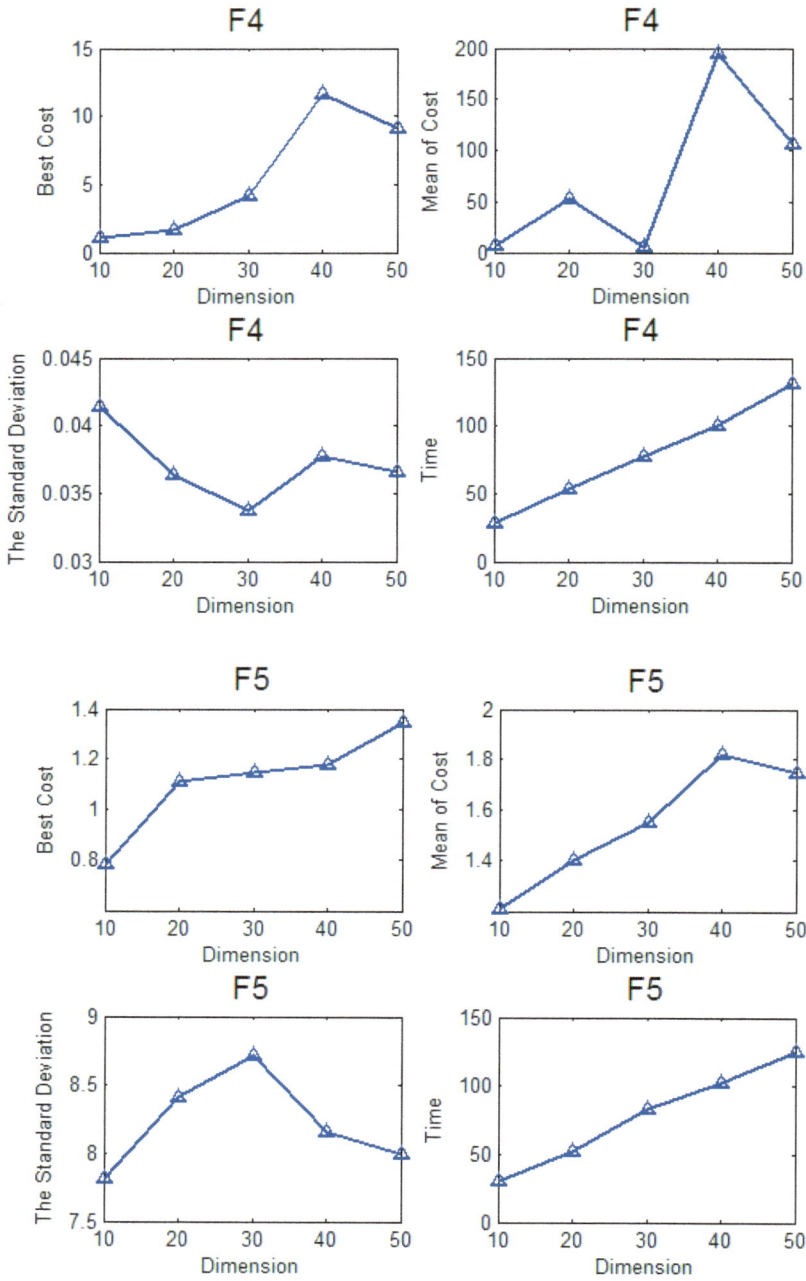

Fig. 48 cont.....

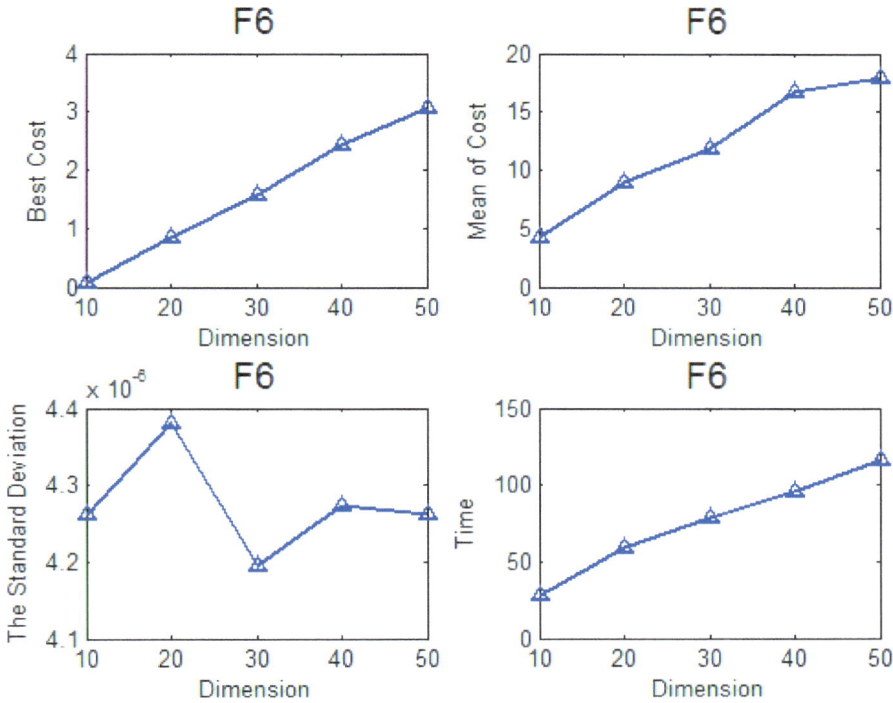

Fig. (48). The diagram for the best cost, mean cost, standard deviation and the implementation time of the proposed method on 14 test functions.

In the last section of the results, the proposed method was compared in Table **38** with identical algorithms published in the last two years. In this section, the function to be tested was the test series CEC 2012. The compared methods were as follows: sinDE, JOA, NPSO and D-PSO-C. 40 populations were assessed 10,000 times. Moreover, there were 30 variables and an average of 51 times on 28 functions.

Table 38. Results of the proposed method and 4 new optimization methods on 28 benchmark functions.

Function	SinDE		JOA		D-PSO-C		NPSO		Proposed	
	Mean	Std	Mean	Std	Mean	Std	Mean	Std	Mean	Std
1	2.23E−14	6.83E−14	1.78E−14	3.33E−14	2.44E−14	4.13E−11	2.52E−14	2.77E−12	1.36E−14	2.18E−14
2	2.16E+06	6.15E+05	2.09E+06	4.36E+05	2.76E+06	1.10E+05	2.22E+06	1.32E+05	2.02E+06	3.46E+05
3	8.49E+04	2.11E+05	8.19E+04	4.31E+05	9.11E+04	1.62E+05	8.57E+04	3.65E+05	8.13E+04	1.33E+05

(Table 38) cont.....

Function	SinDE		JOA		D-PSO-C		NPSO		Proposed	
	Mean	Std	Mean	Std	Mean	Std	Mean	Std	Mean	Std
4	6.38E+03	2.00E+03	5.82E+03	1.80E+03	6.50E+03	3.49E+03	6.47E+03	3.09E+03	4.71E+03	1.77E+03
5	1.14E−13	7.65E−29	1.11E−13	5.14E−29	2.74E−13	4.15E−29	1.22E−13	1.85E−29	1.04E−13	2.64E−29
6	1.46E+01	2.42E+00	1.52E+01	4.38E+00	3.54E+01	3.52E+00	1.76E+01	1.72E+00	1.32E+01	1.24E+00
7	1.21E−01	1.57E−01	1.09E−01	2.18E−01	1.81E−01	4.28E−01	1.34E−01	2.17E−01	4.51E−01	2.45E−01
8	2.09E+01	4.96E−02	1.78E+01	3.54E−02	2.67E+01	3.77E−02	2.13E+01	6.06E−02	1.47E+01	2.14E−02
9	1.52E+01	3.05E+00	1.48E+01	2.31E+00	1.78E+01	2.13E+00	1.50E+01	2.87E+00	1.33E+01	1.09E+00
10	2.04E−02	1.30E−02	1.66E−02	2.19E−02	2.65E−02	3.25E−02	2.19E−02	2.43E−02	1.52E−02	1.22E−02
11	1.95E−02	1.39E−01	1.98E−02	2.55E−01	2.34E−02	2.44E−01	2.00E−02	4.35E−01	0.00E+00	0.00E+00
12	3.02E+01	8.65E+00	2.87E+01	3.44E+00	3.66E+01	4.33E+00	3.18E+01	4.22E+00	2.54E+01	2.75E+00
13	7.33E+01	2.07E+01	7.14E+01	1.87E+01	7.76E+01	4.47E+01	7.40E+01	3.27E+01	7.02E+01	2.09E+01
14	5.04E+01	1.92E+01	5.00E+01	3.52E+01	5.78E+01	5.02E+01	5.16E+01	6.48E+01	4.78E+01	2.02E+01
15	2.95E+03	4.86E+02	2.82E+03	3.21E+02	3.13E+03	3.22E+02	2.97E+03	4.86E+02	2.48E+03	2.00E+02
16	1.74E+00	2.52E−01	1.59E+00	1.45E−01	1.87E+00	3.55E−01	1.75E+00	3.28E−01	1.46E+00	1.50E−01
17	3.37E+01	7.97E−01	3.22E+01	5.79E−01	4.09E+01	3.23E−01	3.59E+01	4.55E−01	3.08E+01	2.10E−01
18	7.86E+01	1.42E+01	7.48E+01	3.56E+01	7.89E+01	3.45E+01	7.55E+01	4.44E+01	7.16E+01	2.33E+01
19	2.24E+00	3.79E−01	2.64E+00	2.12E−01	3.75E+00	2.73E−01	2.33E+00	2.28E−01	2.06E+00	1.23E−01
20	9.99E+00	5.50E−01	9.75E+00	3.22E−01	9.83E+00	4.82E−01	9.81E+00	4.88E−01	9.34E+00	2.71E−01
21	2.87E+02	6.40E+01	2.81E+02	3.91E+01	2.99E+02	6.40E+01	2.91E+02	3.91E+01	2.77E+02	2.38E+01
22	1.49E+02	1.76E+01	1.32E+02	2.90E+01	1.55E+02	4.75E+01	1.57E+02	3.22E+01	1.20E+02	3.09E+01
23	3.14E+03	5.31E+02	3.28E+03	3.22E+02	3.83E+03	4.11E+02	3.20E+03	2.39E+02	3.12E+03	2.88E+02
24	2.00E+02	7.16E−03	2.11E+02	3.44E−03	2.67E+02	4.46E−03	2.52E+02	6.86E−03	1.89E+02	4.79E−03
25	2.49E+02	6.85E+00	2.37E+02	3.63E+00	2.74E+02	3.05E+00	2.51E+02	5.73E+00	2.08E+02	3.66E+00
26	2.02E+02	1.40E+01	1.88E+02	4.43E+01	2.37E+02	5.65E+01	2.12E+02	4.47E+01	1.79E+02	2.72E+01
27	3.01E+02	2.36E+00	3.09E+02	4.65E+00	3.45E+02	7.66E+00	3.20E+02	6.47E+00	2.81E+02	3.31E+00
28	3.00E+02	0.00E+00	0.00E+00	0.00E+00	3.23E+02	2.00E+00	3.54E+02	3.39E+00	0.00E+00	0.00E+00

In the third experiment, the proposed method had a better performance than similar methods during the last 2 years, in terms of finding the best cost more quickly. Except for function F7 in which the JOA approach had the best cost at the end of the specified evaluations, the proposed method found the best cost in other 27 functions. In function F28, too, the JOA algorithm was at the same level as the proposed method and it found the optimal point in this function. Furthermore, the proposed method alone had the best performance in function 26 as well. The standard deviation of the proposed method which was low in most methods indicated that this method had been able to start from a random dispersion and after increasing the dispersion at the end of the assessment, it could converge the most of particles to the general optimum by reducing the level of diversity.

CHAPTER 4

How to Transform the Behavior in Nature into the Algorithm

Abstract: In recent years, recognizing amazing resources in nature can be a way to formulate ideas for optimization problems. First, the ideas are selected in nature, and then the hidden purposeful behavior of these ideas is discovered and expressed as a systematic algorithm. Choosing and observing the order in animals and nature is an art, and researching them is a practical way of analyzing them. The most important part is that these behaviors must be selected in order and then formulated mathematically. This chapter will discuss some techniques for converting ideas into algorithms and a specific framework. Some of the important principles in converting behaviors in nature into mathematical equations are outlined in this chapter If one can find the best and easiest way to transform an idea into a mathematical equation in the form of an algorithm, then one can claim that an efficient algorithm is presented that can solve a complex problem. If some of the principles outlined in this chapter are followed, a good algorithm can be derived from a natural idea. This chapter introduces examples of nature-inspired algorithms presented by authors in recent years. These algorithms all use the source of nature, and the nature and behavior of some animals are the main basis of these algorithms. These algorithms show the orderly behavior of some natural animals and also show how this targeted order can be transformed into an algorithm. Understanding these algorithms can help the reader understand how to transform the idea of nature into meaningful equations. We present some examples of these algorithms in this chapter to familiarize the reader with the order in some natural animals. Also, in this chapter, we can understand how to transform this natural order into meaningful equations. These meaningful equations are introduced in the form of an optimization algorithm.

Keywords: Equations, Formulated, Ideas, Implemented, Mathematical.

Let's first look at some of the algorithms that are inspired by nature with their source of inspiration. These algorithms were later used by researchers in various fields. The source of each was found in nature. These sources have been carefully analyzed by the authors. That order in each source was the main reason for writing the algorithm. Pay close attention to a source and target source system. Understanding this can help you. Table **39** lists some of the nature-inspired algorithms, their source of inspiration, and the idea of algorithm formation.

Rohollah Omidvar and Behrouz Minaei Bidgoli

Table 39. Algorithm, source and target system of source for several famous algorithms.

Algorithm	Source	Target System of Source
PSO	Birds	The order of the birds during the mass flight
GA	DNA	Evolved Gene of Natural Creatures
ABC	Bees	Finding food by bees
HS	Musical Instrument	The order of musical notes in playing a music
ICA	Colonization of countries	How the Colony Countries Relate
ACO	Ants	Ants' behavior in finding the optimal path
SSPCO	See-see partridge	Behavior of See-See partridge Chicks at Risk

This is a small part of the algorithms that are inspired by behavior in nature. Now, let's go back and find some of the behaviors that have not yet been addressed in nature, whether in nature itself or in living things in nature.

Fig. (49). Intrinsic behavior of a dog.

As in Fig. (**49**), the behavior of animals called dogs in nature can be interesting. Dog is famous for its loyalty to its owner. There may be many other interesting behaviors in this animal, but we focus on this feature. This loyalty mechanism has become a win-win game for the dog and its owner. So, the two populations come together in evolution to survive in nature. Why and how the dog's intrinsic loyalty and dog owner's interest in it both contribute to life, and this is a way to achieve a common goal in a system. So, here is a mechanism between two populations that ends in a goal. The secret to this behavior is to be found through the research of biologists and zoologists. It then extended this behavior to the entire population of an algorithm. May be this algorithm is probably able to solve the problem using two-to-two populations.

Fig. (50). The intellectual evolution of humans using one another.

Human development in science can also be of interest to human beings throughout the world (Fig. 50). What is the reason for how science has changed in different parts of the world over the different years? The science in the world has moved from one point to another point based on a specific mechanism. So one has to research and find out why science and civilization in the world have moved from place to place. Here, the geography of the world can be assumed to be the space of an issue, and science is assumed to be elite populations. The relationship between points that have reached competence over time can lead to a specific mechanism.

Fig. (51). Zebra's behavior in covering each other.

Zebra herds move collectively. They merge with their body lines, which mislead predatory animals to hunt (Fig. **51**). So in this fascinating order of zebra, a population-based algorithm can be searched. These populations cover each other to achieve the goal. The purpose of this zebra arrangement is to survive in nature using the appearance. This coverage relationship between populations to move to optimal points can lead to an algorithm.

The snake is deaf and understands its surroundings with the vibrations it receives from the earth (Fig. 52). One can then come up with a mechanism in which a low-population algorithm can move to the optimal point using problem space information. Space information is very important to the snake, and here the problem space is the most important criterion for population movement. This relationship should be explored through research on how the snake obtains ground information. Then we need to put this mechanism in place for the relationship between population and space. This mechanism can work in two-dimensional static functions and complex mathematical functions that have two-dimensional space.

Fig. (52). The snake moves using ground information.

The first step in building an algorithm is to create an initial population or initial state. The initial state shows where an optimization algorithm starts to find the answer to a problem. The initial state for the algorithms is in many forms, but we will focus more on population-based algorithms here. Initial populations are usually random unless states, such as the initial chaos population are used. The initial chaos population has a philosophy that we will briefly discuss below.

4.1. CHAOTIC INTIAL POPULATION

Chaos theory is a theory in mathematical science that is used for systems that have a basic state. This theory causes the initial state to shift from a random state to a target state. It is interesting that in this theory, the initial state has a direct effect at all times when running a system. This theory allows the population to follow the initial state of a population and the search space to influence the population. In general, chaos theory indicates that there is a certain order in disorder. The chaos theory avoids the complete randomization and quantifies the system according to a particular process. There is even a science of philosophy in this theory. Chaos theory, an ancient science, is applied and influenced by various sciences.

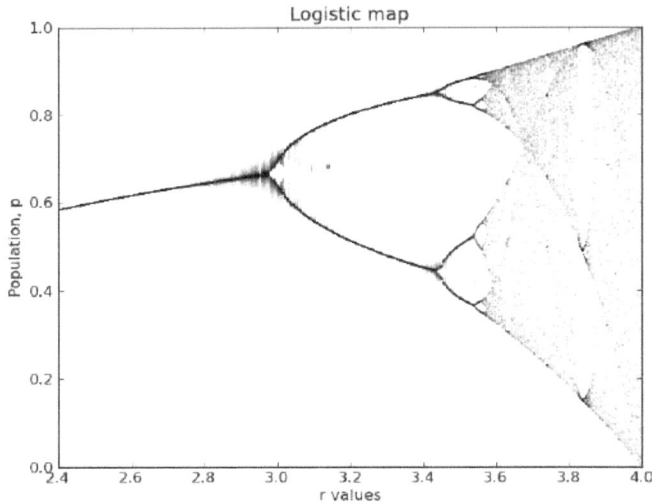

Fig. (53). The sensitivity of a chaotic system at the initial condition.

One of the popular equations of this theory is the equation known as logistics. First, it is a theory of self-adaptation, and secondly, it is sensitive to initial conditions. The most important equation of turbulence theory is the equation which is very effective in optimization algorithms because of these features. Fig. (53) shows the sensitivity of the chaotic logistic mapping system to the initial conditions. In Fig. (53), it is apparent that in a chaotic system, the initial scattering is very well controlled and then propagated in space to the initial conditions.

In addition, according to Fig. (53), the initial population starts in one state and then converges correctly to the same initial population.

In chaotic models, the current state of a system is dependent on its previous state and this leads to the scenario of starting an optimization algorithm from an appropriate state. Applying this theory instead of random initialization makes the optimization algorithm faster to the desired point and leads the population to the desired point. The famous example of the formal logistic mapping is as the equation 67.

$$x_{k+1} = \alpha x_k (1 - x_k), \quad x \in (0,1), \alpha = 4 \tag{67}$$

In the equation 5, x_k is a real number in the interval [0, 1] and parameter $\acute{a}$ that is known as the logistic coefficient leads to the emergence of some unique features in this function. In this paper, the value of parameter *á* has been considered equal to 4. Suppose that parameter *á* = 2.5 and the start point is a number close to 0.025; in this case, different values for the logistic function from the left to right sequences are obtained as following: 0.06093, 0.1430, 0.3125, 0.53063, 0.612527, 0.59334, 0.603216, 0.59836, and 0.600811. In this sequence of numbers, it is observed that in the fifth sequence, the numbers converge to a value of 0.6. There are also other various examples of chaotic systems, which are not about to be introduced here. Fig. (**54**) shows the graph of the logistic function with the parameter = 4.

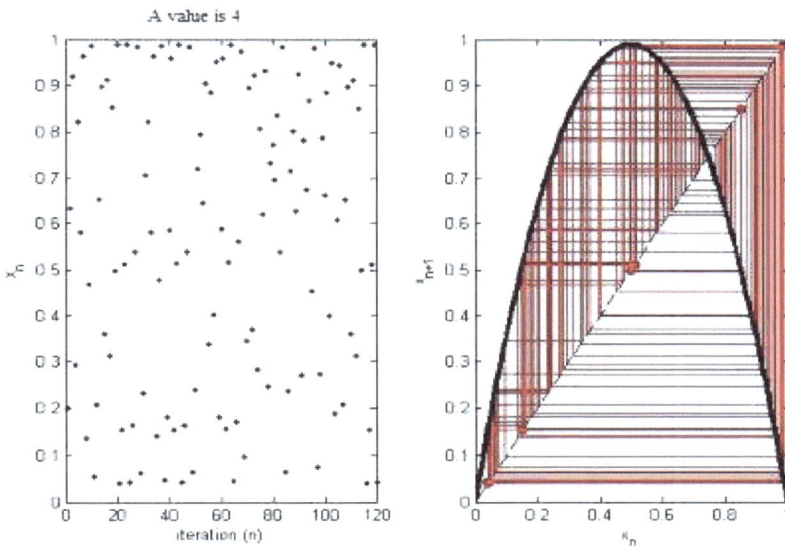

Fig. (54). Logistic function graph with a = 4 where x_n is the nth replicated value.

As shown in this figure, the system has reached a convergence after several replications.

4.2. CHAOTIC CREATION OF FOOD SOURCES

In the standard artificial bee colony algorithm, the initial food sources are randomly created. In the proposed method, unlike the standard artificial bee colony algorithm, the initial food sources are initialized according to chaos theory (*i.e.* logistic mapping). In nature, many systems reveal chaotic behaviors, and in the real world, different complex systems display chaotic behaviors rather than random behaviors. To name a few of chaotic systems, we can list the human brain signals, sea wave, propeller wing movement, tornado, and so on. Initial food sources are generated according to the equation 68.

$$\boldsymbol{Pop}_{ji} = LB_i + (UB_i - LB_i) \times (2\tau_{ji} - 1) \qquad (68)$$

As shown in equation 10, it is observed that the logistic mapping function $\hat{o}_{ji}$ is used instead of random value $\hat{o}_{ji}$. Therefore, the initial food sources are created based on chaos theory.

Fig. (55). Search principle.

Standard algorithms are tested with a random initial population. The initial population is actually the number of solutions that an algorithm proposes to solve a problem.

For example (Fig. **55**), shows how many people want to look for an object in a large building. The number of people looking for that object is the same as the population, and since people are unaware of the location of the object, then they accidentally search for a starting point. The user determines the number of people or population who want to look for the object. This number depends on the space and the problem.

So, we will always create the population number we want, with indexes of that population randomly. This can be almost the same for all ideas. For example, if we have 10 populations, we randomly produce them as follows. If we name the population S, the initial population is as follows:

For i=1 **to** n

$$S_{position} = RANDOM(S_i)$$

(69)

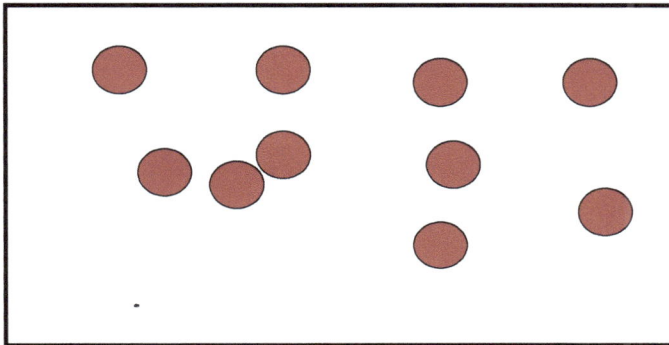

Fig. (56). Initial population.

There are now 10 populations that are randomly assigned to the problem space (Fig. **56**). You will pursue any idea you have in nature and in this way you will produce the initial population.

You have to pay attention to your idea. It may be necessary to define a specific parameter in each idea for each population. These parameters should all be defined for each population. Usually the parameters in the formula with an index for that parameter are shown. For example, parameter B for the previous population would be as follows:

For i=1 **to** n

$$S_B = Define(S_i)$$

(70)

Depending on the idea you are writing for the algorithm you need to select the parameters needed for each population. For example, in the bird algorithm, a parameter called the bird speed is defined as follows:

For i=1 to n

Particle. velocity

(71)

Now this parameter, which specifies the speed of a bird or a population, will be calculated by the following equation:

$$Velocity(i) = w \times Particle(i).Velocity + c1 \times rand(0,1) \times (Particle(i).PBest - Particle(i).Position) + c2 \times rand(0,1) \times (Particle(i).GBest - Particle(i).Position)) \quad \textbf{(72)}$$

Choose the parameters that can properly implement the behavior of that animal or natural structure. Define the parameters by giving the initial numeric value. Parameters such as location, velocity, geographic location, male or female, child or parent, Hunter or prey (Fig. **57**), are part of the parameters that can be defined for an animal in nature.

Fig. (57). Hunting and hunter.

Usually optimization algorithms operate on different iterations or evaluations. In iteration an action is performed by that animal or its natural structure. For example, in iteration the animal moves once to a point or the natural structure changes once. For example, if your idea is an animal, that animal moves from one point to another in a space once a space. Just like the Fig. (**58**):

Fig. (58). Move in space.

By moving the animal to a new location, all animal parameters will be updated. In addition, the cost of the animal or its distance to the optimum points also varies. You can write equations for this transition depending on the animal's behavior or natural structure, which can also be applied in simulator software. Commonly used in population-based algorithms is the mechanical motion equation, in which the current location of the bird is combined with the bird's velocity. It is always necessary to move the population of a given algorithm or natural structure. This move can lead the algorithm to more elite points at higher times. Movements can be in space, batch, colony or group. It's important to Figure out how to set up equations to help the population get to the right points faster.

You have to write in the loop for the whole population the equation of velocity to move the population at one time according to space.

$$\textbf{For } i=1 \textbf{ to } n$$

$$Particle.\,velocity =?$$

(73)

You have to write in the loop for the whole population the equation of velocity to move the population at one time according to space. Try to define the movement of populations relative to each other, that is, populations play a role in moving each other. This is the case in colonies. As in the Fig. (**59**), other birds help the bird move through space. Understanding what parameters are effective in moving a population helps your algorithm to be more integrated and to reach optimal points sooner.

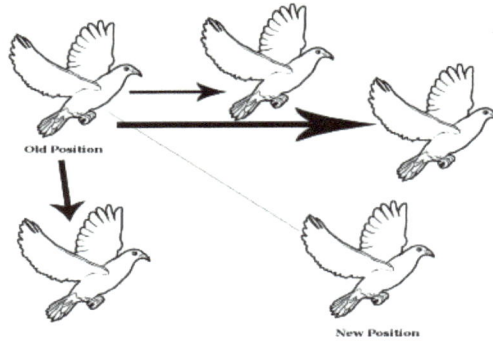

Fig. (59). Neighbour-based movement of the target animal.

Whatever idea you use, you should be able to increase your search space. The structure you want or the animal you want should be able to do the most searching. At midpoint replications, the standard deviation reflecting the dispersion of particles should be as high as possible. This dispersion in the middle iterations should also be considered in the creation of the velocity equation. As in Fig. (**60**), this is an inappropriate search:

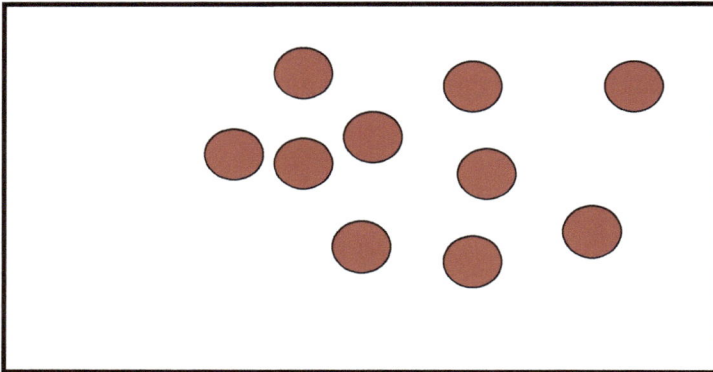

Fig. (60). Low search population.

As in Fig. (**61**), this is a good search for middle iterations:

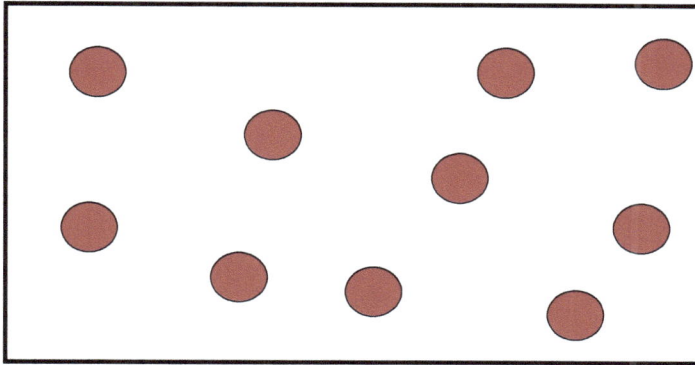

Fig. (61). Population with a good search.

A good algorithm in the last iterations should reduce its standard deviation so that populations converge around the optimal point. If you draw a graph for the search or standard deviation of an algorithm, the best case is a crescent graph. Follow this principle in setting the algorithm's population velocity equation.

The main criterion for measuring an algorithm is the cost rate of a function. Low cost is usually the best case. In static functions, always the least number of a population cost is best suited to solve a function. When the number of evaluations is completed, the least costly population is the algorithm's final answer. Choose an idea that is easy to implement in simulator software. Choose an algorithm that has little complexity and also has a good execution time.

CHAPTER 5

Conclusion

Abstract: Nature-inspired algorithm is types of computing systems use a variety of phenomena in nature to create a coherent mechanism. Designing different systems and creating learning machines as well as optimization are some of the factors that have chosen nature. These systems come from nature and have designed interesting mechanisms. The nature of the search problem is very important in nature and the species of animals and even the natural structures each have a kind of search system inherently. In this book, optimization and optimization algorithms are examined, and solutions are proposed to create a nature-inspired optimization algorithm, and even suggestions are made for natural phenomena that can be transformed into algorithms. The sciences, industry, medicine, and other fields can find algorithms that fit their field by reading this book. Collective intelligence is one of the main phenomena found in nature, and this book also emphasized this. This book first describes optimization, then defines the optimization problem and describes its mechanism. Then nature-inspired optimization algorithms were evaluated and a number of them were introduced. The source of nature was then discussed and explained why nature is a good source of ideas for building an algorithm. A number of authors' algorithms were studied to familiarize the reader with these types of algorithms and then ideas of nature were proposed to the reader. Finally, how to convert an idea into an algorithm is discussed.

Keywords: Ideas, Nature-inspired, Optimization, Order, Source, Swarm.

Change is one of the things that occur in the system over time and the system needs to adapt to it. Relations and computing some of the issues are so complex that they are beyond human ability. Machine learning is one of the new systems that solve these difficult calculations well. Experience and information are very important in machine learning. Proper and efficient use of this information by these systems can lead to the production of efficient algorithms. Optimization systems today in the field of e-commerce can make an economic revolution in the world. In this book, the goal is for the reader to become familiar with algorithms and learning systems and optimizers. Mathematical Optimization is the branch of mathematics that aims to solve the problem of finding the elements that maximize or minimize a given real-valued function. Many problems in engineering and machine learning can be cast as mathematical optimization problems, which explain the growing importance of the field. For example, in a spam detection filter we might aim to find the system that minimizes the number of misclassified emails. Similarly, when an engineer designs a pipe, we will seek for the design that minimizes cost while respecting some safety constraints. Both are examples that can be modelled as optimization problems.

The beauty of optimization is that it allows abstracting from the specifics of the particular problem. For example, once we have transformed the spam detection filter and the pipe design the form of a mathematical optimization problem, we can use the same optimization algorithms to them, abstracting the fact that these are, in origin, very different problems.

In this book, optimization was first defined. Then nature-inspired algorithms were reviewed and their sources of inspiration were announced. Some of the author's algorithms, all inspired by nature, were also explored. Some ideas were introduced in nature that is interesting in order to make an algorithm out of them. Finally, the overall idea of constructing an idea in a framework and algorithm was examined. There are so many interesting ideas in nature that researchers can read through the book to learn how to build an algorithm inspired by these ideas. This book was a small attempt to bring new algorithms into the optimization world research cycle.

The book's most relevant concept is that the reader will be able to turn an idea that he observes in nature and is of interest to him, into a single search mechanism. In this book, we do not intend to confront the reader with a scholarly article. We would love to have a practical book, rather than a compilation book. The optimal concept was defined, then nature and natural phenomena were discussed, and even examples were introduced in nature. This introduction to examples of nature is only for the reader to know what exactly a natural idea means. Here are some examples of nature-inspired algorithms where the reader can see exactly how an idea has been turned into an algorithm. And finally, we came up with solutions that consist of the idea-starting scenario of the algorithm. We have come up with ways to formulate the idea. These guidelines were generalized. However, each idea has its own different demographic, the movement of its components is different, and has a different mechanism. So, we discussed in general and covered most of the ideas.

References

[1]   "The Nature of Mathematical Programming Archived 2014-03-05 at the Wayback Machine," *Mathematical Programming Glossary*, INFORMS Computing Society, 2014.

[2]   D.Z. Du, P. Pardalos, and W. Wu, History of Optimization.*Encyclopedia of Optimization.*, Springer: Boston, pp. 1538-1542.

[3]   J. Clerk, and A. Maxwell, *Treatise on Electricity and Magnetism.*, vol. Vol. 2, 3rd edClarendon: Oxford, pp. 68-73.3rd ed

[4]   I.S. Jacobs, and C. Bean, Fine particles, thin films and exchange anisotropy.*Magnetism.*, vol. Vol. III, Academic: New York, pp. 271-350.

[5]   Y. Yorozu, M. Hirano, K. Oka, and Y. Tagawa, "Electron spectroscopy studies on magneto-optical media and plastic substrate interface", *IEEE Translat. J. Magn. Jpn.*, vol. 2, pp. 740-741. [Digests 9th Annual Conf. Magnetics Japan, p. 301, 1982].[http://dx.doi.org/10.1109/TJMJ.1987.4549593]

[6]   I. Boussaïd, J. Lepagnot, and P. Siarry, "A survey on optimization meta-heuristics", *Inf. Sci.*, vol. 237, pp. 82-117.[http://dx.doi.org/10.1016/j.ins.2013.02.041]

[7]   S. Binitha, S. Sathya, "A survey of bio inspired optimization algorithms", *Intern. J. Soft Comp. Eng.*, p. 1, 2012.

[8]   I. Jr., X. Yang, I. Fister, J. Brest, J. Fister, "A brief review of nature-inspired algorithm for optimization", *Eeletrotehni ski vestnik*, vol. 80(3), pp. 1–7, 2013.

[9]   Yapici. H, Cetnkaya, "An Improved Particle Swarm Optimization Algorithm Using Eagle Strategy for Power Loss Minimization", Hindawi, Mathematical Problems in Engineering, Volume 2017, Article ID 1063045, 11 pages, https://doi.org/10.1155/2017/1063045, 2017.

[10]   I. Rechenberg, *"Cybernetic solution path of an experimental problem"*, *Technical Report.*, Royal Air Force Establishment, .

[11]   I. Rechenberg, *Evolutionsstrategie: optimierung technischer systeme nach prinzipien der biologischen Evolution.*, Frommann-Holzboog: Stuttgart, .

[12]   L.J. Fogel, A.J. Owens, and M.J. Walsh, *Artificial Intelligence through Simulated Evolution*, .

[13]   J.R. Koza, *Genetic Programming: On the Programming of Computers by Means of Natural Selection.*, 1st edThe MIT Press, .1st ed

[14]   L. Yi, "Study on an improved PSO algorithm and its application for solving function problem", *Inter. J. Smart Home*, vol. 10, no. 3, pp.51-62, 2016[http://dx.doi.org/10.14257/ijsh.2016.10.3.06]

[15]   R.M. Storn, and K.V. Price, "Differential evolution–asimple and efficient heuristic for global optimization over continuous spaces", *J. Glob. Optim.*, vol. 11, pp. 341-359.[http://dx.doi.org/10.1023/A:1008202821328]

[16]   J. Kennedy, and R. Eberhart, "Particle Swarm Optimization", *Proceedings of IEEE International Conference on Neural Networks*, pp. 1942-1948.[http://dx.doi.org/10.1109/ICNN.1995.488968]

[17]   N. Wan, and L. Nolle, "Solving a multi-dimensional knapsack problem using hybrid particle", *2 European Conference on Modelling and Simulation*, .

[18]   K.B. Deep, "A socio-cognitive particle swarm optimization for multi-dimensional", *First International Conference on Emerging Trends in Engineering and*, pp. 355-360.

[19]   X. Shen, Y. Li, C. Chen, J. Yang, and D. Zhang, "Greedy continuous particle swarm optimization algorithm for the knapsack problems", *Intern. J. Comp. Appl. Tech.*, vol. 44, no. 2, pp. 37-144.

[20]   H.S. Lopes, and L.S. Coelho, "Particle swarm optimization with fast local search for the blind

travelling salesman problem", *Int.Conf.Hybrid Intell. Sys.,* pp. 245-250.

[21] D. Karaboga, and B. Basturk, "A powerful and efficient algorithm for numerical function optimization: artificial bee colony (ABC) algorithm", *J. Glob. Optim.,* vol. 39, pp. 459-471.[http://dx.doi.org/10.1007/s10898-007-9149-x]

[22] A. Banharnsakun, B. Sirinaovakul, and T. Achalakul, "Job shop scheduling with the best-so-far ABC", *Eng. Appl. Artif. Intell.,* vol. 25, no. 3, pp. 583-593.[http://dx.doi.org/10.1016/j.engappai.2011.08.003]

[23] D. Karaboga, and B. Gorkemli, "A combinatorial artificial bee colony algorithm for traveling salesman problem", *Inter. Symp. Intel. Sys. App.,* pp. 50-53.[http://dx.doi.org/10.1109/INISTA.2011.5946125]

[24] Z. Geem, J. Kim, and G. Loganathan, "A new heuristic optimization algorithm: Harmony search", *Simulation,* p. 60.[http://dx.doi.org/10.1177/003754970107600201]

[25] D.T. Pham, A. Ghanbarzadeh, E. Koc, S. Otri, S. Rahim, and M. Zaidi, *"The bees algorithm", Technical Note, Cardiff University.,* Manufacturing Engineering Center: UK, .

[26] D. Pham, E. Koc, J. Lee, and J. Phrueksanant, "Using the bees algorithm to schedule jobs for a machine", *Proceedings of Eighth International Conference on Laser Metrology,* pp. 430-439.

[27] D.T. Pham, S. Otri, A. Afify, M. Mahmuddin, and H. Al-Jabbouli, "Data clustering using the bees algorithm",

[28] X. Miao, J. Chu, L. Zhang, and J. Qiao, "An evolutionary neural network approach to simple prediction of dam deformation", *J. Inf. Comput. Sci.,* vol. 10, pp. 315-1324.[http://dx.doi.org/10.12733/jics20101559]

[29] L. Cheng, X. Wu, Y. Wang, "Artificial Flora (AF) optimization algorithm", *Appl. Sci.,* vol. 8, p. 329, 2018.; [http://dx.doi.org/10.3390/app8030329]

[30] N. Metropolis, A. Rosenbluth, M. Rosenbluth, A. Teller, and E. Teller, "Equation of state calculations by fast computing machines", *J. Chem. Phys.,* vol. 21, pp. 1087-1090.[http://dx.doi.org/10.1063/1.1699114]

[31] S. Kirkpatrick, C.D. Gelatt Jr, and M.P. Vecchi, "Optimization by simulated annealing", *Science,* vol. 220, no. 4598, pp. 671-680.[http://dx.doi.org/10.1126/science.220.4598.671] [PMID: 17813860]

[32] L.N. De Castro, and F.J. Von Zuben, "Learning and optimization using the clonal selection principle", *IEEE Trans. Evol. Comput.,* vol. 6, pp. 239-251.[http://dx.doi.org/10.1109/TEVC.2002.1011539]

[33] I. Boussaïd, J. Lepagnot, and P.A. Siarry, "Survey on optimization meta-heuristics", *Inf. Sci.,* vol. 237, pp. 82-117.[http://dx.doi.org/10.1016/j.ins.2013.02.041]

[34] I. Fister, X. Yang, I. Fister, J. Brest, and D. Fister, "A brief review of nature-inspired algorithms for optimization", *Elektrotehniski Vestnik,* vol. 80, no. 3, pp. 1-7.

[35] W.C. Graham, Former Minister of Foreign Affairs, Minister of National Defence, leader of the Official Opposition and interim leader of the Liberal Party of Canada, 2000-2014.

[36] F. Zhang, "A. J, C. Sanderson, "JADE: adaptive differential evolution with optional external archive", *IEEE Trans. Evol. Comput.,* vol. 13, no. 5, pp. 945-958.[http://dx.doi.org/10.1109/TEVC.2009.2014613]

[37] N. Hansen, and A. Ostermeier, "Completely derandomized self-adaptation in evolution strategies", *Evol. Comput.,* vol. 9, no. 2, pp. 159-195.[http://dx.doi.org/10.1162/106365601750190398] [PMID: 11382355]

[38] Mirjalili. S, Gandomi. A, Mirjalili. Z, Saremi. S, Faris. H, Mirjalili. M, "Salp Swarm Algorithm: A bio-inspired optimizer for engineering design problems", Elsevier Ltd, 2017.http://dx.doi.org/10.1016/j.advengsoft.2017.07.002

[39] R. Mallipeddi, P.N. Suganthan, Q.K. Pan, and M.F. Tasgetiren, "Differential evolution algorithm with ensemble of parameters and mutation strategies", *Appl. Soft Comput.,* vol. 11, no. 2, pp. 1679-1696.[http://dx.doi.org/10.1016/j.asoc.2010.04.024]

[40] C. Garc'la-Mart'lnez, M. Lozano, F. Herrera, D. Molina, and A. Sanchez, "Global and local real-coded genetic algorithms based on parentcentric crossover operators", *Eur. J. Oper. Res.,* vol. 185, no. 3, pp. 1088-1113.[http://dx.doi.org/10.1016/j.ejor.2006.06.043]

[41] J. Brest, S. Greiner, and C.B. Boskovi, "Self-Adapting control parameters in differential evolution: A comparative study on numerical benchmark problems", *IEEE Trans. Evol. Comput.,* vol. 10, no. 6, pp. 646-657.[http://dx.doi.org/10.1109/TEVC.2006.872133]

[42] H. Gao, and W. Xu, "A new particle swarm algorithm and its globally convergent modifications", *IEEE Trans. Syst. Man Cybern. B Cybern.,* vol. 41, no. 5, pp. 1334-1351.[http://dx.doi.org/10.1109/TSMCB.2011.2144582] [PMID: 21609888]

[43] A.K. Qin, V.L. Huang, and P.N. Suganthan, "Differential evolution algorithm with strategy adaptation for global numerical optimization", *IEEE Trans. Evol. Comput.,* vol. 13, no. 2, pp. 398-417.[http://dx.doi.org/10.1109/TEVC.2008.927706]

[44] A. Draa, S. Bouzoubia, and I. Boukhalfa, "A sinusoidal differential evolution algorithmfor numerical optimisation", *Appl. Soft Comput.,* vol. 27, pp. 99-126.[http://dx.doi.org/10.1016/j.asoc.2014.11.003]

[45] G. Sun, R. Zhao, and Y. Lan, "Joint operations algorithm for large-scale global optimization", *Appl. Soft Comput.,* vol. 38, pp. 1025-1039.[http://dx.doi.org/10.1016/j.asoc.2015.10.047]

[46] L. Zhucheng, H. Xianglin, "Glowworm swarm optimization and its application to blind signal separation", *Math Prob Eng.,* Volume 2016, Article ID 5481602, 8 pages, doi.org/10.1155/2016/5481602, 2016.

[47] X. Xu, Y. Tang, J. Li, C.C. Hua, and X.P. Guan, "Dynamic multi-swarm particle swarm optimizer with cooperative learning strategy", *Appl. Soft Comput.,* vol. 29, pp. 169-183.[http://dx.doi.org/10.1016/j.asoc.2014.12.026]

[48] J.J. Liang, B.Y. Qu, P.N. Suganthan, A.G. Hernndez-Diaz, *"Problem Definitions and Evaluation Criteria for the CEC 2013 Special Session on Real-Parameter Optimization"* , Zhengzhou University, Nanyang Technological University, Zhengzhou, China/Singapore, Technical Report, 2013.

[49] R. Omidvar, H. Parvin, and F. Rad, "SSPCO Optimization Algorithm (See-See Partridge Chicks Optimization", *Fourteenth Mexican International Conference on Artificial Intelligence (MICAI),* IEEE: Cuernavaca, Mexico, pp. 101-106.[http://dx.doi.org/10.1109/MICAI.2015.22]

[50] L. Eduardo, and A. Ruiz-Herrera, "Chaos in discrete structured population models", *SIAM J. Appl. Dyn. Syst.,* vol. 11, no. 4, pp. 1200-1214.[http://dx.doi.org/10.1137/120868980]

[51] L. Dejian, "Comparison study of AR models on the Canadian lynx data: a close look at BDS statistic", *Comput. Stat. Data Anal.,* vol. 22, no. 4, pp. 409-423.[http://dx.doi.org/10.1016/0167-9473(95)00056-9]

[52] R. May, *Simple mathematical models with very complicated dynamics,* .[http://dx.doi.org/10.1038/261459a0]

[53] R. Neal, *The logistic Lattice in Random Number Generation, Division of Methematics,* .

[54] R. Mendes, J. Kennedy, and J. Neves, "The fully informed particle swarm: simpler, maybe better", *IEEE Trans. Evol. Comput.,* vol. 8, no. 3, pp. 204-210.[http://dx.doi.org/10.1109/TEVC.2004.826074]

[55] F. van den Bergh, and A.P. Engelbrecht, "Acooperative approach to particle swarm optimization", *IEEE Trans. Evol. Comput.,* vol. 8, no. 3, pp. 225-239.[http://dx.doi.org/10.1109/TEVC.2004.826069]

[56] J.J. Liang, A.K. Qin, P.N. Suganthan, and S. Baskar, "Comprehensive learning particle swarm optimizer for global optimization of multimodal functions", *IEEE Trans. Evol. Comput.,* vol. 10, no. 3, pp. 281-295.[http://dx.doi.org/10.1109/TEVC.2005.857610]

[57] S. Singh, and S. Sharma, "PEECA: "PSO-Based energy efficient clustering algorithm for wireless sensor networks", *I. J. Comp. Netw. Inform. Sec.,* vol. 2017, no. 5, pp. 31-37.[http://dx.doi.org/10.5815/ijcnis.2017.05.04]

[58] H. Gao, and W. Xu, "A new particle swarm algorithm and its globally convergent modifications", *IEEE Trans. Syst. Man Cybern. B Cybern.,* vol. 41, no. 5, pp. 1334-1351.[http://dx.doi.org/10.1109/TSMCB.2011.2144582] [PMID: 21609888]

[59] T. Sharma, and M. Pant, *SINGH, "Adaptive bee colony in an artificial bee colony for solving engineering design problems", Adv. Mech. Eng. App.,* vol. Vol. P, AMEA, .

[60] D. Karaboga, C. Ozturk, "A novel clustering approach: Artificial Bee Colony (ABC) algorithm", Applied Soft Computing. *Elsevier*, 2009. 10.1016/j.asoc.12.025, 2009.

[61] C.L. Blake, and C.J. Merz, *The University of California at Irvine Repository of Machine,* .http://www.ics.uci.edu/ mlearn/MLRepository

[62] D. Falco, A. Della Cioppa, and E. Tarantino, "Facing classification problems with Particle Swarm Optimization", *Appl. Soft Comput.,* vol. 7, p. 3.[http://dx.doi.org/10.1016/j.asoc.2005.09.004]

[63] http://www.statisticallysignificantconsulting.com/Ttest.htm

[64] J. K. Kruschke, "Bayesian estimation supersedes the t test", *Journal of Experimental Psychology: General* Version of May 31, 2012.[http://dx.doi.org/10.1037/e502412013-055]

[65] J.C.F. De, "Winter, "Using the Student's t-test with extremely small sample sizes", *Pract. Assess., Res. Eval.,* vol. 18, no. 10, .

[66] K. Pathak, and S. Prakash Tiwari, "Travelling salesman problem using bee colony with SPV", *Intern. J. Soft Comput. Eng.,* vol. 2, pp. 410-414. [IJSCE].

[67] D. Karaboga, and B.A. Gorkemli, "Combinatorial artificial bee colony algorithm for traveling salesman problem", *Innovations in Intelligent Systems and Applications (INISTA),* IEEE: Istanbul, Turkey, pp. 50-53.[http://dx.doi.org/10.1109/INISTA.2011.5946125]

[68] R. Omidvar, H. Parvin, and F. Rad, "SSPCO Optimization Algorithm (See-See Partridge Chicks Optimization)", *2015 Fourteenth Mexican International Conference on Artificial Intelligence (MICAI),* IEEE: Cuernavaca, Mexico, pp. 101-106.[http://dx.doi.org/10.1109/MICAI.2015.22]

[69] Q. Zhang, A. Zhou, Sh. Zhao, P. Suganthan, W. Liu, S. Tiwari, "Multiobjective optimization Test Instances for the CEC 2009 Special Session and Competition", *Technical Report CES-487*, 2009.

[70] D.E. Goldberg, *Genetic Algorithms in Search, Optimization and Machine Learning.,* 1st edAddison-Wesley Longman Publishing Co., Inc.: Boston, MA, USA, .1st ed

[71] R. Storn, K. Price, "Differential evolution a simple and efficient heuristic for global optimization over continuous spaces", *J. Global Opt.* , vol. 11, no. 1997, pp. 341–359, 1997.

[72] J. Kennedy, and R. Eberhart, "Particle swarm optimization", *Proceedings of the IEEE International Conference on Neural Networks,* pp. 1942-1948.Perth, Australia[http://dx.doi.org/10.1109/ICNN.1995.488968]

[73] D. Pham, A. Ghanbarzadeh, E. Ko, S. Otri, S. Rahim, and M. Zaidi, The bees algorithm a novel tool for complex optimisation problems.*Intelligent Production Machines and Systems.,* Elsevier Science Ltd: Oxford, pp. 454-459.[http://dx.doi.org/10.1016/B978-008045157-2/50081-X]

[74] M. Cheng, and L. Lien, "Hybrid artificial intelligence based pba for benchmark functions and facility layout design optimization", *J. Comput. Civ. Eng.,* vol. 26, pp. 612-624.[http://dx.doi.org/10.1061/(ASCE)CP.1943-5487.0000163]

[75] F. Wang, Ch. Liu, "A Novel Particle Swarm Optimization Algorithm for Global Optimization", Hindawi Publishing Corporation Computational Intelligence and Neuroscience Volume 2016, Article ID 9482073, 9 pages, 2016.[http://dx.doi.org/10.1155/2016/9482073]

[76] A. Mcnabb, C. Monson, and K. Seppi, "MRPSO: MapReduce particle swarm optimization", *Conference: Genetic and Evolutionary Computation Conference*, GECCO 2007, Proceedings, London, England, UK, July 7-11, 2007.

[77]   L. Titare, P. Singh, L. Arya, and S. Choube, "Optimal reactive power rescheduling based on EPSDE algorithm to enhance static voltage stability", *Int. J. Electr. Power Energy Syst.,* vol. 63, pp. 588-599.[http://dx.doi.org/10.1016/j.ijepes.2014.05.078]

[78]   Y. Liang, Y. Liu, and L. Zhang, "An Improved Artificial Bee Colony (ABC) Algorithm for Large Scale Optimization", *2nd International Symposium on Instrumentation and Measurement,* Sensor Network and Automation (IMSNA), IEEE, 978-1-4799-2716-6/13/$31.00, 2013.[http://dx.doi.org/10.1109/IMSNA.2013.6743359]

[79]   S. He, Q.H. Wu, and J.R. Saunders, "Group Search Optimizer: An Optimization Algorithm Inspired by Animal Searching Behavior", *IEEE Trans. Evol. Comput.,* vol. 13, no. 5, pp. 973-990.[http://dx.doi.org/10.1109/TEVC.2009.2011992]

[80]   X. Yang, and S. Deb, "Cuckoo search *via* Levy flights", *World Congress on Nature & Biologically Inspired Computing (NaBIC),* 10.1109/NABIC.2009.5393690, 210-214, IEEE Publications, 2009.[http://dx.doi.org/10.1109/NABIC.2009.5393690]

[81]   Wang. Ch, Shi. Zh, F.Wu, "An improved particle swarm optimization-based feed-forward neural network combined with RFID sensors to indoor localization", *Information,* vol. 8, p. 9.[http://dx.doi.org/10.3390/info8010009]

[82]   R. Mallipeddi, P. Suganthan, Q. Pan, and M. Tasgetiren, "Differential evolution algorithm with ensemble of parameters and mutation strategies", *Appl. Soft Comput.,* vol. 11, no. 2, pp. 1679-1696.[http://dx.doi.org/10.1016/j.asoc.2010.04.024]

[83]   A. Gandomi, "Bird mating optimizer: An optimization algorithm inspired by bird mating strategies", *Commun Nonlinear Sci,* vol. 19, no. 4, pp. 1213-1228.[http://dx.doi.org/10.1016/j.cnsns.2013.08.027]

[84]   P.N. Suganthan, N. Hansen, and J.J. Liang, "Problem definitions and evaluation criteria for the CEC 2005 Special Session on Real Parameter Optimization", *Nanyang Technological University,* Singapore, Tech. Rep, May. 2005 [Online].http:// www3.ntu.edu.sg/home/EPNSugan/

[85]   Q. Zhang, A. Zhou, Sh. Zhao, P. Suganthan, W. Liu, "Tiwari S.2009. Multiobjective optimization test instances for the CEC 2009 Special Session and Competition", *Technical Report CES-487,* 2009.

[86]   J. Holland, "Genetic algorithms and the optimal allocation of trials", *SIAM J. Comput.,* vol. 2, pp. 88-105.[http://dx.doi.org/10.1137/0202009]

[87]   G. Yuelin,L. Junmei, "A New Differential Evolution Algorithm with Random Mutation", International Conference on Intelligent Computing ICIC 2009: Emerging Intelligent Computing Technology and Applications. With Aspects of Artificial Intelligence, pp 209-214, 2009.

[88]   S. Mirjalili, A. Gandomi, Z. Mirjalili, S. Saremi, H. Faris, and M. Mirjalili, "Salp Swarm Algorithm: A bio-inspired optimizer for engineering design problems", *Adv. Eng. Softw.,* .[http://dx.doi.org/10.1016/j.advengsoft.2017.07.002]

[89]   D.T. Pham, A. Ghanbarzadeh, E. Koc, S. Otri, S. Rahim, and M. Zaidi, "The bees algorithm". *Technical note,* Cardiff University, UK: Manufacturing Engineering Center, 1995.

[90]   X. Xiao, Q. Zhang, "The multiple population co-evolution PSO algorithm", International Conference in Swarm Intelligence, ICSI 2014: *Adv. Swarm Intel.,* pp.434-441.

[91]   N. Sulaiman, J. Mohamad-Saleh, A. Ghani Abro, "New enhanced artificial bee colony (JA-ABC5) algorithm with application for reactive power optimization", *Hind. J.,* Volume 2015, Article ID 396189, 11 pages.

[92]   N. Johari, A. Zain, N. Mustaff, A. Udin, "Firefly algorithm for optimization problem". *Appl. Mech. Mater.,* vol. 421. 10.4028/www.scientific.net/AMM.421.512, 2013.

[93]   H. Gao, and W. Xu, "A new particle swarm algorithm and its globally convergent modifications", *IEEE Trans. Syst. Man Cybern. B Cybern.,* vol. 41, no. 5, pp. 1334-1351.[http://dx.doi.org/10.1109/TSMCB.2011.2144582] [PMID: 21609888]

[94]   R.V. Rao, *"Teaching-Learning-Based Optimization (TLBO) Algorithm And Its Engineering Applications",* Springer International Publishing, Switzerland, 2016.[http://dx.doi.org/10.1007/978-3-319-22732-0]

[95]   J. Ghorpade-Aher, V. Metre, "Clustering Multidimensional Data with PSO based Algorithm", *Soft Computing and Artificial Intelligence*, Third Post Graduate Symposium on Computer Engineering cPGCON2014 Organized by department of Computer Engineering, Computer Science, Neural and Evolutionary Computing, Cornell University, 6 pages, arXiv:1402.6428, 2014.

[96]   A. Gandomi, "Bird mating optimizer: An optimization algorithm inspired by birdmating strategies", *Commun. Nonlinear Sci.,* vol. 19, no. 4, pp. 1213-1228.[http://dx.doi.org/10.1016/j.cnsns.2013.08.027]

SUBJECT INDEX

A

ABC 12, 107, 119
  algorithm 12
  and PSO margins of error 107, 119
  and SSPCO algorithms 107
  methods 107
Algorithms 5, 7, 8, 9, 10, 79, 89, 91, 101, 104, 106, 123, 125, 131, 173, 176, 177, 179, 183
  ants and genetic 123, 125
  artificial bee colonization 10
  artificial bee colony 10
  chaos-based SSOCO 104
  chaotic 79, 89, 91, 101, 104
  differential evolution 9, 131
  low-population 176
  nature-based 5, 7
  plant propagation 5
  popular 8, 9
  population-based 176, 177, 183
  standard artificial bee colony 179
  systematic 173
  two-clustering 106
Algorithm's equilibrium exploration 10
Algorithm SSPCO 14
  algorithm 14
Algorithm Chaotic 41, 91
  ABC 91
  SSPCO 14
Annealing technique 11
Ant Colony Optimization 8
Array 74
  arranged priority 74
  elite 74
Artificial 3, 106, 118
  bee colony clustering algorithm 106, 118
  intelligence technique 3

B

Bat algorithm 8
Bee(s) 5, 10, 179

colony algorithm 5, 10, 179
  elite 10
  multiple 10
  observed 10
  sending 10
  worker 10
Bees algorithm 8, 10, 131, 154
  artificial 10
Behavior 3, 5, 7, 9, 10, 11, 13, 14, 142, 146, 173, 174, 175, 179, 182
  classical conditioning learning 142, 146
  collective 3
  converting 173
  food-seeking 10
  foraging 10
  interesting 174
  mating 10
  orderly 14, 173
  random 179
  social 13
Best cost of 31, 38, 126
  populations 31, 38
  tours in PSO 126
Birds 7, 9, 14, 106, 118, 121, 127, 128, 129, 130, 144, 146, 147, 148, 150, 174, 181, 182
  collective behavior of 106, 118
  dead 127
  first hunted 127, 128, 129
Brain signals 180

C

Calculations 5, 186
  definitive 5
Cancer 106, 107, 108, 111, 112, 113, 114, 118, 119
CCABC algorithm 103, 131
Cellular machines 78
Chaos theory 74, 75, 77, 177, 179, 180
Chaotic 74, 91, 115, 179
  ABC algorithm 91
  creation of food sources 179

T

Target system of source 174
Techniques 2, 7, 106, 107, 108, 109, 111, 112,
   118, 119, 173
  average error clustering 108
  benchmark comparison clustering 107, 118
  data clustering 108
Test(s) 3, 69, 73, 114, 115, 131, 133, 142,
   152, 153, 154, 156, 168
  benchmark Friedman 115
  empirical 3
  nonparametric 115
  statistical 142, 168
   value confidence interval 114
Theory 116, 117, 177, 178
  turbulence 178
Thermodynamics 13
Threshold, defined 146
Thyroid 106, 107, 108, 112, 113, 114, 118,
   119
Travelling salesman problem 14
TSP problem 10
T-Test results 114

V

Velocity 9, 15, 16, 17, 19, 69, 77, 79, 105,
   116, 117, 122, 123, 147, 148, 152, 182,
   183
  bird's 183
  components 105, 116
  high 69
  previous 15, 17, 122
  update chicken's 19, 77, 79, 117
Velocity equation 9, 15, 146, 147, 148, 152,
   183, 184, 185
  algorithm's population 185

W

Wolf search 8

www.ingramcontent.com/pod-product-compliance
Lightning Source LLC
Chambersburg PA
CBHW041658210326
41598CB00007B/458